GW00976361

*V*ictorian
Scandals

*V*ictorian *Scandals*

REPRESENTATIONS
OF GENDER AND CLASS

Edited by Kristine Ottesen Garrigan

OHIO UNIVERSITY PRESS / ATHENS

Copyright © 1992 by Ohio University Press
Printed in the United States of America
All rights reserved
Ohio University Press books are printed on acid-free paper ∞

Library of Congress Cataloging-in-Publication Data

Victorian scandals : representations of gender and class / edited by
    Kristine Ottesen Garrigan.
        p.   cm.
    Includes index.
    ISBN 0-8214-1019-9
    1. Great Britain—History—Victoria, 1837-1901.   2. Great Britain
—Social life and customs—19th century.   3. Scandals—Great Britain
—History—19th century.   4. Social classes—Great Britain.   5. Sex
role—Great Britain.   I. Garrigan, Kristine Ottesen, 1939-   .
DA550.V54   1992
941.081—dc20   92-3945
                                                                  CIP

Contents

List of Illustrations

Chapter 3

Fig. 1. "Lord Cairns to Miss Fortescue," from *The Entr'acte,* 11 Aug. 1883.

Fig. 2. "Mr. Gilbert and Miss Fortescue," from *The Entr'acte,* 15 Mar. 1884.

Chapter 4

Fig. 1. "Holywell Street, Strand," from Walter Besant and G. E. Mitton, *The Strand District* (London: Adam and Charles Black, 1902); by kind permission of Harvard College Library.

Fig. 2. "Madame Vestris," from *Memoirs of the life, public and private adventures of Madame Vestris* . . . ([London]: John Duncombe, [1836]), Harvard Theater Collection extra illustrated volume; by kind permission of Harvard College Library.

Fig. 3. Madame Vestris as Orpheus (swimming), from *English Stars, No. 1*; by kind permission of Harvard College Library.

Fig. 4. An unidentified actress posed as Napoleon, yet emphasizing her crotch; cabinet photo; by kind permission of the Kinsey Institute.

Chapter 8

All figures are albumen prints from collodion on glass negatives.

Fig. 1. David Wilkie Wynfield, "Self-Portrait [?] in Renaissance Costume," 21 cm. × 16 cm., c. 1863–64; courtesy of the International Museum of Photography at George Eastman House, Rochester, New York.

Fig. 2. A. A. E. Disdéri, uncut *carte de visite* portrait of a woman, 19.8 cm. × 23.7 cm., c. 1860–65; courtesy of the International Museum of Photography at George Eastman House, Rochester, New York.

Fig. 3. Unknown photographer, "Thomas Carlyle," *carte de visite*, c. 1861–64; courtesy of the Visual Studies Workshop, Rochester, New York.

Fig. 4. Julia Margaret Cameron, "Thomas Carlyle," 30 cm. × 24.2 cm., 1867; courtesy of the J. Paul Getty Museum, Malibu, California.

Fig. 5. Julia Margaret Cameron, "Alfred Tennyson," 25.3 cm. × 20.1 cm., 1865; courtesy of the International Museum of Photography at George Eastman House, Rochester, New York.

Fig. 6. Julia Margaret Cameron, "Henry Taylor as Rembrandt," 25.3 cm. × 20.1 cm., 1865; courtesy of the J. Paul Getty Museum, Malibu, California.

Fig. 7. Julia Margaret Cameron, "G. F. Watts R.A. in His Studio," 26.2 cm. × 20.8 cm., 1865; courtesy of the J. Paul Getty Museum, Malibu, California.

Fig. 8. Julia Margaret Cameron, "William Holman Hunt," 22.9 cm. × 17.8 cm., 1864; courtesy of the J. Paul Getty Museum, Malibu, California.

Acknowledgements

Slightly different versions of Tracy C. Davis's "The Actress in Victorian Pornography" and Ann R. Higginbotham's " 'Sin of the Age': Infanticide and Illegitimacy in Victorian London" have been published in *Theatre Journal* and *Victorian Studies,* respectively. The current versions appear here by kind permission of the editors of those journals. In Jane W. Stedman's " 'Come, Substantial Damages!' " Arthur Sullivan's holograph diary for 1881 is quoted courtesy of the Beinecke Rare Book and Manuscript Library, Yale University; material from Henry Labouchere's undated letter to George Grossmith is reproduced by kind permission of the trustees of the Pierpont Morgan Library, New York. Joanne Lukitsh's quotations from two of Julia Margaret Cameron's letters to Sir J. F. W. Herschel appear courtesy of the Royal Society, London. Additional acknowledgments are provided in the List of Illustrations.

The editor and contributors express special thanks to Richard D. Altick, Regents' Professor Emeritus of English, Ohio State University, for his invaluable suggestions on shaping this collection and for his confidence in the result.

Foreword:
Decorum, Scandal, and the Press

Kristine Ottesen Garrigan

PANTALOONED piano legs, the censorious Mrs. Grundy, hypocritical worshippers of Respectability like Dickens's Podsnaps and Pecksniffs: in the popular mind, the term "Victorian" still evokes such hackneyed images of prudery. We persist in assuming that the Victorians were easily—in fact, perpetually—shocked by everything from ministry-toppling national scandals to minor breaches of domestic decorum.

Especially over the last two decades, however, vigorous growth in Victorian studies scholarship has generated enlightening revisions, both major and subtle, of the period's stereotypes. The following collection newly demonstrates this continuing process of re-viewing the Victorians. Originally presented in shorter form at the Midwest Victorian Studies Association's 1987 Annual Meeting on the theme "Victorian Scandals: Decorum and Its Enemies," these essays do not deal with standard Victorian *causes célèbres,* such as the fall of Charles Parnell, the Bradlaugh birth control case, or even the Queen's ambiguous relationship with her Scottish groom John Brown. Instead, discussions of lesser-known, richly varied examples of unconventional behavior and its consequences afford a fresh and more spacious reading of the context, nature, and function of "scandal" in Victorian society that cumulatively argues for its broadened relevance.

The opening section, "Disorder in the Court," features three essays centered on specific legal definitions of socially unacceptable conduct. Court cases and other modes of legal action are the most obvious, structured means by which scandals become publicly defined. First, Gail L. Savage surveys divorce cases immediately following the 1857 Divorce Act reforms, suggesting that despite its expense and negative publicity, divorce was sought more often by the middle and lower classes, including women, than has previously been assumed—and certainly more frequently than the act's cautious framers envisioned. Marilyn J. Kurata then examines a chilling series of historical and literary instances in which medical and legal authorities colluded to commit women wrongfully to mental institutions because of their assertive behavior. But the consequences of seeking legal redress for real, as opposed to trumped up, wrongs could prove both unexpected and unwelcome, as Jane W. Stedman shows in recounting the actress Miss Fortescue's 1884 breach of promise suit against her erstwhile fiancé Lord Garmoyle.

The underlying relation in the first section between scandal and sexual politics provides an opening to the second, "The Woman Question/Questionable Women," which examines images of women from the 1850s to the end of the century. Miss Fortescue's resort to legal action had the effect of transmuting her in the public eye from a charming ingenue into a bold, grasping hussy, the latter an image of actresses that persisted to the end of the century, as Tracy C. Davis shows in "The Actress in Victorian Pornography." But women who sought independence through more respectable occupations similarly violated powerful standards of decorum, albeit less spectacularly. As Charles Kingsley discovered when he undertook to pioneer female higher education, once women experience a larger world they will no longer conform to masculine expectations of feminine propriety. John C. Hawley, S.J., explains how such unwomanly independence drove the abashed Muscular Christian to disassociate himself permanently from the "ghastly ring of prophetesses" that his educational schemes had empowered.

Part Three, "(In)decorous Portraits," explores the unsettled criteria for decorum in writers' and artists' depictions of revered Victorians. Teresa Mangum offers evidence of the unease with which reviewers approached George Eliot's "marriage" to G. H. Lewes when they assessed J. W. Cross's life of Eliot. She piquantly details the ingenious strategies reviewers devised to circumvent Cross's reticence even as they approved it—from transforming the relationship into an intellectual "grand romance" to displacing their censure onto the erring women in Eliot's fiction. On the other hand, biographer James Anthony Froude's remarkable candor about Thomas and Jane Carlyle's married life also troubled reviewers, as D. J. Trela illustrates. Froude was praised by some reviewers for a devotion to truth rivaling that of the man who was his subject; he was condemned by others as a traitor to friendship and dismissed as an obtuse, incompetent editor into the bargain. Moving from literary to visual representations, Joanne Lukitsh explores Julia Margaret Cameron's efforts to rescue photographic portraiture from the vulgarizing standards of commercial photographers by employing High Art techniques to render Victorian sages as irreproachable icons—including Carlyle, whose "inner greatness" she tried to capture. Lukitsh fruitfully compares Cameron's timeless, idealized images to *cartes de visite*, the inartistic but highly popular celebrity photos that Queen Victoria herself collected.

The closing section, "The Wages of Sin," focuses on two "great evils" of the Victorian period. Gambling, at least in the view of the crusading National Anti-Gambling League, ultimately led to financial ruin and probable suicide. But the league's view of betting as dangerous and morally degrading was at odds with the Victorian public's more tolerant perception of it, David C. Itzkowitz argues, and thus the league's draconian reform program failed. Infanticide, on the other hand, was believed by the Victorians to be appallingly widespread, a major national scandal. Reviewing infanticide cases tried in London's Central Criminal Court, however, Ann R. Higginbotham challenges the common Victorian presumption that unmarried mothers resorted to murder in order to conceal their shame; she demonstrates that even those who did were often treated leniently by the courts. Finally, Thaïs E. Morgan provides in her afterword, "Victorian Scandals, Victorian Strategies," a masterful retrospective analysis of the major issues of gender and power in these essays from the perspectives of recent critical theory.

At this point, however, a quite practical link among the papers is worth emphasizing. The most common form of documentation among them is not government records, personal letters, memoirs, or other traditional types of historical support. Rather, virtually all these investigations depend directly on, or are vividly fleshed out by, evidence from contemporary periodicals. Two major reasons account for this approach. First, as Michael Wolff has argued,

Newspapers and periodicals occupy an unrivalled position as repositories of the general life of Victorian England. . . . One might almost claim that an attitude, an opinion, an idea, did not exist until it had registered itself in the press, and that an interest group, a sect, a profession, came of age when it inaugurated its journal.[1]

And what an exuberant variety of them are cited in this collection! From established, intellectually dominant periodicals like the *Quarterly Review* and *Blackwood's* to the prurient *Paul Pry* and *Boudoir,* their titles alone suggest the fecundity of the genre, as well as an astonishingly modern segmentation of readership: the *Days' Doings, Once a Week, All the Year Round, Sporting Times,* the *Spiritualist, Moonshine, British Journal of Photography, Journal of the Statistical Society,* the *Adult,* the *Young Woman, Magdalen's Friend and Female Home Intelligencer.* . . . Yet the more than sixty journals noted in these essays are a minute fraction of the estimated fifty thousand that existed, however ephemerally, during the period.

The second and more significant reason for their pervasiveness as sources in our specific context is the crucial role that the press played in the creation, judgment, and perpetuation of scandal. As long as deviant behavior (in the broadest sense) remains private and a superficial moral and social order is preserved, scandal does not exist. Such conduct must be made public before it can shock. Nineteenth-century advances in printing technology, coupled with a more equitably based economic prosperity and the concomitant extension of literacy, made possible the exposure of unconventional behavior on a scale and with an immediacy completely unprecedented. In nearly every essay here, press reaction is central to establishing both the nature and consequences of scandals. Journals could function as arbiters, judging, promulgating, or amending standards of acceptable conduct, whether for biographers, politicians, bettors, or almost any group of women. They could be distorters as well: titillating "fillers" about divorce cases, for example, and lurid accounts of infanticides conveyed faulty impressions of the numbers and classes involved in such scandals. Particularly noteworthy is the extent to which legal cases might be tried in the press. Miss Fortescue's actual court appearance, for example, was anticlimactic after the legitimacy and propriety of her breach of promise suit had been debated among theatrical and popular papers for months beforehand.

That the influence of the press was well recognized is apparent in Kurata's discussion of Rosina Bulwer's publicity-seeking behavior, designed to embarrass her famous husband into acknowledging her legal and financial claims on him. Indeed, her release from a mental institution was achieved partly through the intervention of various London and provincial papers in her cause. Another victim of wrongful confinement, Georgina Weldon, literally "advertised her grievances in the newspapers," as Kurata points out. And of course some Victorians—most obviously Oscar Wilde—skillfully exploited the press in order to achieve celebrity, only to have their success backfire on them when scandal broke.

As a gloss on this power of Victorian journalism to mold public perception, the essays in the comparatively staid third section, "(In)decorous Portraits," are highly pertinent. All deal with problems of image in today's popular sense of the term. Cross's discreet biography of George Eliot and Froude's revealing life of Carlyle presented difficulties to reviewers because both books destabilized, although in very different ways, the "images" of two Victorians whose writings had rendered them exemplars of moral-intellectual greatness. Especially striking is the malleability of such images once the press confronted them. From formidable intellect and moral teacher, Eliot shriveled into a contentedly domestic bourgeois female, helplessly dependent on men's guidance and approval. Carlyle, Victorian sage par excellence, deteriorated into a neglectful, impotent husband, petty and spiteful. Images of whole classes of persons were similarly subject to constant and conflicting revision; women could be anatomized as earnest, modest, chaste, striving after moral goodness, or as loud, flashy, lascivious, thriving on notoriety. The image depended on the ideological agenda and the audience of the journal in which they were described. By contrast, a disparate cluster of images could be conflated; in the National Anti-Gambling League's *Bulletin,* wagerers of all stripes—royalty playing baccarat, matrons at the bridge table, small boys betting with buttons—were depicted monolithically as wayward souls careering toward disaster. Or images could elide, such as those of actresses and prostitutes as "public women."

Meanwhile, the advent of photography promoted the idea of image in a literal sense. Actresses' publicity photos might appear charmingly decorous, but the poses and settings echoed to the initiated the iconography of pornographic illustration, thus reinforcing the identification of actress and whore. (No wonder Miss Fortescue's would-be father-in-law, the puritanical Lord Cairns, allegedly sought to buy up all the photographs of his son's intended.) Both Julia Margaret Cameron's High Art portraiture and the hugely successful *cartes de visite* signaled that individual physical images—immediately accessible, infinitely replicable, and above all, *marketable*—were being transformed into public properties. It is but a short step to private lives in general becoming the regular business of an endlessly curious public.

Today, both the extraordinary popularity of gossip periodicals and tell-all talk shows, and the instant political destruction wrought by media exposure of erring government officials, are logical outcomes of this continuing redirection of interest toward private lifestyles (the very jargon is indicative) and away from public deeds and accomplishments as measures of character. Thus, we see the persistent timeliness of the phenomenon of scandal as it affected an increasingly affluent, pluralistic society from which our own has evolved. Moreover, our morally superior condemnation, on the one hand, of current victims of exposés, and, on the other, our alarm at the specter of a voracious press and public being distracted by the peripheral or irrelevant are not so distant from the ambivalence the Victorians themselves experienced in the presence of scandal. An assessment by the eminent nineteenth-century editor and biographer Leslie Stephen is as disconcertingly apposite now as it was then: "However gravely we may speak, we shall read the next indiscreet revelation, and our enjoyment will only have the keener edge from affectation of prudery."[2]

Notes

1. Michael Wolff, "Charting the Golden Stream: Thoughts on a Directory of Victorian Periodicals," *Victorian Periodicals Newsletter,* no. 13 (September 1971): 26, reprinted from *Editing Nineteenth-Century Texts,* ed. John M. Robson (Toronto: University of Toronto Press, 1969): 37–59.

2. Leslie Stephen, "The Browning Letters," *Studies of a Biographer,* 4 vols. (New York: Putnam, 1907), 3:2, as quoted below by D. J. Trela, who discusses further Stephen's ambivalent views on the legitimacy of public access to details of private conduct.

PART ONE

Disorder in the Court

1 / "Intended Only for the Husband": Gender, Class, and the Provision for Divorce in England, 1858–1868

Gail L. Savage

SAMUEL Wilberforce, sitting in the House of Lords as bishop of Oxford, vigorously opposed the 1857 Divorce Act. The state's providing facilities for divorce, especially if they were made readily accessible to the poor, "would be," he warned, "the opening of the floodgates of licence upon the hitherto blessed purity of English life."[1] Although Wilberforce and the leader of the opposition to the bill in the lower house, William Gladstone, failed to block its passage into law, its enactment did not open these "floodgates." In fact, the annual number of divorces in England did not exceed five hundred before the turn of the century and did not break into four digits until the First World War.

The very low incidence of divorce in nineteenth-century England reflected the determination of lawmakers to protect both the sanctity of the English family and the privileged position of English husbands. Legalizing divorce could further these ends by allowing respectable men to rid themselves of erring spouses. As one supporter of the bill explained to the House of Commons, "a general indissolubility of marriage would inflict a wrong on the injured husband which you have no right to entail upon him."[2] But divorce constituted a potentially dangerous challenge as well. If it were too easy to obtain, divorce would free the lower orders from the discipline of home ties and might as readily be employed *against* husbands as by them. To insure, therefore, that divorce remained the prerogative of the intended beneficiaries, the terms of the act disadvantaged two groups in particular—wives and the poor.

The law recognized only adultery as grounds for divorce. Husbands, however, could sue for divorce on the basis of adultery alone. A wife had to demonstrate that her husband had compounded adultery with some other marital offense (cruelty, desertion, incest, bigamy, sodomy) in order to obtain a divorce. Moreover, the act gave jurisdiction over the divorce procedure to a court situated only in London. This location necessarily raised the costs of proceedings for those who lived outside the home counties. Obviously, many potential litigants would lack the financial resources to bring their cases before the newly created tribunal. The debates[3] on the bill show that legislators clearly understood the political significance of these restrictions and that their inclusion in the statute constituted a self-conscious assertion of power defined by both gender and class.

Government spokesmen characterized the bill as a very limited reform. The attorney general explained to the House of Commons that "the Bill embodied nothing but what had been known to be the law of England for 200 years." English law, as practiced by the House of Lords, already recognized the dissolubility of marriage on the grounds of adultery. Sir George Grey, the home secretary, argued that the bill did not alter the law but simply provided for a tribunal to administer it, thus removing the injustice of denying the poor whatever remedy the law could provide. The bill would not increase the incidence of marital breakdown; it would merely allow the poor and middle classes to divorce as the wealthy already could.[4]

Opponents of the bill, however, did not find credible the government's concern for the poor. They pointed out that the proposed composition of the court, consisting of the highest judges in the land, precluded the possibility that the poor would actually be able to use the new court. As one debater argued, reducing the cost of divorce from two thousand pounds to three hundred pounds would not make it readily available to all. Providing for true social equity in divorce would require giving authority to some local jurisdiction—either the county courts or the assize circuit. But propositions to ease access to the divorce procedure in this way aroused legislators' fears of an unacceptable rise in the incidence of divorce. One speaker, for example, warned that allowing county courts the power to grant divorces would create such opportunities for collusion that divorces would inevitably become common as well as cheap, a result desired by neither the proponents nor the opponents of the bill.[5]

The suggestion that divorce should be made more widely available came, oddly enough, from a group that included those such as Gladstone, who opposed any divorce at all. This inconsistency could hardly escape notice, and the attorney general's sarcastic offer of congratulations to those "hon. Gentlemen opposite for at length so dealing with this Bill as to wish to enlarge and make it accessible to all descriptions of persons" elicited an appreciative laugh. Another speaker more bluntly accused the bill's opponents of trying to make the bill look ridiculous by proposing county courts' jurisdiction.[6] In the end, the government was able to preserve the proposal for a single, centralized court to sit in London—a court everyone assumed would be unavailable to the bulk of the population. Thus, the attempt to block the bill's passage by widening the access to divorce only forced its sponsors to make explicit the social parameters of the court's potential clientele.

Sharp discussion about how the constitution of the court would define access to it reflected the tactical maneuvering of political opponents and did not indicate a rupture within what remained a broad social consensus. In contrast, clashes over the issue of equality of grounds had a greater emotional resonance. Debates on this issue revealed a profound ambivalence about the fundamental nature of women.

Those who argued for unequal grounds defended it as both a proper and necessary exercise of male power. Replying to the claim that adultery was just as much a sin for a man as for a woman, the lord chancellor declared that even so, "every man must feel that the injury was not the same." Sir George Grey insisted that a wife's adultery was "the greatest wrong which a man can suffer." Provision for unequal grounds for divorce was therefore imperative. Otherwise, as a member of the 1850 Divorce Commission, Spencer Walpole, explained, "the other sex, when they feel that be their conduct ever so bad they will still retain their husband's name and their husband's rank, they may be tempted to commit these offenses to a greater extent than when they know that the penalty which hangs over a guilty wife is degradation from her former honourable position."[7] In other words, the threat posed by adulterous wives necessitated framing divorce law to the advantage of husbands.

A similar argument was proffered regarding the threat of merely litigious wives. Lord Campbell reminded the House of Lords that the 1850 Commission on Divorce thought "the most lamentable consequences" would ensue "if the wife, in any case of adultery on the part of the husband, unattended with aggravating circumstances, should have the power to insist that the marriage should be dissolved." These consequences would, of course, include the greatly increased incidence of divorce as a result of wives' suits against adulterous husbands. A proposal that would have at least allowed wives to sue for divorce on the grounds of adultery committed within the conjugal home led the attorney general to argue that any such provision should be narrowly defined so that it clearly referred only to habitual adultery—keeping a mistress in the home—rather than "any occasional and fugitive act once committed in the common residence." During discussion of this amendment in the House of Lords, Lord Redesdale conjectured that "it might enable the wife when so disposed, by putting temptation in the way of the husband, to effect the object which she had in view."[8]

These remarks evoke a vision of sexual relations fraught with conflict, each side giving as good as the other. Men asserted a natural superiority but not a moral one. The weakness of husbands, who might commit "occasional and fugitive" acts of adultery with domestic servants or even collude to commit adultery so that wives could sue for divorce if the law made that possible, did not invalidate masculine authority over the family. The argument mounted by the defenders of unequal grounds portrayed women as active and dangerous combatants, ready and willing to commit adultery themselves or to revenge themselves upon adulterous husbands.

Proponents of the equal grounds side had a much different vision of feminine nature. They pointed out that the law as proposed reflected "a fear that the other sex would take advantage of the equal powers." But such a prospect, they argued, was unlikely. Lord Lynhurst suggested that the ties of home and family would make women reluctant to act. Thomas Collins reassured the House of Commons that "the other sex was patient and long-suffering" and so would not necessarily insist upon exercising any newly granted rights.[9]

Such defenders believed in the moral superiority of women—a superiority that undermined the legitimacy of male claims to the protection afforded by the proposed law. Adultery was, they argued, far more likely to be committed by men than by women. Henry Drummond posed a pointed challenge to members of Parliament: if "adultery was of itself a dissolution of marriage . . . how many men in that House were married?" Gladstone asserted that "the enormous majority of adulteries are adulteries of men," then went still further, declaring that adultery was an even greater sin in men than in women because "where the woman unhappily falls into sin, she does so from motives less impure and less ignoble than those which actuate the man." Either she is repulsed by the cruelty of her husband or animated by an attachment to another. With men, however, "just the reverse is the case; for there is the direct action of sensual desires that causes him to offend." Indeed, the law, rather than buttressing the husband's authority over the wife, ought to do the opposite, because "by arming her with the right of divorce, you would greatly increase her power over him, and you would deter him from the commission of offenses which among husbands are infinitely more common than among wives."[10] Hence, opponents and proponents alike regarded the Divorce Act as an instrument to control illicit sexuality. But they disagreed over which spouse should have the authority to exercise that control, and over the end toward which such control should be directed.

Again and again, opponents of the bill stressed the self

interested nature of the bill's provision for unequal grounds. Lord Lynhurst thought that such a legally sanctioned distinction between the sexes lent force to "the trite, but not altogether unjust observation, that men made the laws and women were the victims." Gladstone commented, "It appears to me that a measure so framed is not so much designed in the spirit of preventing a particular sin as by way of the assertion—I must add the ungenerous assertion—of the superiority of our position in creation." More stridently, Drummond accused lawmakers of being "very much in the situation of Turks legislating for the inhabitants of the seraglio" and added that power "had its duties as well as its rights." Another critic "unfeignedly pronounced this to be a most cowardly Bill: for if he was capable of interpreting the fundamental principles of the English law, it was directed to protect the weak against the strong, while this Bill refused to give the redress to the weak which it gave to the strong." One speaker complained that he "did not understand how, consistently with the principle of common sense, the legislature could refuse to the wife the remedy granted to the husband, the Bill, however, was intended only for the husband."[11] But appeals to a sense of fair play made no more headway than had arguments based upon a presumption of women' s moral superiority. The bill passed into law with its restrictive provisions intact.

The view of women advanced by the defenders of equal grounds conjured up the familiar figure of the "angel in the house," whose power rested upon her exemplifying with long-suffering patience a higher moral standard of sexuality than that adhered to by men. Nonetheless, during the debates on divorce, this image was counterposed to a darker vision of women. Defenders of legal equality presented a case that presumed a profound difference between male and female sexuality. To those who favored unequal grounds, however, the uncontrolled sexuality of women threatened to disrupt the property relations that secured the Victorian family, at least among the well-to-do. Those who defended the double standard based their argument not on differences in the innate sexuality of male and female, but on differences in the social impact (the introduction of "spurious offspring" into the family circle)[12] of the unbridled sexuality of women as opposed to that of men. Both views of women could coexist within the realm of Victorian imagination and myth, but the realities of the political arena necessitated a choice between them in 1857. Then, most members of Parliament preferred to rely on their own resources to protect the interests of men and husbands rather than leave themselves vulnerable to the restraint and mercy of wives.[13] In so doing, they framed legislation which in turn provided an institutional apparatus that constrained and directed the ways in which private conflicts between husbands and wives could be publicly recognized, acted out, and resolved.

The new divorce procedure implemented by the 1857 Divorce Act certainly broadened access to divorce, which had previously been restricted to those who had the resources to finance a private act of Parliament.[14] The limitations of the act, however, led contemporary observers as well as later scholars to assume that divorce would continue to be a privilege of the middle and upper classes. As one commentator noted soon after the passage of the act, "There are two ways of withholding divorce from the poor. One is to say so in words: another is to erect an unapproachable tribunal."[15] O. R. McGregor, in his centenary study of English divorce, described the years up until 1910 as the "period when working-class people, were, in practice, denied access to the divorce court."[16] Although this view is a reasonable surmise, a social profile of those who patronized the Divorce Court shows it to be inaccurate.

The small annual number of divorce decrees up until World War I testifies to the success of those who intended to limit the availability of divorce. Nevertheless, an examination of the actual demand for divorce during the first decade of the Divorce Act's operation reveals that both wives and ordinary working families managed to bring their cases to the court despite the obstacles.

The analysis below, based on a one-in-ten systematic sample[17] of petitions filed before the Divorce Court from 1858 through 1868, first delineates the social profile of litigating couples. It then considers the impact of the location of the court in London on the ability of wives and working-class families to bring marital suits to the court. This approach shows how the systems of representation articulated in parliamentary debate that informed the law in turn framed the social dynamics of the marital conflict weighed by the Divorce Court. The investigation also reveals that the aura of scandal attaching to divorce, which made the subject endlessly fascinating to newspaper readers, in fact misrepresented the mundane reality of marital breakdown in Victorian society. Titillating stories about the loose morals of aristocrats and bohemians did not dominate the Victorian Divorce Court to the same extent that they engaged the Victorian imagination. These analytical steps thus uncover the complex of transformations linking processes of representation and their instantiation in social relations.

A one-in-ten systematic sample of the divorce petitions housed in the Public Records Office produced 338 cases.[18] Although the documentation of each case often consisted of no more than the petition itself and the court minutes, these detailed the particulars of the marriage (duration, number of children) and the suit. Out of the 338 cases, 134 included a copy of the marriage certificate, which named not only the occupation of the husband but those of the husband's father and the wife's father. In addition, the place and date of the celebration of marriage and the current residence of the couple were standard features of the petition.

Who, then, actually took advantage of the newly created court? Not surprisingly, among the sample, the gentry, professionals, and prosperous businessmen filed a substantial proportion of the cases. Twenty litigants were identified only as gentlemen; there were twelve military officers. The professionals included seven solicitors and one barrister, six engineers, two physicians and six surgeons, and four clergymen. Grouped together, this social category totaled sixty-four of the sample cases, or 18.93 percent of the whole. Lower-level white-collar occupations, such as secretary and interpreter, represented an additional 2.9 percent of the sample. Substantial businessmen (planters, manufacturers, merchants, managers) accounted for another thirty-four, or 10.05 percent of the sample. Taken together, these occupational groups represented 31 percent of the cases, which, although a major segment of the sample, does not amount to as large a proportion of the whole as one might expect, given the restrictiveness of the divorce procedure.

The lower-middle class, mainly consisting of clerks (ten) and the proprietors of small businesses (forty-six), accounted for 18 percent of the sample. Working-class families represented a further 23 percent of the total. The shopkeepers included five grocers, four butchers, two tobacconists, two confectioners, and a stationer. Those who did manual labor numbered eleven servants, six laborers, three shoemakers, three compositors, two carpenters, two cabinetmakers, and two soldiers. The more arcane of artisan specialties represented were a piano-key maker, an umbrella maker, a birdcage maker, and a hornbutton presser. Litigants who earned their livelihoods from the sea formed a larger group, including eight mariners, three sailors, three coastguardsmen, two watermen, and a fisherman. Finally, the "other" category consisted of five farmers, four artists, and two comedians.

In eighty-two (24 percent) of the sample cases, the court records did not explicitly identify occupation. Despite this lacuna, however, two different techniques can be utilized to define the upper and lower limits of each social category. One approach makes the assumption that the occupations of those litigants whose occupations went unrecorded follow the same pattern as those whose occupations we do know. Such an assumption does not require a monumental leap of faith. If the reason for the lack of information has no relation to the information itself—that is, if no particular occupation or group of occupations has any greater likelihood of being recorded or overlooked than any other—then this method would in fact provide us with a reliable estimate. Following such a procedure increases the proportionate size of each category. The upper-middle class increases from 31 to 42 percent, the lower-middle class from 18 to 22 percent, and the working class from 23 to 31 percent.

Alternatively, one could judge that the cases with missing information might more properly be placed in a single category rather than distributed among all of them. Many petitions that do not specify the husband's occupation do contain internal evidence indicating that the family likely enjoyed an affluence marking them as upper class or upper-middle class.[19] Adding all the missing cases to that social group results in a somewhat different redistribution of percentages. This alternative increases the percentage of the upper-middle class category to 56 percent and leaves the proportions of the other categories unchanged.

These techniques thus provide us with a guide to the social parameters of the litigants who brought their cases to the Divorce Court. The upper-middle class naturally formed the largest group (41 to 56 percent) and was, of course, the court's intended clientele. The most striking aspect of the profile, however, is the unexpectedly high proportion (23 to 30 percent) of working-class families taking advantage of the court. Certainly, the legislators did not expect this to happen. The English system of law made few concessions to the poor during the nineteenth century. Litigants without sufficient means could perhaps qualify for the cumbersome and stingy *in forma pauperis* procedure, which provided only the remission of court fees to those who owned property worth less than twenty-five pounds.[20] In fact, few took advantage of this option; only five cases among the sample were carried out with the aid of *in forma pauperis*.

Perhaps working-class couples availed themselves of the simpler procedures available at the court, such as protection orders or judicial separations, rather than the more complex and expensive divorce procedure? Considering only divorce petitions decreases the proportion of missing cases from 24 to 16 percent, while increasing the proportion of working-class petitions to more than 30 percent (see graph). The upper-middle class stands alone at 34 percent, or at 52 percent when combined with the missing cases. Distributing the missing cases as discussed above increases the working-class share of the cases to 35.74 percent and the upper-middle class share to 39.14 percent.

Turning now from overall statistics to an examination of individual cases, we can judge how well the act carried out the framers' intent. In light of restrictions on access to the court, it had seemed inevitable that English divorce would remain the monopoly of the affluent, broadly defined. The domestic conflict that led Major John Wilton to petition for

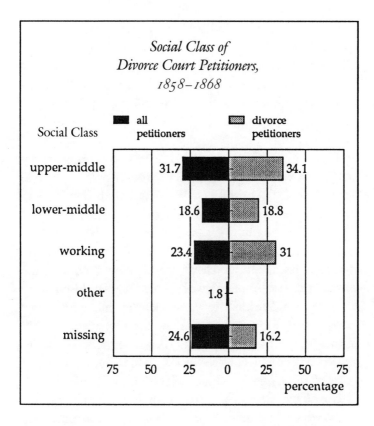

Social Class of Divorce Court Petitioners, 1858–1868

Social Class	all petitioners	divorce petitioners
upper-middle	31.7	34.1
lower-middle	18.6	18.8
working	23.4	31
other	1.8	
missing	24.6	16.2

75 50 25 0 25 50 75

percentage

divorce in February 1859 neatly exemplifies the kind of impasse that lawmakers expected the Divorce Court to resolve. Wilton, after a career in the Indian Army, had retired from the Thirty-sixth Regiment of the Madras Native Infantry. In 1833, while on active service in India, he married Emily Pilkington. The two lived together at various military stations in India as well as in London. The Wiltons had two children, although Major Wilton questioned the paternity of the younger. Wilton's petition accused his wife of committing adultery and bearing an illegitimate child sometime during 1844 and 1845, when she was living in London while he remained at his post in India. Upon his return to London in 1848, Wilton discovered his wife's transgressions and had lived separately from her ever since. Although Major Wilton did not pursue his suit after the court agreed to hear it, his grievance embodied the fear of "spurious offspring" articulated by the parliamentary debates over the 1857 Divorce Act.[21]

The case of William Pettit Dawes also conforms to contemporary expectations about the sort of people who would form the court's constituency. Dawes, described in his petition as a gentleman and a solicitor, had married Annie Mundy, the daughter of a clerk of customs, in 1849. They had lived in London, in Leicester, and after 1855 in Derby. They had four children. Despite these outward signs of domestic success, Annie Dawes formed a relationship with another man. With her lover, she left her husband's home on 9 May 1861, two days after he filed for divorce. With such a straightforward and easily demonstrable case, Dawes obtained his divorce decree in a year. In addition, the court costs of £104.18.2 were billed to the corespondent.[22]

Nonetheless, the quantitative analysis above indicates that in practice many persons in much humbler circumstances also managed to bring their marital grievances before the court, a premise borne out by details of specific cases. For example, William Hunt, a greengrocer from Croydon, filed a petition for divorce in 1862. Hunt, the son of a coachman, had married Sarah Fisher, the daughter of a shoemaker, ten years before. They had spent a decade of married life in Croydon and Lambeth and had six children, three of whom were still living when Mrs. Hunt eloped with another man in January 1862. Mrs. Hunt and her lover defended themselves against Hunt's allegations by accusing him of adultery and cruelty. They charged that he had struck his wife during one of her pregnancies and had also infected her with venereal disease. A jury subsequently found both husband and wife guilty of adultery and accordingly dismissed the petition. Since neither spouse could claim to be an innocent party, the law dictated that neither person was entitled to the relief from the marital bond that divorce provided.[23]

The same year Hunt sued for divorce, John Holmes, an umbrella maker from Bethnal Green, found himself in a similar situation. Holmes, however, had better luck with the outcome of his suit. The son of a weaver, Holmes wed Mary Ann Woobridge, the daughter of a painter, in 1850. They had spent their entire married life in London and had four children. In September 1862 Mrs. Holmes ran away with Samuel Yeats; Holmes filed for divorce in May 1863. The court granted Holmes his divorce and assessed Yeats for court costs totaling £53.0.11.[24] George Hook Page, a whitesmith from King's Lynn, also obtained a divorce from his adulterous wife; the jury assessed the corespondent £100 in damages.[25] Similarly, Timothy Pell, a gardener in Hertfordshire, obtained a divorce in 1866 from his wife of twenty years after she set up a new household with George Borer, a woodman, in 1864.[26]

Such cases, although numerous, generally escaped the notice of both contemporary and subsequent observers. Sir John Bigham, one of the Divorce Court judges, suggested one plausible explanation for this oversight in his 1910 testimony before the Royal Commission on Divorce and Matrimonial Causes: "The popular view . . . is that the Divorce Courts are busy with the affairs of the rich. . . . The newspapers report those cases, and the public form their impressions from what they see in the newspapers. It is a mistake. The poor and the very poor resort to the court and in large numbers."[27]

Statistical evidence assembled for the Royal Commission corroborates Bigham's opinion by showing that working-class litigants accounted for 28.87 percent of divorce cases in 1907 and 26.33 percent of divorce cases in 1908.[28] According to Griselda Rowntree and Norman Carrier's analysis of 1871 divorce petitions, between 41.4 and 53.6 percent were brought by the gentry and between 16.8 and 21 percent by the working class.[29] These figures tend to corroborate what a perusal of the divorce files establishes.[30] Shopkeepers, skilled artisans, and even laborers constituted an important presence among those families who took their broken marriages to the Divorce Court to seek redress.

Wives, like the working class, proved more successful in bringing their cases before the Divorce Court than might be expected, given the legal disadvantages under which they labored. Wives initiated 40 percent of divorce petitions and 92 percent of judicial separation proceedings filed before the Divorce Court from 1858 through 1868. Once a wife managed to get her case to court, she apparently did not suffer any significant liabilities in pressing it to a successful conclusion. In divorce cases, 38 wives enjoyed a success rate virtually identical to that of husbands (68 and 68.42 percent, respectively). In separation cases, wives actually achieved a success rate superior to that of husbands, 36.76 percent compared with 30.18 percent. The Divorce Court dismissed proportionately fewer wives' cases than husbands' cases (6.89 percent as opposed to 9.7 percent in divorce cases, and 13.47 percent as opposed to 24.52 percent in separation cases). On the other hand, a wife's case had a somewhat greater likelihood of lapsing than a husband's case—25.1 percent as opposed to 21.87 percent in divorce actions, and 49.76 percent as opposed to 45.87 percent in separation cases, most likely reflecting the greater difficulty wives had in accumulating the resources to take their cases to court.

The willingness of wives to bring their marital grievances before the court must have proved shocking both to those who claimed that familial sentiment would restrain women and those who believed that the law should protect erring husbands from litigious wives.[31] When all the different types of petitions heard by the court are considered, not just divorces, wives formed a bare majority of petitioners. And they monopolized some kinds of marital proceedings, such as protection orders and judicial separations.

Protection orders, which prevented husbands from seizing any property a wife acquired for herself after her husband's desertion, largely served lower-middle-class women. The 1865 case of Hannah Castle is typical. She had married Thomas Castle in 1844. Due to his weakness for drink, her husband had proved unable to support his family. First, his grocery failed after only two years; then, seven years later, he lost his position at the Post Office. In 1855 Mrs. Castle's mother rented a house and furnished it so that the family could generate an income by taking in roomers. Castle, however, sold all the furniture to get money to buy drink and then deserted. Mrs. Castle testified that she had not heard from her husband since 1856. After his desertion, she took her children to live with her mother and went to work as a housekeeper. After five years of working and saving, Mrs. Castle took a house and furnished it so she could support her reunited family by renting furnished apartments to single men. On this basis, Mrs. Castle asked the court to grant her protection for property valued at £65 and her accumulated savings of £45. The court duly issued a protection order, as it did in most such cases.[32]

Judicial separations, although not the legal remedy of choice for those who wished to free themselves from a spouse, offered wives two advantages. First, judicial separations enabled women who could not demonstrate the combination of marital offenses required by law for a divorce to set up independent households. In addition, separations generally cost less than divorce actions.

The Divorce Act did not recognize acts of cruelty alone as sufficient grounds for a divorce, but cruelty could justify a separation. In 1864 Elizabeth Fielder petitioned for a separation after seventeen years of marriage. She alleged that her husband, a retired shipmaster, had beaten her on numerous occasions. The court decreed the separation and granted her permanent alimony of £1 a week. The court costs for her case totaled only £22.18.4.[33] Charlotte Boot's husband had committed adultery but had not been cruel and had not deserted her. As she explained in her 1866 petition, she had married Richard Webster Boot, a clergyman, in 1859. In 1865 her husband carried on an extended affair with Eliza Brinton. A special jury found Boot guilty of adultery, and the judge decreed a separation. He also granted Mrs. Boot the custody of their three children (although he did allow her husband to have access to them) and ordered the husband to pay the court costs.[34]

Analyzing the cases by the gender as well as the class of the petitioner indicates that working-class wives had the greatest difficulty bringing their cases before the court. Such an analysis also reveals that information about the occupation of the husband was much more likely to be included in husbands' petitions than in those of wives. Of all petitions, only seven (4.43 percent) filed by husbands failed to indicate the husband's occupation. In contrast, seventy-five (41.66 percent) filed by wives lacked that information. Considering only divorce cases reveals a similar pattern; of those petitions filed by husbands, only five (3.57 percent) did not specify occupation, while thirty-two (33.68 percent) of wives' petitions did not. Of all missing cases, 91.46 percent involved wives' petitions; of divorce cases, 86.48 percent of the missing were wives' petitions. The sample cases unquestionably establish the social profile of those couples brought to the Divorce Court by the action of husbands. The much higher proportion of missing information among wives' petitions makes it more difficult to draw such conclusions about social identity with equal confidence.

The number of missing cases bulks so large among wives' petitions that the distribution of these cases by social class must seriously understate the true proportion of each social category. Upper- or middle-class husbands filed 39.24 percent of husbands' petitions. Distribution of the missing cases according to the proportion of known cases changes that figure very little, increasing it to 41.05 percent. On the other hand, the proportion of wives' petitions identifiable as upper class or middle class stands at only 26.66 percent. Distributing the missing cases among the social categories increases this percentage dramatically, to 45.71 percent. These proportions bracket the proportion of petitions filed by husbands of that class. Repeating this exercise for the lower-middle-class category produces the same bracketing. Considering the first two social class categories of divorce petitioners produces a similar result. This pattern suggests that the demand for divorce among middle- and lower-middle-class wives paralleled that of husbands, although fewer wives than husbands actually filed divorce petitions.

The working-class cases show a different pattern. Among husbands, working-class petitions represent 34.81 percent of all cases, or 38.57 percent of divorce cases brought by husbands. Distributing the missing cases changes these proportions to 36.42 and 40.00 percent, respectively. Turning to working-class wives, we find that far fewer managed to bring their cases to court; these women represent just 12.77 percent of all petitions and 17.89 percent of divorces. Distributing the missing cases increases these proportions to 21.9 and 26.98 percent, respectively, but they still remain far below those representing the petitions filed by working-class husbands. Although working-class families appeared before the Divorce Court in greater numbers than anyone expected or believed, husbands probably brought two-thirds of these cases.

Again, the narrative detail of actual cases strikingly fleshes out these statistical distinctions. The 1868 divorce petition of Eliza Jane Edwards shows that even the most respectable middle-class wives could be driven to the Divorce Court. She had married her husband, Joseph Charles Edwards, a clergyman, in 1855. They lived in Leicester, London, and Somerset; they had no children. Mrs. Edwards complained that her husband had been cruel to her by pushing and kicking her out of bed, by frequently talking about murder and suicide, and by pretending to cut her throat. He had also "frequently taunted her with being barren." In 1864 he deserted her and subsequently committed adultery with two different women. Reverend Edwards denied all these allegations, insisting instead that his wife, who apparently had far greater financial resources than he and paid him an annuity after they had agreed to a deed of separation, had been cruel to *him*. A special jury believed Mrs. Edwards's version of events, however, and she obtained a divorce in 1870.[35] The 1861 divorce case of Elizabeth Sarah Harriet Lander demonstrates that the working-class family had no monopoly on domestic violence. Elizabeth Lander had married Eaton

Lander, a surgeon, in 1844. At various times during the course of their married life, Mrs. Lander's husband had threatened her with a bottle of prussic acid, a razor, and a gun; he had struck her with an iron rod. She also claimed that he had committed adultery on more than one occasion. Mrs. Lander, like Mrs. Edwards, succeeded in obtaining a divorce.[36]

Lower-middle-class wives similarly managed to bring their cases to the Divorce Court. For instance, Ann Beecroft, the wife of a butcher from Durham, obtained a divorce in 1868. In her 1866 petition, Mrs. Beecroft, a butcher's daughter, explained that she had married Thomas Beecroft, the son of a grocer, in 1858. They had since then lived in Coshoe, Durham, and had one child. Mrs. Beecroft claimed that her husband had treated her with cruelty by striking her, taking money provided to her by her parents, and depriving her of food and money. In 1860 Beecroft had struck his wife "and turned her out of his house together with her child telling her to go home to her mother which [she] did." Thereafter, her father had provided for her support, and Beecroft had been living with another woman. The court found that this story furnished sufficient grounds for a divorce.[37] The petitions of Esther Levy, the wife of a London butcher, and Frances Robertson, the wife of a London confectioner, in 1864 and 1858 respectively, further illustrate the social range among wives filing for divorce.[38]

Working-class wives, having the fewest resources at their command, found it far more difficult to take advantage of the court's services. Nevertheless, some women overcame formidable obstacles to win a divorce. For example, Elizabeth Monk, the wife of a silkspinner from Huddersfield, York, filed for divorce in 1862. Mrs. Monk, the daughter of a laborer, had married her husband, Edwin Thomas Monk, in 1847. At the time of the suit, two of the couple's three children were still living. Mrs. Monk claimed that her husband had struck her and had committed adultery. The court granted her divorce in February 1863.[39]

The case of Charlotte Coleman, one of the few women who used the *in forma pauperis* procedure to obtain her 1866 divorce, represents an even more extreme situation. Mrs. Coleman had married Walter Cathrow Coleman, a cab proprietor, in 1858. They had since lived in Hackney, Middlesex, and were childless. Her petition tells a harrowing tale. Charlotte Coleman's husband frequently beat her, but when her brother got her separate lodgings for her protection, the husband dragged her home again. Coleman did not work to support his wife. Instead, he depended upon her earnings as a milliner and dressmaker. When Mrs. Coleman's health prevented her from working, "the said Walter Cathrow Coleman vehemently urged [her] to obtain money by prostitution, and threatened her with personal violence if she persisted in refusing to do so. He also argued . . . that other married women did the same thing and there was no harm in it." Mrs. Coleman, "reduced to a state of great bodily fear," succumbed to this pressure. In 1863 she "determined to give up prostitution" and again went to her brother for protection. Although her husband followed her, beat her, and brought her back, she still refused to work as a prostitute. Charlotte Coleman finally managed to escape her husband and, while living with her brother, sued for divorce in 1865. The court gave her case a sympathetic hearing, granting her a divorce in 1866 and billing costs of £35.5.0 to her husband. He did not pay them, however; thus the court subsequently pronounced him "contumacious," issuing a writ of attachment in July 1866.[40] Charlotte Coleman's suit illustrates both the lower limits of the social range served by the court and the severity of the social problems with which the court had to contend.

Situating the court in London undoubtedly limited the opportunity of those who resided outside the area to apply for relief of their marital grievances. Because petitions presented to the court had to specify the residence of the petitioner, it is possible to assess the geographical basis of the demand for the court's services. A majority of petitioners claimed residence in London or one of the home counties; the largest number (112) gave Middlesex addresses. The population of London and its contiguous counties, the home of a slightly smaller proportion of the total population (21.7 percent), provided just over one-half the litigants. Those who lived in Yorkshire and Lancashire, populous regions far removed from London, represented only 11 percent of the petitioners, even though 1861 census figures show that the combined population of these two counties constituted 22.23 percent of the population of England and Wales.[41]

Calculating regional rates of divorce illustrates the impact of geographical realities on divorce litigation. Using the divorce petitions from the sample and the population figures of England and Wales from the 1861 census to create an index of the divorce rate by region produces a rate of 0.1171 per 10,000 population for the country as a whole. In contrast, the divorce rate per 10,000 population was 0.3795 in London and the home counties and 0.0649 in Yorkshire and Lancashire.

The legal exigencies of shepherding litigation through the Divorce Court might, however, have inflated somewhat the number of litigants claiming residence in the London area. Those who could afford to do so might have taken houses for the duration of their suits. Yet of the 176 litigants who recorded London or one of the home counties as their residence, only 35 had been married outside the area. Of these, 7 clearly had their primary residences elsewhere (for example, army officers stationed in India, a merchant from Prussia). Removing all couples who had married outside the London area from the home counties category reduces its percentage from 52 to 41.71 percent, still twice its proportional share of the population of England and Wales at that time. Centralizing the court in London thus resulted in the significant understatement of demand for divorce among those living outside the area.

Nevertheless, the court in London had to service English citizens wherever they resided. Imperial responsibilities and international commerce may have drawn the English to every corner of the globe, but to disentangle their marital difficulties they had to bring their cases back to London for adjudication. The sample cases include twenty-five instances (7.39 percent) of couples identifying their residences as outside of England at the time either of their marriages or their suits. Those couples who lived in India during their marriages represented the largest group, with seven couples, followed by five couples from Ireland, three from Scotland, and two from Jamaica. Couples from South America, New Zealand, South Africa, China, Prussia, Germany, Sweden, and Italy each made a single appearance in the sample.

This group of petitioners, although it does not bulk large among the litigants patronizing the Divorce Court, underlines the way in which the court's London location worked to the disadvantage of wives. Only five such cases represented wives' petitions, and in three of these, the petitioner claimed residence in the British Isles—two in Ireland and one in Scotland.

The divorce action brought by Eleanor Sarah Leigh in the first year of the court's existence illustrates how foreign residence could handicap a wife. Mrs. Leigh married her husband, William, in Valparaiso, Chile, on 1 January 1852. She lived with him for only three weeks. According to her petition, on the day of their marriage her husband asked her to "receive" into their home Emily Courtois, a woman with whom William Leigh had previously formed an "improper and illicit connection." Mrs. Leigh refused. William Leigh promptly eloped with Emily, leaving his wife destitute. Mrs. Leigh remained in Valparaiso for over a year, but her husband did not return to her. Only the kindness of the English community there enabled her finally to go back to her home in Chester, where she lived, totally dependent upon her father.[42]

Geographical proximity thus enhanced the ability of wives to bring their cases to court. Wives represented almost 60 percent of all petitioners who claimed London or the home counties as a residence, but they represented less than one-half of the petitioners who had to travel to London from Yorkshire or Lancashire. Considering divorce petitions only reveals the same pattern, with wives accounting for 44 percent of London divorce petitions but only 35 percent of petitions from Yorkshire and Lancashire.

Looking at social class rather than gender underlines how geographical proximity also increased opportunity for those disadvantaged by class. Whether we consider all petitions or divorce petitions alone, the upper-middle class forms a smaller group among London litigants than the other regional categories. In contrast, they make up the largest group among those resident abroad. Shopkeepers represent a much larger proportion of litigants among London petitioners than among those from the north of England. The working class forms a larger proportion of litigants from the north of England and from London than those from the rest of the country or abroad. These patterns reflect two interacting factors. First and most obvious, distance from London posed a formidable obstacle to potential litigants of modest means. In addition, the regional variation in the occupational structure of England—the industrial economy of the north in contrast to the service economy of London—produced very different social profiles from which litigants were drawn.

The contrast between the social identities of those who sought divorces and the portrayal of the Divorce Court in the press, which Judge Bigham noted, reveals how far the Victorian image of divorce differed from its social reality. No aristocrats and only two baronets appear in the sample. The sample did include four artists and two comedians, 1.7 percent of the whole. In contrast, a sample of divorce cases reports printed by the *Times* of London shows that working-class cases were greatly underreported, and cases of theatrical figures were overrepresented. Working-class families constituted just 10 percent of the cases reported by the *Times;* about 8 percent came from the theater world.[43]

This analysis of the actual basis of the demand for divorce in the decade following the passage of the 1857 Divorce Act points to the restrictiveness of the statute, which served both to limit and disguise the real demand for divorce. The material constraints of geography, gender, and class worked together to shape the social identity of those who sought divorce. The total number of litigants remained small, reflecting the power of social pressures to deter even those with financial resources from taking advantage of the Divorce Court if they wished to do so. Among couples willing to litigate, however, wives did not display the restraint that the defenders of the equal grounds argument had expected of them. In addition, lower-middle-class and working-class families represented a large minority of petitioners despite the burdensome cost of litigation.

The demand for divorce in Victorian England, although latent—constrained by obstacles expressly built into the law for that purpose—nonetheless had a broad social base. Divorce may have been intended as a privilege of gender and class, but a close examination of actual cases shows that in practice, secular divorce could indeed become the ready weapon some had feared. The conflict between husband and wife as exposed to the public in the arena of the Divorce Court provided a material basis for the representation of that conflict in newspaper reports.

Nonetheless, the scandalous aura that surrounded Victorian divorce concurrently served to reinforce the obstacles deterring mismatched spouses from seeking relief from marital impasse. The distortion and misrepresentation of the social realities of marital conflict thus functioned to mitigate the potential threat that divorce posed to the gender and social orders. These transformations of meaning deployed divorce before the public as the weapon legislators had intended it to be, one that buttressed marital order as it stood.

Notes

1. U.K., *Hansard's Parliamentary Debates* (hereafter cited as *Hansard's*), 3d ser., vol. 142 (1856), 1981–82.

2. *Hansard's*, 3d ser., vol. 147 (1857), 885.

3. Discussions of the passage of the Divorce Act include Margaret K. Woodhouse, "The Marriage and Divorce Bill of 1857," *American Journal of Legal History* 3 (1959): 260–75; Mary Lyndon Shanley, " 'One Must Ride Behind': Married Women's Rights

and the Divorce Act of 1857," *Victorian Studies* 25 (Spring 1982): 355–76; Dorothy Stetson, *A Woman's Issue: The Politics of Family Law Reform in England* (Westport: Greenwood Press, 1982), 28–50; Lee Holcombe, *Wives and Property: Reform of the Married Women's Property Law in Nineteenth-Century England* (Toronto and Buffalo: University of Toronto Press, 1983), 88–110; and Allen Horstman, *Victorian Divorce* (New York: St. Martin's Press, 1985), 46–84. In addition, Keith Thomas, in his classic analysis, "The Double Standard," *Journal of the History of Ideas* 20 (Apr. 1959): 195–216, draws upon the divorce debates as an important source. Shanley and Mary Poovey have each placed their analyses of the divorce debates in a larger context. See Mary Lyndon Shanley, *Feminism, Marriage, and the Law in Victorian England, 1850–1895* (Princeton: Princeton University Press, 1989); and Mary Poovey, *Uneven Developments: The Ideological Work of Gender in Mid-Victorian England* (Chicago: University of Chicago Press, 1988). Lawrence Stone has recently provided an extremely lucid narrative of the passage of the 1857 Divorce Act in *Road to Divorce: England, 1530–1987* (Oxford: Oxford University Press, 1990), 368–82.

4. *Hansard's*, 3d ser., vol. 147 (1857), 408, 863, 1041. (In his novel, *Hard Times* (1854), Charles Dickens uses the predicament of Stephen Blackpool to underscore the injustice of denying the poor access to divorce.)

5. Ibid., 743, 1068; 1048; 1069, 1163; 749, 758; 1181.

6. Ibid., 1169; 1173.

7. *Hansard's*, 3d ser., vol. 145 (1857), 813; vol. 147 (1857), 864; 884–85.

8. *Hansard's*, 3d ser., vol. 145 (1857), 814; vol. 147 (1857), 1556, 2016.

9. *Hansard's*, 3d ser., vol. 147 (1857), 1047; vol. 145 (1857), 502; vol. 147 (1857), 1047.

10. *Hansard's*, 3d. ser., vol. 147 (1857), 1268, 840, 1274, 1275. Gladstone opposed all divorce but took the position that if divorce became legal there must be equal grounds for wives and husbands. He declared: "I will offer the utmost resistance to any

attempt to induce this House to adopt a measure which I believe would lead to the degradation of woman" (ibid., 393). Although Gladstone believed in the spiritual equality of men and women, which led him to champion the cause of women in this instance, he did not accept their political equality. See Ann P. Robson, "A Birds' Eye View of Gladstone," in *The Gladstonian Turn of Mind: Essays Presented to J. B. Conacher,* ed. Bruce L. Kinzer (Toronto: University of Toronto Press, 1985), 63–96.

11. *Hansard's,* 3d ser., vol. 145 (1857), 501; vol. 147 (1857), 1274, 1587, 1588, 1600, 889.

12. Ibid., 880.

13. See Walter E. Houghton, *The Victorian Frame of Mind, 1830–1870* (New Haven: Yale University Press, 1957), 342–93, for a classic discussion of the Victorian view of women, love, and sexuality. Houghton sees the "angel in the house" as the dominant motif. Nina Auerbach, in *Woman and the Demon: The Life of a Victorian Myth* (Cambridge: Harvard University Press, 1982), finds a fundamental, powerful (and empowering) unity in the contradictions of the Victorian vision of women. Judith R. Walkowitz, in "Male Vice and Feminist Virtue: Feminism and the Politics of Prostitution in Nineteenth-Century Britain," *History Workshop Journal* 13 (Spring 1983): 79–83, shows how the idea that women provided a moral standard to which men ought to adhere worked itself out in the political process.

14. On parliamentary divorce, see Sybil Wolfram, "Divorce in England, 1700–1857," *Oxford Journal of Legal Studies* 5 (1985): 155–86; and Stone, 301–46.

15. Quoted in C. Gibson, "The Effect of Legal Aid on Divorce in England, pt. 1: Before 1950," *Family Law* 1 (May/June 1971): 90.

16. O. R. McGregor, *Divorce in England* (London: Heinemann, 1957), 36.

17. I included every tenth file in the sample. This procedure approximates a random sample but is often more easily applied to historical documents than is a true random sample, which requires

the numbering of each case before the sample can be selected. See Charles M. Dollar and Richard J. Jensen, *Historian's Guide to Statistics: Quantitative Analysis and Historical Research* (New York: Holt, Rinehart and Winston, 1971), 12.

18. A comparison of the sample to the aggregate statistics on divorce indicates that the sample fairly represents the population of divorce suits. Of the 338 cases selected by the sampling procedure, 235 were divorce petitions and 63 were petitions for judicial separation. The remainder consisted of petitions for nullity, the restitution of conjugal rights, declarations of legitimacy, and protection orders. Divorce petitions filed from 1858 through 1868 totaled 2,435, and separation petitions came to 684. Wives filed 39.91 percent of all divorce and 92.25 percent of all separation petitions (U.K., *Parliamentary Papers*, 1889, vol. 61, "Return of the Number of Suits . . ."). These proportions closely match those found in the sample, where wives filed 40.42 percent of divorce petitions and 90.47 percent of separation petitions.

Family size provides another measure of the representativeness of the sample. The proportion of childless couples among the sample cases is nearly identical to that found by other investigators. In the sample, 38.7 percent of divorcing couples had no children, 44.4 percent had one to three children, and 18.9 percent had four or more children. A study of 1871 divorce cases showed that 38.2 percent of the couples had no children, 46.7 percent had one to three children, and 15.1 percent had four or more children. (See Griselda Rowntree and Norman Carrier, "The Resort to Divorce in England and Wales, 1858–1957," *Population Studies* 11–12 [March 1958]: 226). Statistics compiled for the 1912 Royal Commission on Divorce and Matrimonial Causes indicate that this remained a stable pattern throughout the nineteenth century. Between 1899 and 1909, the proportion of childless families among the divorced varied between 36 and 42 percent. (See *Parliamentary Papers*, 1912–1913, Royal Commission on Divorce and Matrimonial Causes, Report, Minutes of Evidence, appendix 3, table 15, 35.)

19. Rowntree and Carrier also make this observation about their study of 1871 divorce petitions (p. 222).

20. See John M. Maguire, "Poverty and Civil Litigation," *Harvard Law Review* 36 (Feb. 1923): 361–404, for a detailed discussion of *in forma pauperis*.

21. *Wilton v. Wilton*, 10 Feb. 1859, Public Records Office (hereafter cited as PRO), J77/58/W38.

22. *Dawes v. Dawes & Frampton*, 7 May 1861, PRO, J77/14/54.

23. *Hunt v. Hunt & Duke*, 10 Mar. 1862, PRO, J77/25/H127.

24. *Holmes v. Holmes & Yeats*, 30 May 1863, PRO, J77/26/H158.

25. *Page v. Page & Reynolds*, 24 Apr. 1863, PRO, J77/42/P91.

26. *Pell v. Pell & Borer*, 31 July 1865, PRO, J77/43/P125.

27. U.K., Royal Commission on Divorce and Matrimonial Causes, Minutes of Evidence (Cd. 6479), 71.

28. Royal Commission on Divorce and Matrimonial Causes, Report, Minutes of Evidence, appendix 3, table 15a, 35.

29. Rowntree and Carrier, 221–22. The ranges of the percentages represent the different options for distributing the missing cases discussed in the text. These are my calculations; Carrier and Rowntree simply record the proportion of missing cases in presenting their data.

30. Horstman, 98.

31. Ibid., 85–86.

32. *Hannah Castle*, 21 Mar. 1865, PRO, J77/12/C176.

33. *Fielder v. Fielder*, 16 July 1864, PRO, J77/19/F72.

34. *Boot v. Boot*, 29 Mar. 1866, PRO, J77/70/238.

35. *Edwards v. Edwards*, 8 Aug. 1868, PRO, J77/86/887.

36. *Lander v. Lander*, 24 July 1861, PRO, J77/33/L42.

37. *Beecroft v. Beecroft*, 25 Aug. 1866, PRO, J77/67/155.

38. *Levy v. Levy*, 19 May 1864, PRO, J77/34; *Robertson v. Robertson*, 22 Dec. 1858, PRO, J77/44 pt. 1/R37.

39. *Monk v. Monk*, 11 Nov. 1862, PRO, J77/36/M92.

40. *Coleman v. Coleman*, 13 June 1865, PRO, J77/12/C186.

41. Census figures taken from B. R. Mitchell, *European Historical Statistics, 1750–1975* (New York: Facts on File, 1980), 34, 81.

42. *Leigh v. Leigh,* 13 May 1858, PRO, J77/32/L12.

43. Gail L. Savage, "The Operation of the 1857 Divorce Act, 1860–1910: A Research Note," *Journal of Social History* 15 (Summer 1983): 103–10.

2 / Wrongful Confinement:
The Betrayal of Women
by Men, Medicine, and Law

Marilyn J. Kurata

THE threat of wrongful confinement obsessed nineteenth-century England, leading to periodic "lunacy panics." Public anxiety centered on two issues: the technical ease with which a person could be legally incarcerated and kept in a madhouse, and the arbitrary medical basis for diagnosing insanity. Such major feminist studies as Phyllis Chesler's *Women and Madness* (1972), Sandra Gilbert and Susan Gubar's *Madwoman in the Attic: The Woman Writer and the Nineteenth-Century Literary Imagination* (1979), and Elaine Showalter's *Female Malady: Women, Madness, and English Culture, 1830–1980* (1985) have necessarily focused on the madwoman in their documentation of the cultural correlations between femininity and insanity. But sane women could suffer as well. By examining the cases of two real and two fictional Victorian women whose certification as lunatics was clearly unjustified, we can see how men could deliberately invoke the masculine powers of Victorian medicine and law to disarm, discredit, and confine women who refused to suffer and be still.

The first case involves the wife of the novelist Edward Bulwer-Lytton and contributed to the lunacy panic of 1858–59. In 1827, when the then-Edward Bulwer married lively Rosina Wheeler against his mother's wishes, the young couple was forced to live solely upon her eighty pounds a year and on what he could earn as a writer. Rising to the challenge, Bulwer in the next ten years completed thirteen novels; four plays; four volumes of history; and miscellaneous fiction, prose, and poetry to finance their fashionable life in London. But the dual stresses of overwork and financial worries adversely affected the temperaments, health, and domestic happiness of husband and wife. Their letters record passionate accusations and recriminations—and equally passionate reconciliations. The most serious crisis between them began in 1833 over "the ostentatious philandering" of Bulwer and Mrs. Robert Stanhope. Rosina's expectation that her husband's proposed travels to Switzerland and Italy would lead to reconciliation was blighted when she discovered that Bulwer had arranged for Mrs. Stanhope and her complacent husband to meet them on the Channel Packet and tour Paris together. In retaliation, Rosina encouraged the attentions of a Neapolitan prince. Bulwer "flew into a passion, ill-treated his wife with the violence of a lunatic and insisted on an immediate return to England."[1] By 1836, the marriage had broken down so completely that a deed of judicial separation was signed, awarding Rosina custody of their two children and an income of four hundred pounds a year.

The separation, which had been initiated by Bulwer, simply launched a new era of hostility. Rosina attempted to gain public sympathy, revenge, and a supplemental income by writing a series of novels built around victimized, misunderstood women and brutal, profligate husbands. Bulwer retaliated by removing his children from her care, placing them with Mary Greene, "the one true friend of [Rosina's] unhappy girlhood, her confidante and champion in early married life, her only comforter at the time of her separation,"[2] and stipulating that the mother be denied access to them. In addition, he transferred to Greene one hundred pounds from Rosina's income to pay for the children's maintenance.

After Rosina moved to the Continent in 1840, warfare continued at long distance. When Bulwer succeeded to his mother's estate in 1844 on the condition that he add her surname to his own, he had his lawyer inform his estranged wife that she was not entitled to change her name also. Her own solicitor assured her of her legal right to her husband's new name as well as to an increased allowance, which the newly prosperous Bulwer-Lytton refused. Upon returning to England in 1847, therefore, Rosina devoted herself to embarrassing her husband into increasing her allowance. One of her most effective ploys was to address letters, as many as twenty a day, to her husband and his circle. Because the envelopes were covered with violent, obscene inscriptions and were sent to Bulwer-Lytton's clubs, friends' homes, the House of Commons (to which he had been elected), and his private residences, the letters were useful weapons in the connubial war. If he could withhold money and children, Rosina intended to inflict pain and embarrassment.

But Bulwer-Lytton could do more. Although English law made divorce impossible in this case because both partners possessed grounds for divorce, other laws offered means of controlling a recalcitrant wife. In late March 1858, Bulwer-Lytton asked several medical men if his wife's behavior since

their separation provided sufficient proof of insanity to justify placing her under restraint. At least six different physicians provided written opinions that Rosina was insane and
should be committed to an asylum, even though none of
them had examined her and were basing their diagnosis on a
hardly disinterested account of her behavior by a husband
who himself had not seen her in two decades.

The medical establishment's readiness to endorse Bulwer-
Lytton's opinion was a consequence of several factors. First,
as part of Victorian England's sweeping reforms in the treatment of lunatics, asylums had been transformed from prisons
for confining mad people into sanctuaries where sick people
could receive necessary and immediate care; thus, a humani-
tarian concern to ensure curative treatment as soon as possible encouraged physicians to issue certificates of insanity.
Second, the physicians' readiness to pronounce judgment on
mental conditions was backed by the common Victorian assumption that a clear-cut, easily identifiable difference existed
between the sane and the insane. Third, the petitioner was a
rich man, a baronet, a member of Parliament, and a popular
novelist. Finally, of course, the alleged lunatic was a woman.
As Elaine Showalter has demonstrated, "the prevailing view
among Victorian psychiatrists was that . . . women were
more vulnerable to insanity than men because the instability
of their reproductive systems interfered with their sexual,
emotional, and rational control."[3]

Bulwer-Lytton's conduct throughout this period indicates
that his primary concern was neither Rosina's mental condition nor her well-being. The "evidence" for insanity was an
account of Rosina's consistently hostile behavior since the
separation. There was no suggestion that Rosina had suddenly become deranged. Hence, if Rosina was mad, her
husband was guilty of gross irresponsibility toward both his

wife and society, having allowed a lunatic to run loose for years—a point Rosina made in her subsequent meeting with Hale Thomson, the man sent by Bulwer-Lytton to certify her as insane. If, on the other hand, Rosina was sane, the husband was guilty of much worse. This perception would become a rallying point of the newspapers that were instrumental in Rosina's obtaining her ultimate release from confinement.

Even the biography written by their grandson reveals that selfish reasons prompted Bulwer-Lytton's rash invocation of the lunacy laws:

> The knowledge that it was the sacrifices which he had made for her sake, the love which he had once felt for her which gave this woman the power to wound him so deeply; the realization that the chains by which, in defiance of his mother's warnings and advice, he had bound himself to her could never be loosed; that it was his money which she was paying to unscrupulous lawyers, obscure publishers, and newspaper editors for the purpose of defaming his character; that it was his name which she was dragging through the mire—all this was peculiarly bitter to a man of Bulwer-Lytton's temperament. . . . In these circumstances, and as much for the protection of his friends as of himself, Sir Edward began to make inquiries as to the powers which he might possess of placing his wife under restraint.[4]

Bulwer-Lytton is presented throughout this book as victim and sufferer, but the language in the above passage reveals more than merely where the sympathies of its author lie. The ubiquitous masculine possessive pronoun reflects the Victorian world view that man is central, woman peripheral. More particularly, in a world defined by his sacrifices, his love, his chains, his money, his character, his name, his protection, and his powers, Rosina (or any wife) was but another chattel of the man recognized by tradition and law as the family's sole arbiter. Divorce as a legal means for discarding an unwanted wife may have been blocked, but the law offered the husband an alternative.

Lytton states that his grandfather finally had Rosina certified as insane because her harassment became unendurable. But Bulwer-Lytton's inquiries into the lunacy laws coincided with the March 1858 formation of the new government under Lord Derby, the resignation of Lord Ellenborough, the appointment of Lord Stanley to Ellenborough's vacated seat, and Lord Derby's invitation to Bulwer-Lytton to succeed Stanley as secretary of state for the colonies.[5] Both the magnification of his political profile and the promise of greater advancement likely prompted Bulwer-Lytton to seek out a means of temporarily gagging and permanently discrediting his worst critic. As an article in the *Spectator* had pointed out, "A party detained on a charge of insanity may be acquitted and restored to liberty; but we all know that this is a question of such a nature that it cannot even be raised without attaching suspicion ever after to the individual to whom it relates."[6]

Before Bulwer-Lytton could act on the medical opinions he had solicited, however, he endured a mortifying encounter with the woman whose sanity he was challenging. Hearing of her husband's inquiries, Rosina decided to defy her enemy personally and publicly.[7] Bulwer-Lytton's appointment to the newly formed ministry necessitated an uncontested election at Hertford on 8 June; Rosina therefore had printed and posted placards inviting the electors to come hear her speak. On the day of the election, Rosina, outfitted in the colors of the opposite party, interrupted her husband's speech to his constituents. Bulwer-Lytton retired in complete confusion and humiliation, leaving the field to his heckling wife, who then accused him of every villainy and concluded, "How can the people of England submit to have such a man at the head of the Colonies, who ought to have been in the Colonies as a transport[ed felon] long ago?"[8] According to Rosina, her forthright denunciation of her husband was enthusiastically received, "the people waving their caps and handkerchiefs and crying, 'God bless you! God prosper you, brave noble woman! You'll defeat the wretch yet. He could never buy what you have won to-day.' "[9]

But Rosina's triumph was short-lived. Four days later, at Bulwer-Lytton's request, Hale Thomson, Dr. Woodford, and a keeper from the local madhouse called upon Lady Lytton. The object of the two medical men was to issue the two certificates of insanity legally necessary for a person's confinement as a lunatic. After a prolonged interview with Rosina, however, Thomson refused to issue such a certificate because he could not agree upon the alleged unsoundness of her mind. Later, however, he and another physician did provide the necessary certificates. When Rosina arrived by appointment at Thomson's house on 22 June, she was physically overpowered and taken to Inverness Lodge, Brentford, one of several private asylums operated by Dr. Robert Gardiner Hill. As the former possession of the Duke of Cumberland, Inverness Lodge boasted beautiful grounds and fine rooms; Hill was one of the first advocates of nonrestraint in the treatment of lunatics.

Nevertheless, Rosina was understandably more outraged at her wrongful confinement than pleased by the consideration her husband had shown her in his choice of asylum. Although Rosina had been guilty of unorthodox, unwise, even illegal behavior, the difference between derangement and her mental condition is reflected in the following recorded exchange between the head of the asylum and its latest inmate:

"Mr. Hill," said I, "I sent for you to *order* you to remove those two keepers from my room, for I am *not* mad, *as you very well know*, and I won't be driven mad by being treated as a maniac, and as for walking out with or associating with those poor creatures out there, if they really are insane, I'll *not* do it, if I am kept in your madhouse ten years."

"Madhouse! madhouse! Nonsense, Lady Lytton! This is no madhouse, and those are my children."

"Then you must be a perfect Danaus," said I, "for there are about forty of them."[10]

As Lady Lytton pointed out to the Commissioners in Lunacy who came to examine her during the second week of her detention, Dr. Hill's willingness to let his young daughter be her constant companion, even during solitary walks and rides, argued that he did not perceive her to be a dangerous lunatic. Nevertheless, Lady Lytton was not released until her friends were able to arouse a public outcry against her wrongful confinement. .

On 6 July 1858, a public meeting was called in Taunton, the town where Rosina had resided for the preceding three years. The meeting resulted in a set of resolutions expressing alarm at Lady Lytton's confinement and asking for justice to be done. This cry was taken up by the local press, especially the *Hertford Mercury* and the *Somerset County Gazette,* the latter proclaiming itself the injured lady's champion:

> There is, we say, a firm belief that Lady Lytton is the subject of a horrible and appalling injustice and wrong; that while perfectly sane she has been shut up in a lunatic asylum, merely in order that a woman who has, no doubt, been a constant source of annoyance to her husband may be prevented for ever [*sic*] from again giving him similar trouble, or again molesting him in any way. In ascribing to her the character we have given, we desire to avoid the indication of any opinion as to her conduct towards Sir Edward, or as to his general treatment of her. We only state a fact, that people among whom she has resided during a period of three years—to many of whom she is well and intimately known, and most of whom have had frequent opportunities of seeing

her—believe that though sent to an asylum for lunatics, her intellect is perfectly sound.[11]

The outcry in the press for a public enquiry spread to the London papers, most notably the *Daily Telegraph*, which severely criticized the new colonial secretary and, by association, the ministry that had appointed him. This response, coupled with written appeals by Rosina's solicitor to the Commissioners in Lunacy for her case to be tried before a judge and jury,[12] threatened the type of sensational scandal that could force Bulwer-Lytton's resignation and destroy faith in the new ministry. The wife wanted her release, her debts paid, and a larger income; the husband wanted to avoid a judicial investigation with all its attendant publicity and opportunity for Rosina's exhibitionism; Lord Derby wanted the press to stop its oblique attacks on his government. A compromise settlement began to be negotiated.

On 14 July the *Times* quietly announced, "We are requested to state upon the best authority that all matters in reference to [Lady Lytton], about whom certain statements have appeared in some of the public journals, are in process of being amicably settled by family arrangements to the satisfaction of all parties concerned."[13] Other newspapers were less easily reconciled to the apparent demise of what had promised to be a spectacular scandal. The *Daily Telegraph* continued to castigate Bulwer-Lytton even after Rosina was finally released on 17 July, three and a half weeks after she had been forcibly abducted. On 19 July, the *Times* published a letter from Rosina's son, who claimed that "the statements which have appeared in some of the public journals are exaggerated and distorted, and . . . they are calculated to convey to the public mind impressions the most erroneous and unjust." Robert Lytton insisted that his father had been motivated throughout by the best and kindest concern for his mother, that "she was never for a moment taken to a lunatic asylum" but had been a guest in the private home of Dr. Hill, and that Rosina was, "at her own wish," to travel abroad immediately, accompanied by him and a female friend she had chosen. He then appended brief letters, which both approved Rosina's release and condoned the original confinement, from Dr. Forbes Winslow and Dr. John Conolly, two prominent physicians specializing in mental diseases. Robert's letter, with accompanying medical testimonials, appeared in the *Times* as well as the *Observer,* the *Daily Telegraph,* and the *British Medical Journal.* But questions raised by the case continued to agitate the public and contributed to the lunacy panic of 1858–59. As the *Daily Telegraph* stridently announced, many people confidently believed

> that the lunatic asylums of this country are frequently applied to the same uses as the Bastille, where the Man in the Iron Mask was immured for life and buried in secrecy because his pretensions were considered dangerous by claimants to estates and title, or perpetrators of unsearched crimes.
>
> But a social question of far more universal importance is connected with the deplorable disclosure in the case of Sir Bulwer Lytton. The baronet's wife may be released from the terrible captivity to which, by the practical confession of her persecutors, she never ought to have been for a moment consigned, and from which we have made no unsuccessful effort to deliver her; but what of humbler persons? What of the domestic victims in whose name no publicity is invoked?[14]

The phenomenal success in the following year of Wilkie Collins's novel, *The Woman in White,* was partly owing to Collins's exploitation of the horrifying questions raised by the *Daily Telegraph.* The novel centers on Walter Hartright's efforts to establish the rightful identity of Laura Fairlie Glyde, who has been declared dead. Actually, Laura has been the victim of a plot devised by her husband, Sir Percival Glyde, and his friend Count Fosco. Having discovered that Laura bears a remarkable physical resemblance to Anne Catherick, a young woman Glyde has had confined to a private asylum, they arrange for an exchange of identities between sane Laura and certified-as-insane Anne. When Anne dies, she is buried as Lady Glyde. Meanwhile, Laura's mental and physical health are so undermined by her experiences in the asylum that only Hartright and her half-sister, Marian Halcombe, believe in her true identity, which forces them to resort to illegal means to secure her release and maintain her freedom. As Barbara Fass Leavy has pointed out, *The Woman in White*, when examined in light of its historical background, "does not merely involve the substitution of a sane woman for a deranged one in a lunatic asylum, but rather the substitution of an obviously unjustifiably confined woman for another whose commitment is also questionable."[15] It was not accidental that the serialization of *The Woman in White* in 1859–60 coincided with the meetings of the special Parliamentary Select Committee appointed in response to the lunacy panic of 1858–59, for Collins was exploiting contemporary concern over the legal and medical abuses that could—and did—lead to such cases of wrongful confinement as that of Lady Lytton.

Although Anne Catherick is clearly feeble-minded, Collins suggests that her confinement as a lunatic is unjustified. When Hartright learns that the stranger he has befriended has escaped from an asylum, the question of Anne's mental condition is raised, not answered. Repeating the words he has overheard, "She has escaped from my Asylum," Hartright asserts:

> I cannot say with truth that the terrible inference which the words suggested flashed upon me like a new revelation. Some

of the strange questions put to me by the woman in white, after my ill-considered promise to leave her free to act as she pleased, had suggested the conclusion, either that she was naturally flighty and unsettled, or that some recent shock of terror had disturbed the balance of her faculties. But the idea of absolute insanity which we all associate with the very name of an Asylum, had, I can honestly declare, never occurred to me, in connexion with her. I had seen nothing, in her language or her actions, to justify it at the time; and, even with the new light thrown on her by the words which the stranger had addressed to the policeman, I could see nothing to justify it now.

What had I done? Assisted the victim of the most horrible of all false imprisonments to escape; or cast loose on the wide world of London an unfortunate creature whose actions it was my duty and every man's duty, mercifully to control?[16]

Everything Hartright learns about Anne underscores the rightness of his first instinctive feeling that neither her language nor her actions justify her confinement. First, Hartright discovers that eleven or twelve years earlier, Anne had been befriended by Laura's mother, who arranged to have her examined by a physician when she discovered that Anne's scholarly accomplishments and aptitude were inferior for her age. The physician's opinion that Anne would "grow out of it" indicated no cause for alarm. Or, as Mrs. Fairlie assured her husband, "you must not imagine, in your offhand way, that I have been attaching myself to an idiot" (49–50). Although the years have proven the medical diagnosis wrong—Anne has not developed mental powers appropriate to her years—Mrs. Clements, the elderly friend who shelters Anne after she escapes from the asylum, similarly considers her mental infirmity a cause for sympathetic concern, not confinement. Although she admits that Anne was "always queer, with her whims and her ways," she simultaneously maintains her to be "as harmless, poor soul, as a little child" (82). Anne's fancy for dressing in white excites "a certain amount of sympathy" (496) from the people of Welmingham who, quick to jump upon a neighbor's transgression, would hardly have allowed their despised neighbor Mrs. Catherick to keep a lunatic in their midst.

Thus Anne's certification as a lunatic and her subsequent confinement to a mental institution are neither demanded by society nor rendered necessary by her mental condition. She lives in uncriticized freedom until she awakens the anger of Sir Percival Glyde, who comes to visit her mother. Glyde orders Anne to leave the room. Anne not only refuses to obey but also challenges his reiterated order to leave by threatening to reveal his secret. Mistakenly convinced that Anne knows of his bastardy, Glyde insists "on securing his own safety by shutting her up" (497) in an asylum. Anne's unwomanly defiance of male authority is punished with incarceration.

Although Fosco and Glyde execute their Machiavellian plot against Laura Fairlie for financial gain, Laura's placement in an asylum as a lunatic is prompted by a comparable unwomanly defiance of Glyde's will. To relieve his most pressing debts, Glyde desires a loan from her private fortune, which is being held in trust for her unborn children. To secure this loan, he needs her signature. When she asks what document she is being commanded to sign, Glyde scoffs at any woman's ability to understand business. Laura's response that the family solicitor always explained things to her evokes the sneer, "I dare say he did. He was your servant, and was obliged to explain. I am your husband, and am *not* obliged." When Laura still refuses to sign a document she has not read, he exclaims, "A wife [cannot be] right in distrusting her husband!" and "it is not part of a woman's duty to set her husband at defiance" (221, 223).

Superficially, Laura's defiance of her husband is based on

moral scruples. She has assured her half-sister, Marian Halcombe, that she will do nothing unknowingly that might expose herself to future shame, and she already has reason to doubt the honor of her husband. In the middle of the confrontation with him, however, Laura expresses her willingness to sign the unread document if *Marian* tells her to, an act that transforms the nature of her rebellion from ethical to domestic. The central crisis precipitating Laura's wrongful confinement revolves around her refusal to act like a proper English wife, "a civil, silent, unobtrusive woman" (195) like the totally repressed Madame Fosco. This explains the seemingly unnecessary scene that immediately precedes the one in which Laura refuses to obey her husband. Glyde has asked Marian to replace Madame Fosco as one of the two required witnesses to Laura's signature. Although Glyde explains that the law of England allows husband and wife to act as separate witnesses, the count sends his wife out of the room, insisting, "we have but one opinion between us, and that opinion is mine" (219). As well as being legally irrelevant, the count's scruple is literally irrelevant because Laura refuses to sign the document anyway. By introducing this paraphrase of the popular saying, "In law husband and wife are one person, and the husband is that person,"[17] Collins renders the scene ambiguously for his Victorian audience. On the one hand, we have a high-minded heroine thwarting a despicable villain. On the other, we have an undutiful wife defying the expectations of a paternalistic social and legal system.

At the end of his famous confession, the count asks, "What is the secret of Madame Fosco's unhesitating devotion of herself to the fulfilment of my boldest wishes, to the furtherance of my deepest plans?" and then responds, "I ask if a woman's marriage-obligations, in [England], provide for her private opinion of her husband's principles? No! They charge her unreservedly, to love, honour, and obey him" (570). Fosco's definition of the married Englishwoman's conjugal duties underscores Laura's failure to feel, think, and act as a wife should. Personal allegiance, not money, is at the heart of Laura's resistance and Glyde's violence. Subconsciously, she has never accepted him as her husband, a fact that Marian had already discerned from the letters Laura wrote during her honeymoon.

> I cannot find that [Percival's] habits and opinions have changed and coloured hers in any single particular. The usual moral transformation which is insensibly wrought in a young, fresh, sensitive woman by her marriage, seems never to have taken place in Laura. She writes of her own thoughts and impressions, amid all the wonders she has seen, exactly as she might have written to some one else, if I had been travelling with her instead of her husband. I see no betrayal anywhere, of sympathy of any kind existing between them. . . . In other words, it is always Laura Fairlie who has been writing to me for the last six months, and never Lady Glyde. (180–81)

Ironically, Laura is *not* Lady Glyde, because her husband's claim to the title is fraudulent. But fraudulent misrepresentations of birth, social position, and fortune were not recognized by English law as grounds for vitiating a marriage contract. Thus Laura *is* Percival's wife and he expects her to behave accordingly.

When Laura, like Rosina Bulwer-Lytton, flagrantly defies her husband, Glyde can justify his subsequent actions; her behavior vindicates the prompt institutionalization recommended by Dr. John Conolly for "young women of ungovernable temper, subject, in fact, to paroxysms of real insanity; and at other times sullen, wayward, malicious, defying all domestic control; or who want that restraint over the passions without which the female character is lost" (9–10). This diagnosis explains the significance of Glyde's final taunt to his wife when she refuses to sign the document: "It is rather late in the day for you to be scrupulous. I should have thought you had got over all weakness of that sort, when you made a virtue of necessity by marrying *me*" (223). As Laura later explains to Marian, the oblique accusation is that Laura and Walter Hartright had been lovers in every sense of the word before she married Glyde. It is easy to overlook the fact that Laura is later confined in an asylum not because everyone thinks she is Anne Catherick but because she can be, and has been, certified as insane. The two medical men whom Fosco introduced to her separately in London and who "startled and confused her by some odd questions about herself" (392) provide the two certificates of lunacy required by law for any person to be placed under restraint. New certificates would not be necessary to return Anne Catherick, a previously certified lunatic, to her asylum. Although Laura's wrongful confinement occurs simultaneously with a criminal exchange of identities, her incarceration is legally and medically valid, independent of true or false identities. Of course, certification as a lunatic discredits whatever Laura says, and—this is the point made by the *Daily Telegraph*—her transformation from baronet's wife to humble commoner further reduces her chances of redress.

How much Collins's novel may have been affected by the Bulwer-Lytton scandal is uncertain,[18] but such influence would explain the novel's emphasis on Percival's exact claim to his title—"Knight, or Baronet?" questions Hartright (65). The mechanics of Collins's plot would be served with a villain of either rank. Is it merely fortuitous, therefore, that both Glyde and Bulwer-Lytton are baronets, when one speculates on the probability of Collins's familiarity with the widespread coverage given to the real-life baronet's committal of his unwanted wife? In particular, the *Daily Telegraph*'s equation of Rosina's wrongful confinement with the Man in the Iron Mask's imprisonment in the Bastille by "claimants to estates and title, or perpetrators of unsearched crimes" may have suggested the pivotal element in Collins's sensational plot, because the Man in the Iron Mask was popularly believed to be the secret twin of the king of France. Moreover, Collins's villain bases his false claim to estate and title on the crime of forgery. There is also a sly familiarity in Mrs. Catherick's boast that her daughter was placed in a "Private Establishment, of the sort which my genteel neighbours would choose for afflicted relatives of their own," and was "treated (as I took care to mention in the town) on the footing of a Lady" (498). What lends credence to the probability of Collins's familiarity with and subsequent adaptation of the Bulwer-Lytton scandal is that Collins was researching asylum conditions during the summer of 1858, the time of Rosina's wrongful confinement, for his play *The Red Vial*. (Bulwer-Lytton himself hated *The Woman in White* and denounced it as trash to mutual friends.)[19]

Later in the century, publicity pilloried another husband who, "tired of a wife of strong will and definite purpose who renders his life uneasy, determines to get rid of the bother by putting her into an asylum."[20] Like Edward and Rosina's, Harry Weldon's wedding to Georgina Treherne in 1860 occurred despite bitter parental opposition. In this case, however, the bride's father rather than the groom's mother cut off financial support and quit speaking to the errant couple upon news of their secret union. The resulting burden of providing the means for the London season, foreign trips, and niceties of life necessary to a fashionable society couple devolved upon the resourceful wife, who kept meticulous account books, courted generous friends, and repaid country-house hospitality by lending her considerable musical talents to amateur entertainments.[21]

The death of Harry's grandmother relieved their greatest financial worries, but continued disagreements about money, fidelity, and Georgina's admitted unconventionality resulted in their eventually leading separate lives. As Windsor Herald, Harry continued to enjoy the mildly hedonistic lifestyle of a man accepted into the best social circles. Georgina pursued a more original course, collecting stray children from the streets to establish an orphanage, setting herself up as a music teacher and singer, and writing for the *Spiritualist*. Georgina became professionally and personally involved with Charles François Gounod, the French composer, and in her usual forthright, careless manner laid herself open to charges of infidelity, although it is unlikely that she was ever anything more than indiscreet. As her only biographer convincingly argues on the basis of her diaries, Georgina was "one of those women whose emotions are much more passionate than their actions."[22] Harry himself pursued more serious extramarital attachments; as in the Bulwer-Lytton case, divorce proceedings were thus impossible. Finally in 1875, they agreed to separate, Georgina retaining the use of their London house and an income of a thousand pounds per year.

The next three years witnessed Georgina's continued involvement with orphans, musical education, and psychical research. Unfortunately, she also first befriended and then became intimate friends with a questionable Belgian couple, Anacharsis and Angele Menier, and invited them to live with her. They soon made themselves indispensable in her schemes to set up and fund an orphanage devoted to teaching children to sing according to the Weldon Closed-Mouth

Method. The events of the next publicity-filled years are too complicated to recount here, but they resulted in Anacharsis and Georgina falling out and in Menier retaliating with vicious gossip, including rumors that Georgina murdered her orphans for a thousand pounds apiece.[23] Eventually, Harry found his unconventional wife such an embarrassment that he decided to commit her to a private asylum run by Dr. Forbes Winslow.

On 14 April 1878, Winslow and his father-in-law, Dr. Winn, visited Georgina at home, introducing themselves as Shell and Stewart, gentlemen interested in spiritualism. After a cordial discussion of Georgina's psychic experiences and her work with orphans, the two men left. That evening another pair of medical men associated with Winslow's private asylum in Hammersmith invaded her house under the same false names. When Georgina pointed out that, being neither blind nor forgetful, she could *see* that they were not the men she had met earlier that day, the two men answered that because they came on behalf of Shell and Stewart, they had given their names. Nonetheless, Georgina good-naturedly engaged in another conversation on her psychic experiences with these suspicious strangers. Only later did the real oddity of her visitors strike her. By that time, the second pair of Shell and Stewart had, on the basis of their visit, signed the necessary certificates of lunacy. That night a man in Winslow's employment and two asylum nurses unsuccessfully attempted to enter Georgina's house. By the time they returned the next morning with the medical certificates and an order under the Lunacy Acts signed by Harry Weldon, Georgina had enlisted the support of Louisa Lowe, a prominent member of the Lunacy Law Reform Association. She barricaded herself behind locked doors and with the aid of loyal servants and Mrs. Lowe (herself a discharged mental patient who in

1872 had brought a wrongful confinement suit against the Commissioners in Lunacy) was able to persuade the neighborhood police to obstruct the asylum people long enough for her to escape. After spending one night with a friend, she spent the next within a few hundred yards of Winslow's asylum, making her escape from this dangerous neighborhood disguised as a Sister of Mercy.

Then, for perhaps the first and last time, Georgina acted prudently. She had herself examined by two physicians and pronounced sane before coming out of hiding and launching herself into a public career in lunacy reform. Knowing that publicity was the key to both her continued freedom and effective changes in the law, Georgina was determined not to lose the limelight. She published a series of books and pamphlets, including *The History of My Orphanage; or, The Outpourings of an Alleged Lunatic* and *How I Escaped the Mad Doctors,* which clearly emphasized that certification as a lunatic was the punishment her independent conduct had elicited from an angry spouse. She also advertised her grievances in the newspapers. She hired St. James's Hall to deliver a two-and-one-half-hour monologue on her personal experience with lunacy law abuse, to which she invited Forbes Winslow. (He declined.) She delivered popular lectures and sang at meetings of the Lunacy Law Reform Association. Georgina offered a series of widely advertised "intimate" entertainments at her home every Tuesday afternoon and Wednesday evening, at which she sang musical selections, recounted her dramatic escape from the asylum keepers, and collected financial and moral support for her crusade. Public feeling was so strongly in her favor that Forbes Winslow felt obliged to publish a defense of his conduct in a letter to the *British Medical Journal,* emphasizing the legality of his part in the attempt to commit Mrs. Weldon.

One of the most frightening aspects of what happened to Rosina, Anne, Laura, and Georgina is that their certification as lunatics and attempted incarceration in madhouses was sanctioned by law and medicine. In other words, the men who invoked the lunacy laws of England in order to effectually do away with sane women were able to act without fear of punishment because they were careful to observe the legal and medical formalities outlined by the Lunatics Act of 1845. They might lay themselves open to public disapproval, as in Bulwer-Lytton's case, but they were not subject to criminal charges. Sir Percival Glyde conveniently dies before his villainies are exposed, but had he lived, he could not have been charged with false incarceration—the letter of the law had been observed. The "sanctity" of a man's invocation of the lunacy laws was augmented when the alleged lunatic was a spouse, because generally neither a wife nor a certified lunatic could institute law proceedings in her own right and certainly not against her own husband.[24]

The Weldon case is particularly significant because later Georgina was able to turn the patriarchal forces of law and medicine upon the very men who had attempted to commit her. In 1882, Parliament passed the Married Women's Property Act, which allowed a married woman to file a civil action in her own right as a *feme sole*. This act and the statute of limitations made it possible for Georgina to seek legal redress for what had occurred in 1878. That redoubtable woman promptly filed multiple law suits against Harry Weldon; Sir Henry de Bathe, a family friend who had countersigned the order for removing Georgina to an asylum; Mr. Neal, Harry's solicitor; Drs. Winslow and Winn, the owners of the asylum to which Harry had committed her; and Drs. Semple and Rudderforth, the medical men who had signed the medical certificates of lunacy. De Bathe, for example, was charged with trespass, libel, slander, and assault; Dr. Winslow, as employer of the asylum staff who forced her to flee her home, was accused of libel, assault, wrongful arrest, false imprisonment, and trespass. Her master stroke, however, was against Harry, whom she successfully sued for restitution of conjugal rights.

The other actions achieved varying legal success, but they and Georgina kept the legal columns of the *Times* filled for months. The trials, retrials, and appeals became Georgina's most effective promotion for lunacy law reform, because repeated testimony illustrated with frightening clarity that the lunacy laws—and, consequently, physicians—promoted concern merely for the technical correctness of the certification process, rather than the establishment of the medical need for confining the person being certified as insane. Simultaneously, the arbitrary medical basis for diagnosing insanity was exposed. Among evidence offered by specialists in mental disorder as conclusive proof of Georgina's madness were her spiritualist activities, her pursuit of interests incompatible with her duties as a wife, and her belief that she, a woman, could make the Albert Hall a profitable establishment. The various physicians' definitions of insanity became so all-inclusive that one medical witness finally confided to the presiding judge, "All persons except your lordship are in a sense or to some extent unsound in mind."[25]

The laughter this comment evoked in the courtroom may have been tinged with apprehension, for Georgina, as Rosina and Wilkie Collins had done before her, made the public aware that no one was quite safe from the asylum. These real and fictional cases of wrongful confinement, however, signaled that the most vulnerable person was a woman who refused to submit to the authority and control vested in a husband by a patriarchal society. Rosina, Anne, Laura, and

Georgina were lucky to escape from what was seen as the worst of living hells by attracting sympathetic attention to their plight. Many were not so fortunate. As early as the 1700s, Daniel Defoe had charged that madhouses often served as receptacles for unwanted wives. New, and significantly more alarming, in the nineteenth century's abuse of the lunacy laws with respect to women was that the medical profession sanctioned it. Even worse, the powers of law and medicine could be—and were—invoked by vindictive men to permanently disable, disarm, and discredit sane, but rebellious, women.

Notes

1. Michael Sadleir, *Bulwer: A Panorama* (London: Constable, 1932), 169, 171. Contemporary biographies of Edward Bulwer-Lytton tend to gloss over the marriage or reproduce the "facts" of the two-volume biography written by his grandson, arguing that Rosina was mad and Edward much put upon. Rosina's biographer goes to the other extreme, presenting her as an innocent martyred by an arrogant, violent man. The most balanced account is that of Sadleir, who acknowledges that in their mutual maltreatment, both Edward and Rosina were guilty of the violence and irrationality of lunatics.

2. Victor Alexander Lytton, *The Life of Edward Bulwer, First Lord Lytton,* 2 vols. (London: Macmillan, 1913), 2:263.

3. Elaine Showalter, *The Female Malady: Women, Madness, and English Culture, 1830–1980* (New York: Pantheon, 1985), 55. Showalter argues that

> alongside the English malady, nineteenth-century psychiatry described a female malady. Even when both men and women had similar symptoms of mental disorder, psychiatry differentiated between an English malady, associated with

the intellectual and economic pressures on highly civilized men, and a female malady, associated with the sexuality and essential nature of women. Women were believed to be more vulnerable to insanity than men, to experience it in specifically feminine ways and to be differently affected by it in the conduct of their lives. . . . It was also at this time that the dialectic of reason and unreason took on specifically sexual meanings, and that the symbolic gender of the insane person shifted from male to female. (7–8)

4. Lytton, 2:267–69.

5. Ibid., 2:268–69.

6. Quoted in Peter McCandless, "Liberty and Lunacy: The Victorians and Wrongful Confinement," in *Madhouses, Mad-Doctors, and Madmen: The Social History of Psychiatry in the Victorian Era,* ed. Andrew Scull (Philadelphia: University of Pennsylvania Press, 1981), 342.

7. Louisa Devey, *Life of Rosina, Lady Lytton* (London: Swan Sonnenschein, Lowrey, 1887), 285, 292.

8. Quoted in Lytton, 2:270.

9. Quoted in Devey, 286.

10. Quoted in Devey, 299.

11. Quoted in Devey, 313.

12. Devey, 310–11. In the Minute Books of the Commissioners in Lunacy (Public Record Office, Kew), entries on 7, 9, and 14 July 1858 relate directly to this case. These entries indicate the repeated attempts by Rosina's solicitor to force a public inquiry into her case and the great concern of Bulwer-Lytton to be immediately informed of the commissioner's opinions as to his wife's mental state and any intended action on their part.

13. Quoted in Devey, 310–11.

14. Quoted in Devey, 320.

15. Barbara Fass Leavy, "Wilkie Collins's Cinderella: The History of Psychology and *The Woman in White,*" *Dickens Studies Annual* 10 (1982): 98.

16. Wilkie Collins, *The Woman in White* [1860] (Oxford: Oxford University Press, 1981), 22 (hereafter citations appear in parentheses in the text).

17. This saying was generally ascribed to the eighteenth-century jurist and Oxford professor of English law, Sir William Blackstone, whose *Commentaries on the Laws of England* (1765–69) provided the basis for interpreting common law relating to marriage throughout the nineteenth century; it surely underlies the count's praise for Madame Fosco's unquestioning support of all his schemes and actions.

18. In an interview reproduced in the *World* (16 Dec. 1877), Collins claimed that the two sources of inspiration for his novel were a letter he had recently received asking for his help in a case of wrongful confinement and an account of an eighteenth-century crime perpetrated against a Madame de Douhault (reprinted as appendix C in the Oxford University Press edition of *The Woman in White*). Leavy, however, points out that "while, to my knowledge, no one has challenged the veracity of Collins's claim to have received such a letter, neither has anyone proven its existence" (137 n. 18).

19. Frederick Lehmann to Mrs. Lehmann, 13 May 1861, quoted in Nuel Pharr Davis, *The Life of Wilkie Collins* (Urbana: University of Illinois Press, 1956), 230.

20. "*Weldon v. Semple,*" *Journal of Mental Science,* October 1884, 413. This is one of three alternative interpretations offered by the editor of this journal for the events surrounding Georgina Weldon's certification as a lunatic. Not surprisingly, this periodical for physicians specializing in mental disorders dismisses such an interpretation as improbable because in the Weldon case, any indictment of the husband's motivation implied criticism of the actions and integrity of the medical men involved.

21. Edward Grierson, *Storm Bird, the Strange Life of Georgina Weldon* (London: Chatto & Windus, 1959), 43–44.

22. Ibid., 30.

23. Ibid., 160.

24. Technically, a married woman had the legal right to institute certain law proceedings against her own husband, but historically the courts did not uphold this right when the case came to trial, except occasionally in divorce proceedings, suits for separation, or exceptional assault charges.

25. Quoted in Grierson, 214.

3 / "Come, Substantial Damages!"

—W. S. Gilbert, *Trial by Jury*

Jane W. Stedman

"THERE has been a great deal of interest about the scandal of Lord Garmoyle and Miss Fortescue," the eighteen-year-old Beatrix Potter wrote in her journal on 10 February 1884.[1] By twentieth-, even by later-nineteenth-century, standards, it was an innocent enough scandal, involving no illicit sexual relations, no guilty secrets, no financial double-dealing. And yet the jilting of a young actress by the son of a leading political figure raised issues upon which the press seized with righteous, if inconsistent, indignation, especially after the actress sued for breach of promise. Although the engagement of the young couple had followed lines approved of in many Victorian dramas of backstage life, the lawsuit violated the expected happy ending and was seen as an unwomanly assertion of rights. That Lord Garmoyle's father had twice been lord chancellor in Conservative governments and that Miss Fortescue was a protégée of the dramatist W. S. Gilbert enlarged the scope and intensified the emotions behind these journalistic portrayals. The Garmoyle-

Fortescue case was a political and theatrical event, as if George Bernard Shaw had grafted an act of "New Drama" on to the stock of a Dion Boucicault play.

In April 1881, May Fortescue (née Emily May Finney) began her stage career by creating the small role of Lady Ella in Gilbert and Sullivan's *Patience* at the Opera Comique in London. When Arthur Sullivan auditioned her, he had noted: "no voice to speak of—but very intelligent, somewhat 'emancipist,' " adding in the German he occasionally used, "Laf Haare auf den Zähnen!" (she has hair on her teeth), meaning "she can take care of herself."[2] Indeed, she intended to take care not only of herself but of her mother and younger sister as well after their father's bankruptcy. (That shadowy father was variously described as a brewer, a coal merchant, and, much later, a country gentleman. Miss Fortescue was also said to be related to John Tenniel, the *Punch* cartoonist and illustrator of the *Alice* books.)

D'Oyly Carte engaged Miss Fortescue, and at a subsequent hearing Sullivan thought her voice had improved. But even if she had almost nothing to say or sing, she so intoxicated audiences with her demure look as a Gilbertian rapturous maiden that a *Sketch* reporter remembered the effect for years.[3] When *Patience* moved to D'Oyly Carte's newly built Savoy Theater during the following October, Miss Fortescue went with it; when its run ended a year later, she created the role of Celia, a fairy, in *Iolanthe,* opening 25 November 1882. Reviewers found her efficient, fascinating, and particularly pleasing in pose and demeanor. She was often referred to as "the beautiful Miss Fortescue." (It was a respectable eccentricity of hers never to use her given name but always to be billed and reviewed as "Miss." Later she was to become the notorious Miss Fortescue and "the forsaken ⌐iry.")

In late June or July 1883, she became engaged to Lord

Garmoyle, second and eldest surviving son of Earl Cairns, Disraeli's friend and colleague, who had recently helped to pass the Married Women's Property Act of 1882. Lord Cairns had risen through the ranks of the peerage entirely by merit. His powers of incisive logic, however, were combined with such piety that the *Freeman's Journal* would call him "the most ostentatiously religious man among the prominent statesmen of the day,"[4] and many journalists disliked him.

On Disraeli's death, Lord Cairns might have succeeded to the Conservative leadership had it not been for his own ill health and, perhaps, his strict evangelicism. He was so Low Church, the comic weekly *Moonshine* jestingly remarked, that the High Church faction threatened to go over to the Liberals.[5] To this lifelong Sunday School teacher, the theater was of course anathema; had he known the plot of *Iolanthe,* he would have been doubly horrified at the prospect of a daughter-in-law-elect who appeared on a stage where George Grossmith sang, "I'm *such* a susceptible chancellor."

Against this parental austerity, Lord Garmoyle seems to have reacted stereotypically, going to playhouses, affecting the peculiar enunciation of a young swell,[6] and visiting the Cigar Club.[7] Harry Furniss, the *Punch* cartoonist, considered him "curious-looking,"[8] but Miss Fortescue seems to have loved him, believing that "there would never be another person right for her."[9]

Although the young couple intended to keep their engagement secret, Miss Fortescue told W. S. Gilbert almost at once that she was to be married and would leave the stage when *Iolanthe* ended its run.[10] Meanwhile, her mother prudently insisted that Lord Garmoyle inform his parents. The earl was on the Continent, but telegraphed his son, "expressing, not perhaps in cordial, but rather guarded terms, approval of the engagement."[11] Lady Cairns, however, wrote more kindly, trusting that God would bless the young people. On 26 July, after Lord Garmoyle had visited his father in Switzerland, the engagement was formally announced, and his other relatives made friendly overtures to his fiancée. *Moonshine* immediately told its readers that "Lord Cairns is said to have, with great anxiety, collected the photographs of Miss Fortescue which are likely to be published"—a futile precaution, since the *Era*'s gossip column three weeks later estimated that some ten thousand pounds' worth of her pictures had been sold.[12]

Journalists immediately capitalized on the resemblance between Miss Fortescue's stage role—that of a peri who marries a peer—and what seemed to be her life role. The irrepressible *Moonshine,* for example, burst into congratulatory verse:

> Away with the tinsel and void unreality,
>> Glamour and glitter of life on the boards,
> Giving to Gilbert's creation vitality,
>> Singing your ballads to Sullivan's chords.
> ....
>
> Now that you've settled that you'll have no *more on it,*
>> Gilbertian Earls are but beings of air;
> You have accepted a true noble coronet,
>> One of the right sort—no stagey affair.
> Then may your happiness turn out solidity,
>> Lasting unchequered till silver old age;
> And may life's sweets have no tinge of acidity,
>> Unlike the sweets that we see on the stage.[13]

The title of this effusion was "Shadow and Substance." Its slightly denigratory attitude toward the stage as artificial and meretricious accorded with the ambivalent tone of many Victorian plays about theatrical life in which virtuous young actresses marry above their own social rank and leave the illusion of painted "flats" for the reality of marble halls. Miss Fortescue's engagement satisfied, therefore, the dramatic expectations of the age and showed that life was catching up with art, even though the press generally considered that Lord Garmoyle's social superiority was a mere technicality.[14]

To render the actress more attractive to his parents, and perhaps at their insistence, Lord Garmoyle asked his fiancée and her sister (then contemplating a stage career) to give up the theater. When they did so, Lord Cairns became more gracious (see fig. 1). Miss Fortescue was introduced everywhere in her new role; her lordly lover "bound her to the wheels of his cab all over London," as the *World* put it later; "She exchanged the mock fairyland of the world behind the footlights for the real fairyland of social delights—for judiciously chaperoned dinners . . . and for a brilliant apprenticeship to the glittering glories of her future sphere." James McNeill Whistler gave one of his Sunday breakfasts "in honour of two happy couples, Lord Garmoyle and his fairy queen, and Oscar [Wilde] and the lady whom he has chosen to be the *châtelaine* of the House Beautiful."[15] Miss Fortescue was invited to Lord Cairns's shooting place; the marriage date was discussed.

At this point Lady Cairns suggested that because Lord Garmoyle was intended for a military career, the wedding might be postponed until he finished Sandhurst. Again Miss Fortescue agreed. The young people exchanged affectionate letters, in which Miss Fortescue showed herself a true emancipist by asking her betrothed not to send her expensive presents.

> We are a sensible man and woman, who, having found out that they care for each other more than for anyone else in the world, have settled to pass their lives together. For this to be successful, the man must not be in the habit of thinking the woman a

LORD CAIRNS TO MISS FORTESCUE:—"DELIGHTED, MY DEAR, THAT MY SON HAS SHOWN SUCH GOOD TASTE!"

Fig. 1. "Lord Cairns to Miss Fortescue," from *The Entr'acte,* 11 Aug. 1883.

pretty plaything on whom jewels and toys are to be lavished, and that these things make her happiness. . . . You see I'm not simply a pretty brainless doll whose spurious kind of "love" . . . needs to be kept aflame by all sorts of appeals to her vanity as her strongest point.

She hoped that by doing "something a little out of the way," they would set an example for other men and women who wanted to take "their lives into their own keeping. . . . And it seems to me it is rather a good thing in life to have been able to help other people a little by being strong, and brave, and doing right." Conscious, perhaps, of Lord Garmoyle's weakness, she reminded him what "you have told me about being the only woman who ever wanted you to do that."[16]

Lord Garmoyle's parents waited. An occasional rumor drifted by, but four months later the young couple still "looked quite happy and desirably spooney" at the Lyceum.[17] Chaperoned by her mother, they appeared in a box at the first performance of Gilbert and Sullivan's *Princess Ida* on 5 January 1884, while his father prepared to preside over the annual meeting of the Church Missionary Society on 7 January. When Miss Fortescue went with her sister and mother to Brighton, Lord Garmoyle visited them for more than a week, behaving with his accustomed affection. Then he went home to write a letter breaking their engagement. Although protesting that he still loved her, he was, he said, "acting upon the suggestion of others," who had asserted that his relations and friends could not receive an ex-actress socially. (It seems likely that these "others" were his fellows at Sandhurst, who would have pointed out that such a marriage precluded his joining any of the crack regiments.)

Sullivan heard the news from D'Oyly Carte on 28 January, including the possibility of Miss Fortescue's bringing a breach of promise suit. Carte, in turn, may have heard it from Gilbert, who had continued in her confidence. By this time Lord Garmoyle had left England for more exotic climes. On 2 February the *Era*, the theater's own weekly, announced in its gossip column: "We hear, on good authority, that the marriage arranged between Miss Fortescue and Lord Garmoyle is broken off."[18]

Henry Labouchère, politician and editor of *Truth*, immediately dashed off a note to George Grossmith, asking for full details so that he could denounce Lord Cairns. "It really is a little to [*sic*] impudent for this holy man to object to his masher of a son marrying a girl because she is an actress," added Labouchere, whose own wife was a former actress—and his former mistress.[19] The recently appointed editor of the *Evening News*, Frank Harris, gave two front-page columns on 27 February to an exposition of Miss Fortescue's wrongs.[20] The *World*, however, did not wait that long. In "The Forsaken Fairy" (6 February) and "Garm-Oyling the Waves" (13 February), it indicted the parents' lack of humanity and their son's lack of chivalry. Yet even while treating Miss Fortescue as the victim of a heartless policy, the *World* inconsistently referred to a social fusion between women "of every degree of virtue and of want of virtue" and men of all ranks "from the peer to the counterjumper." This connection was established by the Gaiety Theater and other houses that permitted men easy access backstage, according to the *World*, which suggested that stage fairies should teach mashers a lesson learned from the present case.[21] Much more antagonistic were two unpleasant paragraphs in the *Sporting Times* accusing Miss Fortescue's relatives of anticipating a large sum in damages and explaining that Lord Garmoyle's being heavily mulcted was a recognized consequence of getting mixed up with actresses.[22] Thus almost from the first, the press began a moral campaign against both parties.

Journalistic sympathies were at first, however, largely on Miss Fortescue's side. On 12 February the *Freeman's Journal* happily abused Lord Cairns as a ranting religionist. On 13 February *Under the Clock* asked what else could have been expected, given Lord Garmoyle's lack of pluck. His antecedents were attacked—he was said to be the great-grandson of a butler, the grandson of a tradesman or of an apple woman. Then, on 16 February 1884, the *Era* took the defense of Miss Fortescue upon itself in an editorial which declared that her only "crime" was possessing grace and beauty "without the concomitants of money and position." Commenting on the Savoy Theater's widely known reputation for backstage decency, the *Era* asserted that the actress and the lord had fallen in love "under exactly similar circumstances as though he had become enamoured of a duchess at a Belgravian ball"—except that Miss Fortescue's stage costume was less revealing than a duchess's décolleté. The periodical congratulated her upon escaping "so weak-minded a husband" but warned that she would reflect more credit upon her profession if she renounced the rumored "material retaliation."[23]

Dignified seclusion was the *Era*'s advice, a position endorsed by such journals as the *Stage* (29 February), which counseled absolute rest and quiet, telling "this distressed maiden" to wait, hope, avoid any legal action, and not return to the stage.[24] Nonetheless, the wronged emancipist declared her determination to go before the court and the public as soon as possible. Almost certainly, she did so on the advice of W. S. Gilbert. Such a proceeding, aimed at vindicating both the actress and the theater in general, would be completely characteristic of the dramatist, who had a penchant for lawsuits and whose 1874 play *Ought We to Visit Her?* had already satirized the social hypocrisy of ostracizing an actress. And Miss Fortescue's solicitors, Bolton & Mote, were also Gilbert's.

Meanwhile, not having an income, Miss Fortescue went back to the stage. Because Mrs. Beerbohm Tree was unable to take the role she had been offered in a revival of Gilbert's serious drama *Dan'l Druce* at the Court Theatre, Gilbert arranged for Miss Fortescue to play Dorothy Druce at eight pounds a week, opening 6 March. He himself coached her in this character, which Marion Terry had created under his direction eight years earlier. Although *Under the Clock* (20 February) had anticipated that Miss Fortescue would "return to fairyland and be a star," it cautioned readers on 5 March that her powers as an actress were yet to be discovered. A week later, it dismissed "Miss Fortescue, the forlorn" as having no pretensions to being considered an actress—yet.[25]

Unfortunately, other reviewers agreed, even while conceding her physical attractiveness in the role and her clarity of enunciation. Tarnished was the image of the "clever actress," who had been praised for winning "the respect and esteem of all who know her."[26] Instead, she had become "a young lady on whose domestic relations a not very enviable light of publicity has lately been thrown."[27]

On the whole, however, serious periodicals and daily newspapers treated Miss Fortescue more tolerantly than did the comic and theatrical weeklies. Kindest of critics, the *Academy*'s reviewer praised her for more than average grace, humor, and pathos, asking "why it is that we have not seen her earlier in some such part."[28] The *Morning Post* (7 March) commended her understanding of literary dialogue. But most

MR. GILBERT AND MISS FORTESCUE.
GIVING HER A HELPING HAND.

Fig. 2. "Mr. Gilbert and Miss Fortescue," from *The Entr'acte,* 15 Mar. 1884.

reviews were decidedly mixed. The *Athenaeum* (15 March) declared her performance of a not-very-exacting role creditable and pretty but noted her constraint in big emotional scenes. The *Times* (7 March) similarly described her as playing "prettily enough" but found her acting "colourless and empty" next to Hermann Vezin's powerful rendering of the title role—a rather unfair comparison. Praising with faint damns, the *Standard* admitted that although she was better than expected and had been carefully drilled, she was stiff and self-conscious. The *Graphic* (15 March) said she was pretty, interesting, nervous, scarcely equal to the demands of the role, but sympathetic.

Nervousness and constraint were clearly the defects of her performance, and in an antagonistic review, Clement Scott of the *Daily Telegraph* (7 March) hammered away at them. She was, he said, "conspicuously over-trained and over-taught"—"a mere machine, instructed to carry out the ideas of someone else." If she wished to succeed she must occasionally forget her tutor and show that she understood the emotions she was called on to portray. Scott's biting criticism thus attacked both Gilbert as a dramatic coach and a girl whose private life had very likely introduced her to too much emotional experience.

The comic papers treated Miss Fortescue with clumsy jocularity as they did most topicalities, considering it amusing to call her "Miss Finney." Her former eulogist *Moonshine* printed a verse filler (22 March) on the question of whether her stage name should be pronounced like "burlesque." She found herself parodied in the provinces as "Kate Buckingham, leading actress at the Saveloy Theatre . . . who made such a hit in *I. O. U. Lanthy.*" This was in a burlesque, *Posterity; An Operatic Andissipation,* in one act by Moore and Lutz, produced at the Theatre Royal, Newcastle, on 10

March. The scene is set in a future England where women rule and work and men are weaker, tea-drinking vessels—another implicit connection between Miss Fortescue and female emancipation.

But the unkindest cuts of all were given in a slashing campaign that the *Era,* so recently her defender, mounted against Miss Fortescue. On 8 March a paragraph in its gossip column noted that *Dan'l Druce* was being put on "under circumstances of peculiar interest." A second paragraph said she should be grateful to Lord Garmoyle for her chance to be a star "run after by fashionable crowds." (The social status of her first-night audience was a sore point with more than one journalist.) When her engagement had been announced, the *Era* referred to Miss Fortescue as one of the cleverest members of the Savoy company. Now she was held up as "another illustration of the fact that a little notoriety, from the commercial point of view, is to be preferred to talent."[29]

Two pages later, a long review developed this theme: "We are inclined sorrowfully to admit now that, so far as the stage is concerned, notoriety is better than brains, and to be plaintiff in an action for breach of promise of marriage of more value than artistic excellence." The critic wrote, however, more in anger than in sorrow. He deplored the audience's flocking to see Miss Fortescue as they did a fashionable society beauty turned actress—a scarcely covert allusion to Lillie Langtry. Falling back on a favorite Victorian complaint, the *Era* declared that Miss Fortescue's performance lacked sympathy, although she was "a pretty young lady who had learnt a pretty lesson and was able to go through it prettily." Her performance was merely that of an intelligent amateur, and the writer wanted it clearly understood that the applause she enjoyed had "nothing whatever to do with art or artistic ability." Later in the same review, Charles Hawtrey, the romantic lead in *Dan'l Druce*, was dismissed as "almost painfully amateurish," but the *Era* did not belabor his insufficiencies as it did Miss Fortescue's.

Two weeks later, with *Dan'l Druce* still running, the *Era* reported that the plaintiff's solicitors had entered cause for trial in the Queen's Bench Division, that the case would not likely be heard before next summer, and that Lord Garmoyle was said to be in Constantinople. It also ran a long editorial inveighing against untalented and notorious persons on stage. Again, an unnamed but "well-known 'professional beauty'" was linked with Miss Fortescue, who bore the brunt of the attack. Abandoning references to her intelligence, the *Era* dismissed her performance as puppetlike and asked rhetorically, "What would not many a hard-working and meritorious young artist have given for the opportunity now offered (and offered, as far as any artistic achievement goes, in vain) to Miss Fortescue!" Once more there was an oblique thrust at Gilbert: the editorial described Miss Fortescue's training as her "having been taught to repeat by rote, some six or eight lines of commonplace prose."[30]

This was too much. Gilbert himself now entered the lists with a letter to the editor, dated 24 March and published on the 29th. Ascribing the *Era*'s tone to "a complete misapprehension of the facts," he set out "to explain away the erroneous and highly injurious impression that is likely to be conveyed by your leading article of last week." Gilbert then pointed out that Miss Fortescue had *been* a hard-working young artist at the Savoy, that she had played small roles only because her singing voice was not strong enough for larger ones, and that she remained at the Savoy because it was a permanent engagement which would support her mother and sister. Carefully he rejected the comparison between Miss Fortescue and Mrs. Langtry, whom he named; the former, he said, had been a professional actress before appearing at the Court, while the latter turned to the stage only after making an international reputation outside the theater. As for the role Miss Fortescue was now playing, it was paid fifteen pounds a week at the Court Theatre.[31] Gil- voice, an attractive appearance, and a quiet, gentle, graceful manner. Nor had Marion Terry been a widely experienced actress when he cast her in the original production.

The question of salary had been a sore point with some members of the press, who reported that Miss Fortescue was paid fifteen pounds a week at the Court Theatre.[31] Gil- bert's letter gave her salary at the Savoy as six pounds, hav- ing risen from three pounds, her starting wage. At the Court she was receiving eight pounds a week for three months. Fi- nally, Gilbert asked the *Era* what actress of those available at the time would it suggest for Dorothy Druce in preference to Miss Fortescue.[32]

On 5 April the *Graphic* summed up Gilbert's letter for its readers; on the same day, the *Era* doubled its attack with an impertinent letter and yet another editorial. The *Era* letter, addressed to the editor from "The Caught Theatre" and signed "AL. BUNKUM," sneeringly set out to demolish Gilbert, "the great Pan-jam," by means of the misquotation, quibble, and chop-logic dear to comic journalism and yet so ineffectual as argument. BUNKUM suggested that D'Oyly Carte paid Miss Fortescue six pounds a week simply because he knew the worth of a beautiful woman on stage. The accompanying long editorial, "A Matter of Opinion," gave a top-lofty, self-righteous, but evasive answer to Gil- bert's letter. Only the courtesy due a leading dramatist, said the writer condescendingly, had made him return to a sub- ject on which he and the theatrical profession were already agreed. Ironically praising Gilbert's knight errantry in defense of "a very weak case," the editorial repeated the familiar accusations of Miss Fortescue's lack of talent, parrotlike training, and overpayment. It did, however, make one valid point in rebuttal by pointing out how Marion Terry had had provincial experience, which Miss Fortescue lacked. But it declined to suggest a better actress for the present production and offered the foolish suggestion that *Dan'l Druce* should have been postponed while a search was made.[33]

The next week the *Era* was back again with a paragraph referring to "that young lady of vast experience . . . [and] transcendent talent" having refused a part in the Court's next production. A few issues later, after Weedon Grossmith's portrait of Miss Fortescue was hung in the Royal Academy exhibition, the *Era* again referred to the attractions of notoriety, and commented, "there can be very little doubt that Miss Fortescue has a high estimate of her own attractions, which are greatly flattered by the complimentary artist."[34]

Paradoxically, however, while the press was busily depreciating Miss Fortescue, it did not, compensatorily, appreciate Lord Garmoyle. He was rechristened "Gumboil."

Why this attack on a young woman in whose defense a thousand journalistic swords had so recently leapt from their scabbards? First, her action was not only contrary to their endless advice but unwomanly as well. As the *Era*'s inveterate editorialist would put it when the trial came on, "when a woman brings an action of this sort she places herself beyond the pale of delicacy and sympathy. . . . It is just as if one were to interfere between a woman and a ruffian who was beating her and then find the lady suddenly putting one aside, squaring up in scientific style, and inflicting severe punishment on her injurer."[35] If Miss Fortescue lacked

friends big and strong enough to "explain" to Lord Garmoyle, she should have left him to the punishment of public
opinion. The *Era* was pleased that her connection with the
stage had been so slight, "for we should have been sorry to
have seen an actress in the real sense of the word bring such
an action."[36]

This withering judgment suggests a second reason for the
animosity that theatrical papers displayed. Constantly under
fire not only from the Lord Cairnses but its own members as
well, the Victorian theater was extremely edgy about its
moral reputation. When F. C. Burnand, the burlesque writer,
published articles in the *Nineteenth Century* (1882) and the
Fortnightly (1885) alluding to the almost inescapable temp-
tations surrounding young ladies who embraced the "quasi-
profession" of actress, the *Era* flew into abusive tirades.
Furiously it reminded him that both his wives had been
actresses and that he had earned thousands of pounds by
writing pieces which exploited women's legs.[37] When Miss
Fortescue had seemingly been accepted as a daughter-in-law
by an evangelically strict earl, she enhanced the reputation
of the stage; jilted and suing, she was a liability to be classed
with the girls from the Gaiety Theatre who cut a swath
through the younger aristocracy.[38] She was also, as we have
seen, used as a means of attacking Mrs. Langtry, whose
own reputation had not enhanced that of the stage even if
she drew curious audiences. As the comic character Ally
Sloper put it two years later, to be a Society Actress, a girl
*"must either have not got married to a lord or must have got de-
vorced [sic] from a commoner."*[39]

A third cause of the outrage was the Court Theatre itself.
Responding to a large box-office demand, the theater had
without warning converted part of its pit to higher-priced
stalls, thus offending regular playgoers, who protested dur-

ing the performance. Although their temporary disturbance was not directed specifically against Miss Fortescue, the incident confirmed the assumption by the theatrical press that the managers were exploiting the actress with her own connivance. This, according to the *Stage*, showed "questionable taste on the part of the lady who lends herself to such a scheme." The fact that what the press repeatedly called a "fashionable audience" had come to see her also told against Miss Fortescue.[40]

Finally, there are the imponderables. How good or bad an actress was she at this point in her career? She had been away from the stage for more than six months and was very nervous. Clement Scott saw her lip tremble and tears fill her eyes at her first entrance—her only natural expression during the evening, he said. But even had she been at ease, it is unlikely that she could have avoided invidious comparisons with Marion Terry. Moreover, although under Gilbert's tutelage she must have played the role rather as Terry had, it is true that the style of acting so deliciously fresh in 1876 was no longer a surprise in 1884. Or again, how many unpleasant paragraphs resulted merely from the snowball effect whereby a victim was rolled to death by the mindless momentum generated by the need for "fillers"?

Dan'l Druce ran till the end of April. Miss Fortescue then went to the Strand, where she played Mary Melrose in a revival of H. J. Byron's record-breaking comedy, *Our Boys.* The *Graphic,* the *Stage,* and *Under the Clock* took exception to her "painted eyes"; the *Graphic's* objection was mild, but the *Stage* (6 June) reminded her that she was not playing a " 'mistress.' " The Playgoers' Club officially considered that some papers had treated Miss Fortescue somewhat discourteously.[41]

Assisted by the presence of popular actor David James in his original role, *Our Boys* played through the summer and autumn. Meanwhile, interest in the pending lawsuit was kept alive in the papers by paragraphs giving a succession of possible court dates, promising that eminent witnesses would be subpoenaed, and speculating on the amount of damages to be awarded. (Figures from four thousand to fifty thousand pounds were mentioned.) In September, *Under the Clock* published a so-called American rumor that Lord Cairns was anxious for his son to marry the daughter of an (unspecified) illustrious nobleman. In October, *Judy* reported that curiosity-seekers had mobbed Miss Fortescue "on Prayer-book Parade" in Scarborough.

In the midst of this titivation by "filler," an event occurred that temporarily gave the press a new victim, while very likely strengthening its feeling against Miss Fortescue. In late September 1884, Mrs. Kendal, the highly respectable, highly praised actress, read a paper at the Congress of the National Association for the Promotion of Social Science, held at Birmingham. Here she discussed the influence of the theater as teacher, the happy fact that actors were now considered gentlemen, the relation of a pure stage to a pure public, and the profession's charitable willingness to welcome all men and women regardless of their pasts, even though Puritans condemned such tolerance. Mrs. Kendal criticized the stage itself for suggestive French importations and the players for undignified self-advertisement. Then she turned to the press, particularly the "so-called theatrical papers . . . where insolent and generally untrue gossip and tittle-tattle take the place of honest criticism." The press, she said, did not truly foster the drama's welfare: "Existing critics generally rush into extremes and either overpraise or too cruelly condemn."[42] She warned reviewers that their great power would cease if playgoers found them untrustworthy guides but also admitted that public interest in seeing notorious persons on stage degraded the theater. It is likely that Mrs. Kendal was thinking not of Miss Fortescue at this point but of Lillie Langtry, who was playing Kendal roles.

Scarcely waiting to be touched to the quick, the *Era* rushed fighting into the field (27 September). Beginning with a gender slur at Mrs. Kendal's "charming *ex cathedra* style which is so characteristic an attitude of the sex, be their theme what it may," the editor fancied that most of her observations had already been made by male critics and took her equally to task for having said elsewhere that she hoped to earn enough money to retire. Again the *Era* raised the cry of self-interest— of coining one's own profession—of assuming "a Pharisaical superiority" while making "spiteful allusions" to her fellow players.[43] The *Era* professed itself shocked to learn that an actress it had praised looked upon her profession merely as a lucrative trade.[44]

Punch joined in with a punning article, "The Stage by Kendal-light," which began "What! at it again? This talented Histrione is coming out as the Great Irrepressible! . . . Mrs. KENDAL (bless her!) is becoming quite a Premier in Petticoats." After many plays on the words Kendal and candle, all derogatory, the writer—who must have been the editor, F. C. Burnand—seized upon the actress's assertion that actors were considered gentlemen. Taking the line he had pursued in the *Nineteenth Century,* Burnand announced that "a young lady by birth and education, pure in mind, and refined in taste" would be utterly disgusted with the "atmosphere of the theatre" and would leave it at once. If she persisted in becoming an actress, she would unconsciously deteriorate, "and then?—*histoire banale!*" If she were born into the profession, her everyday life would be revolting to a homebred English girl. Since *Punch* writers, including himself, had always been connected with the theater,

Burnand was obviously willing to foul his own stage in order to give Mrs. Kendal her comeuppance. (He did, however, protect himself by stipulating that he referred to ordinary actresses without Mrs. Kendal's or Ellen Terry's great ability.) An accompanying cartoon showed the actress's face in a candle flame about to be snuffed, with the caption, "Out, out, brief (?) Kendal!"[45]

When *Finney v. Cairns* was finally heard on 20 November 1884, the trial proved an anticlimax. Neither the defendant nor the rumored witnesses were on hand. Lord Garmoyle admitted via his attorney that he had refused to marry Miss Fortescue and consented to a ten thousand pound judgment against himself, the highest award of its kind hitherto recorded. His counsel remarked that while many persons would shrink from bringing a breach of promise suit, there was perhaps some justification in this instance. Interestingly enough, the defense referred to the plaintiff as "Miss Finney" throughout, while her own counsel called her "Miss Fortescue."

Mr. Punch was disappointed in what he named "The New Play at the Royal Courts" or the "Comedy-Tragedy of *Finney v. Garmoyle*," the plot of which was "extremely uninteresting and devoid of incident."[46] Indeed, Lord Garmoyle had described Miss Fortescue's conduct during their engagement as always that of a high-minded English gentlewoman. The comic press made what capital it could out of the fact that a revival of Gilbert and Sullivan's *Trial by Jury* was currently running at the Savoy, while on the night of the trial an anonymous domestic drama, *Lottie,* had opened at the Novelty Theatre, dealing with the seamy side of stage life and including an actress who married a baronet. Predictably, the *Era* refused to hail Miss Fortescue's damages with "joyful satisfaction"; instead, the paper repeated the familiar charges.[47]

When, perhaps unwisely, Miss Fortescue gave Pear's Soap a paid testimonial, the *Theatrical Programme* suggested: "HAPPY THOUGHT for Miss Fortescue in her new profession of testimonial-writer . . . 'I can with pleasure testify to the excellent quality of your sixpenny diamond rings. They are much finer than any Gummy ever gave me.' "[48] The year closed with a summary in *Moonshine:* "Lord Garmoyle perpetrated a coal scuttle; Miss Finney was valued at £10,000 per sack."[49]

Nevertheless, Miss Fortescue emerged from her "scandal" with dignity; pictures in illustrated papers show her as quiet and rather sad. She continued to act in increasingly serious roles, she toured the provinces, and Gilbert sent her to America with his Faust play, *Gretchen,* in 1886. Thereafter she appeared sometimes in London (a special 1887 engagement as seduced second lead in Robert Buchanan's *The Blue Bells of Scotland*), sometimes in America, even in South Africa. She assembled her own company to tour on a regular basis, financed by Lord Garmoyle's ten thousand pounds—which no doubt came from his father's pocket, Lord Cairns thus subsidizing a profession he loathed. It is also ironic that had Lord Garmoyle waited a year, he might have been free to wed his fairy, for his father died in April 1885. The new earl's accession to his title prompted a brief revival of Fortescue-Garmoyle cartoons, but he ceased to be fair game when he married in 1887.

Year by year, and especially after the early death of the second Earl Cairns in 1890, the notorious Miss Fortescue slipped into the past while the beautiful Miss Fortescue came forward again. She portrayed Galatea in Gilbert's *Pygmalion and Galatea,* and several of his serious heroines—Clarice, Jenny, Mrs. Van Brugh, Selene—in revivals he directed. From time to time, she also played Lady Teazle, Frou-Frou, Juliet,

Rosalind, Julia in *The Hunchback,* and Vere in *Moths.* Richard Le Gallienne was overwhelmed by "her radiant loveliness" as Hypatia.[50] She had always to contend with a certain stiffness in acting style, but provincial critics found her constantly improving and capable of strong emotional effects, as in her delivery of Hypatia's dying speech, which brought down the house in Sheffield.[51] Developing a competent, even a breezy manner, she became a complete manager, even to conducting rehearsals herself.

Miss Fortescue never married, remaining a model of propriety, always with an attendant chaperone. She did not return to the stage of the Savoy but did continue an informal association with its triumvirate, especially with Gilbert, who wrote and directed *The Fortune Hunter* for her. Described beforehand as a strong modern drama with a somewhat unconventional plot, it depicted an independent Australian heiress, whose father was a merchant, falling in love with an aristocratic French cad. His parents, however, repudiate his behavior toward her and accept her. Unfortunately, Gilbert's dialogue suggested the late 1860s rather than the late 1890s; *The Fortune Hunter* was a success only at its 1897 Birmingham premiere, although Miss Fortescue played it elsewhere on that year's tour.

A year later, and more successfully, a love story resembling Miss Fortescue's own again appeared on stage, this time in Arthur Wing Pinero's *Trelawny of the "Wells"*—and with a happy ending. Here Rose Trelawny, an actress, falls in love with the grandson of a puritanical former lord chancellor and is taken off the stage to be sanitized. She melts the grandfather by arousing his adolescent memories of Edmund Kean; the grandson goes on stage as a gentlemanly actor.

The new century saw Miss Fortescue playing in London

productions of social comedies: the Duchess of Strood in Pinero's *The Gay Lord Quex,* the Dowager Countess of Drumdurris in a revival of *The Cabinet Minister,* and Lady Faringford in St. John Hankin's *The Return of the Prodigal,* the latter a role that the no-longer hostile *Era* (4 May 1907) said she acted "with the necessary acerbity and hauteur."[52] Of her performances, the *Illustrated London News* critic wrote: "Miss Fortescue . . . has an inalienable right to the role of the conventional *grande dame.*"[53] At last!

Notes

1. *The Journal of Beatrix Potter from 1881 to 1897: Transcribed from Her Code Writing by Leslie Linder* (London: Frederick Warne and Co., 1966), 65.

2. Sullivan's summary of the year 1881 in his holograph diary for 1882; quoted by kind permission of the Beinecke Rare Book and Manuscript Library, Yale University.

3. "A Chat with Miss Fortescue," *The Sketch,* 20 Dec. 1893, 416.

4. *Freeman's Journal,* 12 Feb. 1884; taken from the D'Oyly Carte press cuttings books, which do not necessarily record page numbers. Unless otherwise noted, all periodical articles for which no page number is given come from this collection (now in the Theatre Museum, London), used by kind permission of the late Dame Bridget D'Oyly Carte.

5. *Moonshine,* 14 May 1881, 230.

6. Potter, 65.

7. Lord Garmoyle dated a letter to George Grossmith "21st Sept: 1883," from the Cigar Club; Grossmith family papers in the possession of the late Phyllis Bevan.

8. Harry Furniss, *Some Victorian Women: Good, Bad, and Indifferent* (London: John Lane, 1923), 58.

9. Quoted by her niece, Dr. Mary Mayeur, in "Breach Girl

Leaves £6800," *Evening Standard*, 21 Nov. 1950; press cutting in the Enthoven Collection, Theatre Museum, no page given.

10. Autograph letter signed W. S. Gilbert to Richard D'Oyly Carte, 7th July [1883]; D'Oyly Carte papers now in the Theatre Museum.

11. *Times*, 21 Nov. 1884. In this account of Miss Fortescue's day in court, she and Lord Garmoyle are said to have met in society, where she also met Gilbert and Sullivan.

12. *Moonshine*, 1 Sept. 1883, 104; *Era*, 22 Sept. 1883.

13. *Moonshine*, 11 Aug. 1883, 64.

14. "It is true that Miss Finney is at least Lord Garmoyle's equal in birth; but . . . he is, as heir to an earldom, her social superior" (*World*, 13 Feb. 1884). Several papers pointed out that it was, however, a very new earldom.

15. *World*, 6 Feb. 1884 and 26 Dec. 1883.

16. The letter was published by the *Times*, 21 Nov. 1884, in its account of *Finney v. Garmoyle* (p. 4). It was also published by the *Era* on 22 November (p. 10).

17. *Entr'acte*, 15 Dec. 1883, 4.

18. *Era*, 2 Feb. 1884, 8.

19. Undated; in Grossmith's letter book of autographed letters sent him; Gilbert and Sullivan Collection, Pierpont Morgan Library, New York, quoted by kind permission of the trustees. Labouchere's wife was Henrietta Hodson, who became Lillie Langtry's dramatic coach and accompanied her to America. In July 1887, Miss Fortescue played Hermia in *A Midsummer Night's Dream*, performed at a Saturday party given by the Laboucheres. G. A. Sala played Bottom; minor roles were filled by Whistler, Burnand, and Pinero (*Musical World*, 23 July 1887, 580).

20. Frank Harris, *My Life and Loves* (New York: Grove Press, 1963), 364.

21. *World*, 6 and 13 Feb. 1884.

22. *Sporting Times*, 11 Feb. 1884.

23. *Era*, 16 Feb. 1884, 15.

24. *Stage*, 29 Feb. 1884, 13.

25. *Under the Clock*, 20 Feb. 1884, 7; 5 Mar. 1884, 6; 12 Mar. 1884, 5.

26. *Musical World,* 11 Aug. 1883, 500.

27. *Athenaeum,* 1 Mar. 1884, 290.

28. *Academy,* 22 Mar. 1884, 212.

29. *Era,* 8 Mar. 1884, 10; the *Era* had noted Miss Fortescue's engagement in its 28 July 1883 issue.

30. *Era,* 22 Mar. 1884, 9.

31. In some stories, her salary was said to be fifteen guineas, which would raise the estimate to nearly twice the sum she was actually paid.

32. *Era,* 29 Mar. 1884, 8.

33. Ibid., 5 Apr. 1884, 13.

34. Ibid., 12 Apr. 1884; 10 May 1884, 7.

35. When Lydia Thompson and Pauline Markham cowhided a Chicago editor for abusing them personally in print, English and American journalists were outraged by their unwomanliness. Thompson, in a 27 Mar. 1870 letter to the *Daily Telegraph,* defended their action as intended "to call attention to the fact that even actresses have some rights that journalists are bound to respect."

36. *Era,* 22 Nov. 1884, 15.

37. Ibid., 7 Feb. 1885, 13.

38. The Gaiety was, or was thought to be, the opposite of the Savoy in the accessibility of its chorus ladies. The Savoy protected theirs from stage-door Johnnies, and an often-repeated anecdote tells how Gilbert personally ejected a young man who sent a soliciting note to Jessie Bond, the Savoy soubrette. Allen Horstman has pointed out another such incident, this involving Miss Fortescue. In this case a young officer of Hussars, on 24 and 25 Oct. 1882, "intentionally allowed a member of [the Raleigh] Club to infer that I had passed the night with Miss Fortescue. . . ." Gilbert forced an unqualified apology from him and a written admission that this was not true (Hesketh Pearson, *Gilbert: His Life and Strife* [London: Methuen & Co. 1957], 124). Pearson characteristically does not give a source for this document, which he publishes almost in full, and I have been unable to find it among the Gilbert Papers deposited in the British Library. Evidently no word

reached the press, because it was not used against Miss Fortescue, whose chastity her critics did not impugn. The Raleigh Club was well known for pretended familiarity with actresses, as a parody in *Judy* demonstrates (16 July 1879, 36). Its members evidently affected the peculiarities of "swell" enunciation.

Several years later, however, Miss Fortescue may have been more seriously involved with Edward Fairfield, Rebecca West's uncle, who was allegedly "enjoying a happy affair" with the actress. (See Philippa Pullar, *Frank Harris* [New York: Simon and Schuster, 1976], 130.) Again, there seems to be no documentary evidence and no gossip. Finally, in a letter to F. C. Burnand on 27 Oct. 1888, Henry Irving remarked that the editor Harry Quilter, who incited George Moore to attack the stage in the *Universal Review*, had once been engaged to "the fair Fortescue" (Laurence Irving, *Henry Irving: The Actor and His World* [New York: Macmillan Co., 1952], 496). The press said little about such an engagement, except for a couplet in the *Entr'acte* (1 Mar. 1884, 5): "He spoke fair words, and then did jilt her,/Which made her sorry she quitted her Quilter."

39. *Entr'acte Annual,* 1886, 19.

40. *Stage,* 14 Mar. 1884, 14.

41. *Stage,* 20 June 1884, 15.

42. Mrs. Kendal, *The Drama: A Paper Read at the Congress of the National Association for the Promotion of Social Service, Birmingham, September 1884* (London: David Bogue, n.d.), 17. Mrs. Kendal's paper went into four editions.

43. Kendal was widely (and erroneously) assumed to be attacking Ellen Terry.

44. *Era,* 27 Sept. 1884, 13.

45. *Punch,* 4 Oct. 1884, 165.

46. *Punch* reviewed the trial throughout as if it were a play, commending a juryman's makeup and the admirably acted scene between the two counsels and the judge, but objecting to the absence of a supporting cast (29 Nov. 1884, 254).

47. *Era,* 22 Nov. 1884, 15.

48. *Theatrical Programme,* 13 Dec. 1884, 2.

49. *Moonshine,* 27 Dec. 1884, 312.

50. Lecture delivered by Le Gallienne at Pembroke Chapel, Liverpool, on 15 Apr. 1894. He referred to Miss Fortescue's company then playing at the Shakespeare Theatre as "able and cultivated men and women "who" had made the fifth century live again" (*Era,* 21 Apr. 1894, 10).

51. Provincial review in the *Era,* 31 Mar. 1894, 11.

52. *Era,* 4 May 1907, 18.

53. *Illustrated London News,* 18 May 1907, 746.

PART TWO

The Woman Question/ Questionable Women

4 / The Actress in Victorian Pornography

Tracy C. Davis

> Oh! it is absurd to have a hard-and-fast rule about what one
> should read and what one shouldn't. More than half of mod-
> ern culture depends on what one shouldn't read.
>
> —Oscar Wilde, *The Importance of Being Earnest*

DECADES before the theories of conditioned
reflexes and behavior modification were expounded in England, moral reformers recognized that to control passions
in the Victorian theaters, passionate stimuli must be checked.
Yet only a few reformers—those who understood these stim-
ulants and the nature of the passions they aroused—were
eager to eradicate a socially approved source of so much
erotic pleasure. If the great majority of playgoers were indifferent to the sensual marketplaces inside the variety theaters'
promenades and outside the legitimate theaters' colonnades,
they wholeheartedly defended the sensual content of performance and patronized it faithfully.

In burlesque, opéra bouffe, pantomime, music hall, musical comedy, ballet, and extravaganza, conventions of costume, gesture, and theatrical *mise-en-scène* insured that the

most banal material was infused with sensuality—sensuality that was deliberately manipulated to arouse male spectators. These theatrical conventions, deeply encoded in the sexual language of society, embodied and reinforced a view of the theater and particularly of actresses, because the objects as well as the subjects of arousal were gendered. The encodings, almost certainly invisible and unintelligible to many spectators, were explained in Victorian erotic books, periodicals, and illustrations widely available to men. Thus, while erotica [1] included images of the theater and its practitioners, the theater persistently contained elements of the erotic, to the consternation (or more often the delight) of knowing spectators.

The erotic components of performance catalogued in 1839 by Dr. Michael Ryan were constant features in almost all theatrical genres throughout the nineteenth century:

> Who has not seen actresses appear in . . . dresses as white as marble, and fitting so tightly that the shape of their bodies could not be more apparent, had they come forward on the stage in a state of nature? Again, the opera dancers appear nightly before crowded moral audiences, in dresses made for the express purpose of exposing their . . . figure, while the style of dancing is such as to excite the most wanton thoughts and lascivious desires. The attitudes and personal exposure of these females are most disgusting to every really modest mind, and more suited to an improper house than to a public exhibition. . . . Were the scenes and figures depicted in prints and drawings [instead of on the stage], and offered for sale, they would be considered outrages on public morals.[2]

Ryan exclusively identifies actresses, not actors, as the sexually evocative components of performance and explicitly compares them to illustrated erotica. Women were the bait and men the appointed victims, as described in an 1888 series of articles on "Tempted London":

The youth . . . becomes more or less enamoured of a "singing chambermaid" or the "leading lady," both of whom display their personal attractions with more regard to them being fully comprehended than to any old-fashioned ideas of modesty; and when the latter appears in some thrilling scene clad in a white robe, her hair flowing loosely in extravagant luxuriance down her back, her white arms bared to the shoulder, her neck and bosom by no means jealously guarded from the vulgar gaze, he loses his head in the enchantment of her presence, and carries away a mental impression of her which can do him no good and may do him much harm.[3]

The harm in this "temptation" began with the young man's vigil at the stage door and then his pursuit of the elusive actress down the thoroughfare of vice—the Strand—which, as "almost every Londoner knows," was the precinct of the trade in nocturnal prostitution, terminating at its eastern end in Holywell Street, the British Empire's infamous marketplace for "loose reading."[4] (See fig. 1.)

This sort of lurid imagery helps explain why an American minister, the Reverend S. M. Vernon, could warn that the theater's moral influence, imparted through "the half-dress, the indecent attitudes and postures, the lascivious looks and embraces, and the unfolding of a plot for the corruption and overthrow of the pure and innocent," infected men like a contagion, which "may carry death to the most healthy, robust natures." This allusion to venereal diseases (at worst) or masturbation (at best) is a delicate caution against putting opportunity in the way of arousal, and it suggests that the damage from even a single visit to the theater could be lifelong.[5]

Dr. Ryan, Vernon's fellow clergyman, is less circumspect in his moralizing. Putting aside the question of how Ryan came to know enough about "dirty pictures" to recognize the living versions, it is surprising that he stopped short of

HOLYWELL STREET, STRAND
(*Demolished* 1901)

Fig. 1. "Holywell Street, Strand," from Walter Besant and G. E. Mitton, *The Strand District* (London: Adam and Charles Black, 1902); by kind permission of Harvard College Library.

noticing that the stage was indeed "depicted in prints and drawings, and offered for sale" in the most objectionable of formats and places. The author of "Tempted London," on the other hand, did observe the coincidence: "The ordinary spectator will notice in the window [of a Holywell Street shop] pamphlets with long titles, promising entertainment of a certain kind, bad photographs of dancers, and a few books."[6]

Research in the Private Case as well as nonrestricted materials in the British Library, and in the collections of the Kinsey Institute for Research in Sex, Gender, and Reproduction, reveals that the theater in general and actresses in particular appear frequently in Victorian erotica—so frequently that acting was the most often particularized occupational type for women.[7] The content of Victorian erotica verifies in a fictive (and therefore for readers, a real) sense that the actress was inseparable from the whore and was synonymous with sex—and that she, not other women, is the signified partner. Examples in various media abound throughout the Victorian era, so that sufficient evidence exists to reveal the traditions of publishing, writing, and illustrating in this highly ephemeral genre and to permit generalizations about them. Surviving examples have been found from every decade, including the 1890s, when the knighting of male actor-managers was considered due recognition of their service to British society and art; they had lost their historical taint as rogues and vagabonds. This development shows that the stigmatization of the actress was a product of widespread and enduring fantasies about *her* and was not contingent upon the general stature of the theater or of performing in it.

Until the last years of the century, in fact, the very term "actress" remained scatologically associated with "scandal." Irrespective of changes in the socioeconomic, educational, or moral background of recruits and despite the theater's increasingly sympathetic reception, popular culture continued to ascribe immorality and sexual indiscretion to actresses; the stigma existed on the level of common knowledge or the folkloric. An examination of Victorian erotica, however, provides an attitudinal and empirical link between the cheap press's relish of rumors and trial proceedings and the widely held assumption that actresses were impure. Most importantly, it demonstrates how constant reiteration of the concept of the lascivious actress in pictures and in print affected living actresses, bearing out Andrea Dworkin's view that "the definition of women articulated systematically and consistently in pornography is objective and real in that real women exist within and must live with constant reference to the boundaries of this definition."[8]

Such a definition may not have had reality beyond the minds of the consumers, but it did have consequences. Because the Victorians viewed work as sober, serious, and rational, they no doubt had difficulty believing that acting was a serious vocation for anyone, let alone women. Furthermore, because actresses were precluded from showing the laborious side of their work, projecting instead a light, frivolous, and amusing image of the theater, the Victorian public could readily question the integrity and chastity of actresses. An actress's public profession implied impurity even when her costumes, roles, and gestural idiosyncracies did not. As Beatrice Headlam noted in 1880, men, like Muslims, have no respect for women unless they are closely veiled: "For such as these no dress is modest."[9] The prevailing eroticization of actresses in performance and print probably discouraged performers from objecting to it, for to do so might only call more attention to the phenomenon and develop among an ever-larger population the ability to decode performance.

Serials

The illustrated weekly serial is undoubtedly the oldest and most influential format for English erotica depending heavily on theatrical motifs and personages. Judging by the prices (as low as one penny for a copy of *Paul Pry* in 1848 or *Photo Bits* in 1898) and circulation figures (400,000 copies a week by 1902)[10] for this mass-produced material, the erotica richest in theatrical imagery was accessible to a broad socioeconomic range and can be regarded as a consistently cheap complement or competitor of the stage itself. The title of the earliest relevant serial, the *Crim. Con. Gazette* (1838-40, four pence), is a euphemism for adultery: the contents are risqué, vicious, and racy, featuring (in a falsely moralizing tone) biographical sketches of actresses, particularly specialists in breeches roles or those involved in affairs with notable men.

The *Exquisite* (1842-44, four pence) has copious theatrical content in addition to hints about venereal diseases, features on saloon singers, erotic fiction, translations from Du Châtelet and Montaigne, and reports of famous sex trials. The succession of cover illustrations clearly demonstrates the interchangeability of clothed female performers with other erotic stimuli. The series begins with Madame Vestris as Venus, dressed in a light gown gathered at the front to reveal her lower leg and knee; the ensuing numbers 2-7 each feature a well-known dancer in short skirts.[11] Two allegorical scenes follow—"L'Amour Corrige" (Love Corrects) and "L'Amour Vainquer" (Love the Victor). Mrs. Honey is featured in knee-length skirts in number 10 and in above-the-knee skirts in number 14.[12] Fifteen of the next nineteen plates depict famous ballerinas *pas seul* or in *pas de deux* with men, while Rachel (in exotic Oriental harem trousers), Mrs. Nisbet (in a man's fencing costume),[13] and Celeste (in breeches) are featured intermittently. The last theatrical portrait occurs in number 36 (Taglioni). The remaining twenty-four issues have titles such as "Do You Like it This Way? Eh!" and "I hope nobody's coming," which accompany depictions of sentimentally "classical" nudes, coy bedroom scenes, lesbian displays, and women in partial undress suggestive of birching. The costume of Mrs. Nisbet recurs both in "How do you like me now?" (number 41), which depicts an anonymous woman in a top hat, long skintight trousers, an unbuttoned blouse falling over her shoulder, and in the composition and decoration of "Stay, Oh Stay" (number 51), which is also related to number 8, depicting a nude woman using a bunch of flowers to flog a naked cupid. Number 45, "What are you thinking of," reiterates Titian's *Venus of Urbino,* anticipating by twenty years Manet's *Olympia;* a variant pose—clothed, of course—is used frequently in actresses' publicity shots, as in the cases of Pauline Markham, Miss Moore, Miss Fowler, and Finette.

If it is true that the clothed female performer was interchangeable with other erotic stimuli, particularly nudes, how did the eroticism of the actress's clothes function? The *Exquisite* relied on costume fetishism—borrowed wholesale from the theater—to attract men. Theatrical costume flagrantly violated the dress codes of the street and drawing room, flaunting the ankles, calves, knees, thighs, crotch, and upper torso. Cross-dressing as males was sometimes the pretense, highlighting rather than disguising sexual difference. But even when dressed as animals or inanimate objects, female performers were costumed as gendered objects of display. In the Victorian theater, adult female performers were never sexless: sex was always apparent in gendered costume, whether through tights, breeches, skirts, corsetted silhouettes, hairstyles, or headgear. Femininity was intractable and the point was to reveal it.

Like the American *National Police Gazette,* the *Days' Doings* (1870–72, three pence) emphasized murder, suicide, vengeance, and incredible feats by daring and unusual persons (much as the *News of the World* and *National Enquirer* do today). Frequent references to the theater and a regular column on "Dramatic Doings" served to reinforce stereotypes and retain the theater within the realm of the bizarre and sensational sexualized world. The innocence of the "Gallery of Public Favourites," which includes cover illustrations of the actresses Nellie Farren, Nelly Power, Teresa Rutado, and Mrs. John Wood, are counteracted by the copies of "classical" paintings and sculptures similar to those found in the *Exquisite* (minus the captions) as well as illustrations inspired by the theater itself (such as an Astley's production with Amy Sheridan as Lady Godiva, dressed in an apparent but minimal costume). The theater is rarely depicted without invoking sexual connotations. The "Strange Presentation to a Judge," for example, portrays at least eight chorus girls in tights, diaphanous skirts, and bloomers, presenting an inkstand to a short, stout, dignified judge; one girl exchanges looks with two of the barristers seated near her, confirming the implication of sexual complicity and conspiracy. The Christmas number for 1871, entirely devoted to "Behind the Scenes," reiterates in several illustrations the theme of the sexually evocative actress observed by men: men in the street watch the silhouettes of women in their dressing room; a man bursts into a room full of chorus girls to claim his scantily clad wife; a row of pretty legs is observed through the grid as they rise to stage level; a leading lady's dress is caught in the curtain roller, pulling the fabric backward and between her legs.[14] In *Here and There*, a direct successor to the *Days' Doings*, a curious tale of Sassi's snake dance is described as "the nastiest thing . . . yet heard of":

> To a slimy, creeping tune she glides up to an urn of flowers, and drags therefrom a hideous, cussed snake. She shakes the torpid wretch until he slowly unfolds himself, runs his forky tongue out, and wags his scaly tail in long-meter fashion. Then she dances and winds the clammy worm about her neck, and if there's a man in the audience wants to make her acquaintance after [this] exhibition it's some man that owns an anaconda and wants to have it educated.[15]

Interpreters do not require the assistance of the psychoanalytic theory of displacement to appreciate the *Days' Doings;* it was anything but subtle.

The infamous limited circulation monthlies of 1879–83, *Pearl, Cremorne,* and *Boudoir* (priced from two to fifteen shillings), are not as attentive to the actress as three mass-produced weeklies emanating from one publisher in the 1890s: the *Mascot,* the *London Illustrated Standard* (both three pence), and *Photo Bits* (one pence). These magazines are packed with posed photos of living pictures (a common music hall entertainment); portraits of burlesque and music hall artistes in tights; and acrobats, equestriennes, and actresses in dexterous contortions, sometimes but not always "candid." What do these swinging, kicking, reclining, bending performers suggest to prospective theater audiences? And what does the inclusion of short paragraphs of theatrical news or illustrated interviews with legitimate performers like Ellaline Terriss[16] suggest about actresses in general and the interviewees in particular? As reported in 1896 by the National Vigilance Association, an umbrella group of conservative Christian organizations campaigning against pornography and theatrical licentiousness, these are "illustrated journals of a very objectionable kind":

> Many of the pictures are vulgar in the extreme, and obviously printed in order to pander to a vicious and depraved taste. They are not what would be termed legally indecent, and cannot therefore in the present state of the Courts and of public opinion to which they respond, be stopped. Such publications are most demoralising, and tend to deprave the mind by their unwholesome and lewd suggestions.[17]

Because the sexualized context relies on references to more overtly pornographic literature (particularly fetishistic literature) and a long pictorial tradition of inferred sexuality in the subject, the knowing reader of these illustrated weeklies sees more than appears to be represented. Thus a photograph that gives an excuse for a lifted skirt or a posterior view alludes to rape or invites sodomy; dancers' high kicking in the aftermath of "Ta-ra-ra-BOOM-deay" is a contest for male attention and a metaphor of male arousal and fantastic potency; "sisters" acts and catty hair-pulling episodes stand in for lesbian sex scenes; the innocent or debutante is a virgin ripe for defilement; allusions to an actress's or dancer's tights refer more to the contents of the tights than to the tights themselves (which, unlike stockings, encase the pelvis). The message comes across repeatedly that these images are sexy, frivolous, and interchangeable.

Photo Bits recalls actresses' constant violation of public decorum and the similarity of their particular traditions of attire to those of prostitutes. As in the *Days' Doings,* actresses are satirized for wearing cosmetics: in one 1898 Archie Gunn cartoon, a ballet girl bends at the waist and says to a man, "Come dear, kiss my cheek and make it up," to which the gent replies, "I'll kiss it, but I don't think it wants any more making up."[18] Actresses' costumes reminded more than one country cousin of the Garden of Eden,[19] and their erotic value is caught by a caption beneath a picture of a pretty woman clad in tights: "It makes you shiver to see a girl without a flannel petticoat in this cold, damp weather." In an 1898 spoof on the vogue for disrobing acts, one cover of *Photo Bits* demonstrates that if scenery were abolished, nothing would impede the audience's view of the tiers of dressing rooms that rim the stage.[20]

These periodicals were definitely entertainment for men. One cartoon series depicts Farmer Haystack in raptures of delight during the ballet, while his wife covers her eyes.[21] Direct juxtapositions of illustrations of actresses and pictures of streetwalkers are common. Advertisements offer everything for the fully equipped roué, including pornographic playing cards, books, and photographs; rubber appliances; stereoscopic slides; spyglasses with a thousand-times magnification; false mustaches; cures for red noses; hair restorers; "Rose's Famous Female Mixture" (presumably an abortifacient); and birth control literature. Amid such props, women are idealized erotic objects for the use and enjoyment of men.

While the minor genre of the theatrical novel verifies that the social stigma about actresses outlasted the nineteenth century, erotic serials portray the stigma being acted upon again and again, and are as forthright and unwavering in the depiction of sexuality as Victorian novels are circumspect. Male spectators must have observed performance and performers in the light of the erotic jokes, cartoons, and short stories that "documented" social judgments about real and imaginary actresses, particularly because the erotic props that were recognizable to the pornographically literate were flaunted in the presence of (and often by) actresses. Unlike the generalized and anonymous "schoolgirls," "wives,"

"maids," "prostitutes," and "ladies of fashion" that also pop-
ulate erotica, the actress could be particularized. Her reality
verified the existence of the fantasized underworld of perpetually loose chemises, easily spread thighs, double enten-
dre, and militarily erect penises. Even when the actresses in
erotica were not real, they were a type that could be observed for a modest fee in hundreds of theaters and music
halls without any censure befalling the libertine *manqué*.
Because both in periodicals and in performance actresses
excited lust, they were obliged *en masse* to take the credit.

Printed Books

None of the full-length theatrical erotica are very "good,"
but neither authors nor buyers demanded literary excellence.
Unlike most serials, however, the elegantly bound editions
of illegal erotic books were accessible only to Holywell
Street's most prosperous customers: the frequenters of theater stalls, boxes, and dress circles rather than pits, upper
circles, and galleries. This material makes use of privileged
playgoers' stereotypes about women performers, and especially their costumes (or lack thereof), exhibitionism, relationships with agents and other promoters of professional
advancement, supposed sexual promiscuity, stage door liai-
sons, and late-night debauches. Yet none of the themes are
entirely unique to printed books. Ballet girls (who also appeared in pantomime, burlesque, extravaganza, and musical
comedy) are often featured in erotica, although any formal
occupational distinction between dancers and actresses was
probably irrelevant to both readers and playgoers. The breast,
leg, and buttocks fetishism associated with dancers relates
to the more general costume fetishes and voyeur fantasies

associated with all types of female performers, but the printed book's principal reliance on prose rather than pictures frequently led to more blatant referencing. The sadomasochistic themes so prevalent in English erotica of the period appear with special force in connection with female dancers (possibly through an erotic association between balletic training and other forms of postural "correction") and are drawn out in this format to their fullest extent. Representative examples reveal the common themes and variations in printed books.

One such work is *Crissie: A Music-Hall Sketch of To-Day* (1899), which purports to be based on the experiences of a dramatic agent, Edward Piddlewick, who panders to aristocrats' taste for music hall beauties—after satisfying himself, of course. If a virgin responds to his advances with compliant lustiness, Piddlewick concludes: " 'She'll make a rattling good artist.' "[22] There is some question as to which art these novices are actually being trained for, but it is resolved by the synonymity of the lusty whore and the successful actress. Readers are told that after a single session with Piddlewick, a novice

> had now the gratification of knowing that she had not only the expert opinion of her famous tutor and agent as to her suitability for the stage, but she had also the satisfaction of having received his first great lesson in the art of becoming rich and distinguished in the profession. . . . She was not aware that she had so far received any professional instruction from him whatsoever; but . . . she afterwards learnt that these elementary "facings" he had so energetically put her through, really constitute the alpha and omega of most of our pretty girls' successes as popular footlights' favourites.[23]

The sexual compliance and erotic effect of Piddlewick's women is explicitly described in an episode set at a dress rehearsal involving the corps de ballet of the Pandora Palace of Varieties. The women attract attention to themselves by performing acrobatic feats; the business of rehearsing is abandoned when they retire to all parts of the theater building to couple with admirers (including mashers, musicians, and the chairman of the Theatres and Music-halls Committee—who is a London county councillor). The title character, Crissie Cazarotti (the "Pandora Prostitute"), combines her occupation as prima ballerina with her vocation as a nymphomaniac. During one performance, Crissie's petulant refusal to go on stage has to be dealt with by five men who endeavor to satisfy her voracious sexual appetite.

Piddlewick's and Crissie's operatic counterparts are found in *Pauline the Prima Donna; or, Memoirs of an Opera Singer* (1898). Here, a young singer is given advanced instruction in more than vocal technique by her Viennese tutor, following a girlhood initiation into both heterosexual and lesbian lovemaking.[24] Other actresses personify lust in *The Confessions of Nemesis Hunt,* a popular work that appeared in various attenuated editions following publication of the original three-volume set of 1902–06. At the age of sixteen or seventeen, Nemesis is caught by her father *in flagrante delicto,* thrown out of the house, and forced to find her own living. She considers becoming a typist,

> but I had heard a typewriter's position in this great metropolis [of London] entailed a good deal of sitting on the knees of elderly employers, what time the trousers of the said employers were not at all in their proper decorum. If I was going to lead an immoral career I judged it better to do it on the stage.

Nemesis learns that success depends not only on complying with managers' sexual requests but also on knowing how to use sex to achieve professional and technical perfection. A famous soprano, for example, always keeps two young fellatrix with her to lubricate the vocal mechanism and improve her singing, and Nemesis is advised to fellate the comedian in a pantomime if he is getting the better of her on stage. (Her performance will improve while his declines.) While observing from a stage box, she notes that among a line of choristers,

> one of them, the biggest, had so tightened and pulled up her trunks that the outline of her cunt was plainly visible. You could see the little creases made in the silk by the hairs of her bush. I wondered at that time how she could have the daring to stand and smile into the rows of opera glasses point blank levelled at so conspicuous a portion of her body. How many members of the men watching had, I wondered, been into that sanctum so slenderly veiled from the public gaze?

The attraction of actresses like Nemesis even in the least elevated products of the stage, such as burlesque, is explained by a gentleman to his male companion:

> You *may think* it trash, though I know you've been at least a dozen times, but the public love it, and the public deserve to be catered for. Take the men in tonight's audience. They had worked hard during the day, and they had dined heavily when their work was over. They did not want to *think,* their tummies were much too full. They wanted to laugh easily, and, above all, to see lots of pretty girls, and feel their old jocks stiffen; . . . cunt, my dear Annesley, cunt, and lots of it, is what the greater part of this blessed nation wants. There's a certain proportion of the stalls who can take the cunt they see on the stage out to supper afterwards, and block it, and a much larger proportion who wish they could, but who go home and block their wives or mistresses instead.[25]

Voyeuristic fantasies of venturing behind the scenes into the secret realm supposedly forbidden to the public are common; no doubt this is the rationale for much theatrical erotica. In *Intrigues and Confessions of a Ballet Girl* . . . (1870) the reader/voyeur is treated to an episode in which the novel's heroines, aspiring dancers Emma and Maria, present themselves before the ballet mistress of Drury Lane Theatre to have their legs scrutinized. The eroticization of the situation and costumes is obvious:

> What a novel scene; here were girls of all ages, from ten to twenty; had all their practice, each dressed as their fancy pleased them; some with short skirts barely reaching to the knee, others with loose drawers, without skirt at all; most of them had light polka jackets made either of cotton or silk, and all with fleshings that reached from the waist downwards. By this style of dress their limbs were as free as when they appeared on the stage at night.

Costume is a crucial element in Maria's success; her fuller and shorter skirts are admired by male dancers, actors, and spectators alike: "Her pirouettes were divine, and brought down thunders of applause, and what caused no small portion of the enthusiasm she created, was her style of dress, which, was far more 'a naturelle' than most dancers indulge in."[26] Whether the forbidden zone was backstage or up a skirt, the theater provided a situational excuse and a plausible toilette for the voyeuristic journey. By facilitating a private fantasy in the public, or semipublic, loci of the theater, the voyeur metaphorically penetrated the most public yet most private site of womanhood. The realization of his quest (in erotic fantasy) prostituted the characters and fictionalized all female performers who reminded him of his fantasy. Their seeming willingness to participate in their own debasement—that is, their continuing to perform—served to justify his low opinion of actresses; instigate repeated imaginary defilements; and eroticize all aspects of their realm, including training, auditions, costume fittings, greenrooms, dressing rooms, and stage doors. Because in erotica anything is capable of carrying sexual overtones, and because sexual disinclination is never believed, prose was restricted by neither plausibility nor truth.

The sadomasochistic *Memoirs of a Russian Ballet Girl* (1901) is a case in point.[27] It chronicles the life of Mariska, a serf born into a household of aristocrats who spank, whip, and birch all the servants from a very young age. After being apprenticed to a dressmaker and witnessing the flagellations in the "House of Corrections" associated with that establishment, Mariska is sent to an orphan asylum that functions as a juvenile brothel. Next, at the age of fifteen, she is sold into a Grand Duke's dancing academy. The fitting of her costume—a stiff skirt, tights that will split at the rear when she bends, and a bodice revealing three-quarters of her large breasts—takes an entire chapter. The academy's rehearsals are open to aristocratic spectators; here the dancers wear very stiff short skirts, bodices entirely revealing the bosom, and silk stockings arranged so the thighs and buttocks are mostly bare. Corporal punishment is meted out by the ballet master during private lessons, while public whippings always follow rehearsals and performances; the whipped girls then disappear for a few hours or overnight in the company of the courtiers. During such absences, Mariska acquires a reputation for being sexually responsive, so she is much in demand. When she turns twenty-one, Mariska's contract expires and she is sold as a concubine to an old man who makes money by renting out his regiment of ballet girls (including ten-to-twelve-year-olds whom he requires to fellate him before he sodomizes them) to theaters that cannot afford a regular troupe. Mariska is finally bought by a captain of the Guards, to whom she is a willing sexual slave until her liberation. Throughout the narrative, the ballet school and theater are suffused with sadomasochism that supplies excitement for rich spectators. The dancers are indentured serfs, a role which the "good" ones revel in. Excellence is measured by the size of girls' buttocks and breasts (both preferably large and very white), and by their wrigglings under the birch. Male and female spectators alike attend rehearsals and performances in order to view the girls' bodies. Curiously, there is no mention of principal dancers in this book—the corps de ballet seems to be everything.

If Pauline, Nemesis, Maria, and Mariska are too sensationalized to seem convincing, it is worth mentioning that actual stage actresses were also heroines in books of this type. Three spurious memoirs and a fictitious autobiography of Eliza Vestris are similar in tone and episodes to *Intrigues and Confessions of a Ballet Girl*, but based loosely—very loosely—on her theatrical career. One of the earliest, John Duncombe's edition of *Memoirs of the life, public and private adventures of Madame Vestris. . .* , begins prophetically: "To write of the life of a Woman of the *Town* is difficult; you can scarce keep from obscenity, and seldom arrive at the truth." This is borne out in later pages, not only with respect to Vestris but also through imputations of Harriet Mellon, Madame Mercandotti, and Maria Foote. Although she was popular in her original line as a singer, Vestris's fame and erotic appeal were substantially attributed to her appearance in breeches roles, such as Macheath (see fig. 2) and Giovanni.

> A man may well exclaim thus when he sees a woman all but in a state of nudity; the lightness and colour of the dress often being made to appear like nature, unblushingly exposing herself to fulsome admiration. But whether the taste be bad or a good one . . . Madame Vestris no sooner appeared in *breeches*—no

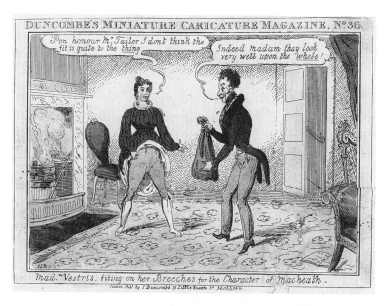

Fig. 2. "Madame Vestris," from *Memoirs of the life, public and private adventures of Madame Vestris . . .* ([London]: John Duncombe, [1836]), Harvard Theater Collection extra illustrated volume; by kind permission of Harvard College Library.

> sooner had she committed this *breach* of female modesty, than every buck and blood in London crowded to the theatre to see her.[28]

Verses reprinted from the *Amatory Biography No. 7* emphasize the point:

> What a breast—what an eye—what a foot, leg, and thigh!
>   What wonderful things she has shown us.
> Round hips, swelling sides, and masculine strides—
>   Proclaim her an English Adonis! . . .
> Her example so gay leads all the young astray,
>   And the old lick their lips as they grin;
> And think, if she would, mayhap, they still could
>   Have the pleasure and the power to sin. . . .
> Then be breeches on the go, give me the fur below,

Which appears with such grace upon many;
But V. to please must her lovely limbs squeeze
In the pantaloons of Don Giovanni.[29]

The misdating of an 1840 volume, *Memoirs of the Life of Madame Vestris,* as 1830 implies an attempt to recall and inflame Vestris's early notoriety before she had settled into matrimonial domesticity with Charles Matthews.[30] The publication of *Confessions of Madame Vestris . . .* in 1891 suggests that the attempt was long-lived.[31] (And compare, for example, fig. 3.)

Maudie. Revelations of Life in London and an unforeseen denouement, a final example published in London in 1909, represents the most complex achievement in the genre and the simplest paradigm of its characteristics. One of the rooms in Maudie's country house is a photography studio hung with countless pictures of erotic scenes. Theater managers from London and Paris have equipped the studio with the full stage apparatus in which the photos are taken and then displayed, but under the auspices of a private club, Maudie also exhibits real life on her stage for her clients' entertainment. One such play consists of a courtship, rivalry, seduction, marriage, pregnancy, and birth, all of which are enacted before the audience's eyes. Maudie explains:

> "Of course we were lucky in having a girl who was not only a very good actress, but happened to be like that, and was strong enough to play right through. It was Miss _____," naming a very well-known player. . . . "Yes, that's how she spent her time when the papers said she was touring in Italy."[32]

Many playtexts of the sort of private erotic theatricals described in *Maudie* survive from French, Dutch, and English presses dating back to 1782.[33] The Edwardian counterpart to Hefner's mansion and Rops' illustrations to *Le Théâtre Gaillard,*[34] Maudie's studio is the nexus of both production and

MADME VESTRIS AS ORPHEUS.

"Euridice! Euridice! Euridice!"

Fig. 3. Madame Vestris as Orpheus (swimming), from *English Stars, No. 1*; by kind permission of Harvard College Library.

supply, image and action, fantasy and experience, functioning as the consummate playground of the erotically theatrical, the complete gallery of relevant photographic imagery, the documentary arena for the actress at "work." It might be argued that in such a setting, as in the studios of early-twentieth-century photographers of Arabic women,

> the whole array of props, carefully disposed by the photographer around and upon the model (trompe l'oeil, furnishings, backdrops, jewelry, assorted objects), is meant to suggest the existence of a natural frame whose feigned "realism" is expected to provide a supplementary, yet by no means superfluous, touch of authenticity.[35]

The erotic book sets its own standards of truthfulness while flouting the very notion of truth. The theatrical apparatuses of Maudie's studio are authentic stage devices, but the theatrical object is never the real thing, and in this setting the fakery that is the actress's natural milieu is even further removed from its usual degree of inauthenticity. The actress plays herself while standing in for all her compatriots, as well as for all of harlotry; in either guise she is a dissembler, yet in Maudie's play her passion and procreation are as authentic as the reader's imagination can allow. Like pornography itself, the actress displays what is cloaked (anatomically and experientially), supposedly revealing truths about womanhood, role-playing, sexuality, and morality, promulgating a mystery as deep and as artificial as the colonial photographer's penetration into the Oriental harem.

Photographs

Once technology permitted them, both illustrated serials and printed books utilized photographs—literally in the case of *Photo Bits* and figuratively in *Maudie*. In erotic prose, the theater did not function as a blank backdrop but was a very particular milieu wherein illusion enhanced attractiveness and provided a ready-made imaginative context for erotic fantasy. Erotic photographs, particularly cabinets and cheap postcards, borrowed this semiotic whenever the theater was invoked by models or settings within otherwise "blank" photographic studios (see fig. 4). The social environment for sexual adventure was significant and crucial to enjoyment.

Two types of invocations were common. In the 1870s, six pence could purchase a set of the *London Lounger's Album* of cabinet photographs advertised as "The Pretty Girls of London—Regent Street, Holborn Casino, Ballet Girls at Theatre Royal Drury Lane, Bond Street, *danseuses* at Alhambra, and the Argyll Rooms." Additional series included a set exclusively of the Alhambra Palace Theatre, with portraits of the lessee and orchestra conductor "surrounded by the ballet's stars, [along with] the glove stall lounge, wine saloon, cigar bar lounge, supper room, [and] American Bar"; a second Alhambra set took the camera backstage. These little portfolios may have been either charming souvenirs or titillating tours—the evidence has vanished and it is impossible to be sure. "Polly, Adelina, and Belinda, the Pet, the Gem, and the Belle of the Ballet" (six and a half pence per photograph, or two shillings, six and a half pence for a set of six) was almost certainly, however, a tour of fantasy.[36] These concoctions of "theatrical" photographs usually emanated from Paris, but distinctly English subjects, such as the Alhambra dancers and "the Original Mikado Maids" were not unknown.[37]

During the last years of the Victorian period, the tenor of naughty postcards featuring actresses and theatrical backdrops changed as scenes of explicit sex became more readily

Fig. 4. An unidentified actress posed as Napoleon, yet emphasizing her crotch; cabinet photo; by kind permission of the
Kinsey Institute.

and inexpensively available in the marketplace. In the 1870s, six pence bought a series of Alhambra Palace photographs, a set of stereotyped scenes behind the curtain, or poses by the acrobat Lulu ; their competition consisted of dressed seaside postcards, windy weather shots, and Girls of the Period.[38] But by the 1890s, postcard sets depicted a nude female gymnast on the swing and trapeze (thirty-six poses, one shilling, six pence per cabinet photo, or fifteen shillings a dozen), and "Behind the scenes at the Ballet, startling revelations" with fifteen "highly erotical scene[s] between a well known abonnetand [and] the first star of the ballet" (in cabinet and *carte de visite* sizes). Now their competition became scenes with naked prepubescent girls, interracial sex, and intergenerational lesbianism.[39] The theater's unconsummated dramatic narratives of Oriental exoticism, classical mythology, fairyland; melodramatic threats of defloration; callypiges (a pornographic invention denoting women who were remarkable for their fleshy buttocks), shepherdesses, painters' models, and cocottes could not vie with consummated versions of the same fictions attainable at a bookseller's or stationer's for roughly the price of admission to a West End playhouse. The gossamer Graces, chain-mail Valkyries, and cross-dressed swashbucklers on late-Victorian theatrical postcard sets filled in much of the narrative continuity that on stage was the responsibility of the playgoer. Such pictorial eroticism may have become more enticing and satisfying precisely because it legitimated both partners in the voyeuristic erotic encounter. One French set entitled "La Loge de l'Actrice," depicting a woman's transformation from "undress" in street skirt and unfastened corset to "dress" in breeches, waistcoat, sword, eighteenth-century coat, and feathered hat, concludes with the caption: "Tonight I'm going to put everything into my part! But not for you, the public, for him! for my lover! For love commands through two lovely eyes—and man the slave must obey!"[40]

The second type of invocation was the legitimate publicity photograph of real performers. The vast majority of these photographs (very likely including those of Miss Fortescue) are as decorous as anything from Julia Margaret Cameron's studio. Unlike Cameron's subjects, however, the photograph of an actress carried a blight of erotic associations—what Susan Griffin calls "the pornographic idea of a female, and of female sexuality,"[41] or what John Elsom describes as "the weight of their context." "Because this girl has appeared at the Gaiety or the Alhambra, her photograph was fair game for our fantasies: and the significance of these photographs is that they subtly controlled the fantasies, hinting at possibilities in one direction or another."[42] As on stage, the photographed actress remains acutely aware of the spectator, for without him she is not an actress. Easily identifiable through her nocturnal occupation, she was transformed by the publicity photograph into an icon—perhaps of glamour, certainly of sex. Through the postcard, the tabooed icon could be collected and displayed in an album as a household amusement or private harem. The reduction to a regular format, the eight-by-thirteen-centimeter postcard, with a point of sale common to similar postcards of politicians, royalty, authors, and artists, suggests that the medium eliminated the stigma of the actress's profession. But at the same time, erotic periodicals printed actresses' images (probably unauthorized but nonetheless flagrant) and French postcards flowed into Britain, causing erotic visual encodings to become more widely understood than ever.

In *fin-de-siècle* and new century English and French postcards, costume jewelry, see-through draperies, strings of beads, mirrors, flowers, ewers, vanity tables, paintings, cushions, carpets, lutes, swords, and cups and saucers carry erotic weight. Fairies, flowers, Amazons, bathers, living statuary (sometimes realizations of paintings), and Oriental exotics are common guises. The congruencies of conventional theater sets and props with the erotic postcard "narrative," and of character personae in postcards with pantomime, ballet, tableaux vivants, and drama, are striking. The unnaturalness of these habitats is natural to actresses. By association, all the models became actresses and all actresses became models.

As on the stage, actual nudity was not a requirement for sexual titillation. Simulated nudity (with tights or maillots) was just as powerful and, by Victorian aesthetic standards, much more beautiful. Scandal arose by association: posing with a man, posturing indecently (one foot on a chair, one leg highly elevated, an ankle crossed over a knee, dorsal views, contortions), or through activity (bicycling, climbing, arranging the toilette). Momentary deferment of nudity is the message of the photograph.

Feminist art and film theory argues that the male spectator possesses "the Look";[43] nineteenth-century erotica demonstrates that this privilege was also extended to the Victorian male playgoer, not only through the directness of his gaze but also through his power to ascribe meanings to the objects of his gaze. Two hypotheses follow from this principle. As public nocturnal women, actresses and prostitutes depended for their livelihoods on successfully suing for men's attention—on being recognizable and therefore eligible for the gaze. These women routinely violated conventions of dress, makeup, gesture, and association that distinguished "respectable" women from the demimonde. Their function as the senders of erotically stimulating messages is confirmed and reinforced by the behavior, ideology, and literature of the male receptors. But in the theater event, the skulking illicit voyeur had no role; a man's attendance at the theater was a public act and his looking was direct, legitimate reception of the sexual semiosis. His gender dictated that he entered the theater with a particular semiotic history that determined his ability to perceive and appropriately understand the significant sexual messages. Without him, the erotic transmission—or *gest*—of the actress was sexually meaningless.

For those who lacked the semiotic history of the contemporary masculine culture, the performance had less than full meaning. Although puritanical and female spectators sometimes regarded the actress as a woman warranting social ostracism, their objections to the Empire promenade, for example, were misdirected because they could not fully participate in the semiosis. The real problem in the Empire music hall was not that men made assignations with prostitutes there (because assignations were made in all sorts of public places) but, rather, that the whole interior of the building housed a sexual system that was consistent within itself and harmonious with the Leicester Square and West End neighborhoods. Both Dr. Ryan in 1839 and the National Vigilance Association's journal editor Laura Ormiston Chant in 1894 recognized that they could neither close the theaters nor eliminate the sexiness of performance; their only recourse was to warn audiences away and prevent aroused spectators from having ready access to the ladies of the promenade.

The second hypothesis concerns conventions of performance. Like nineteenth-century erotica, much nineteenth-century theatrical fare was repetitive in structure, content, and presentational style. David Mayer postulates that the pantomimic formulas of sexual cross-dressing supplied "a mechanism for dealing with real and immediate and acute anxieties in disguised form." His theory that male unemployment was the trauma behind the first adolescent pantomime boy in 1819 and the first voluptuously proportioned pantomime boy in 1831 would benefit by his attending more to the expressed fantasies of pornography and relying less on psychoanalytic generalities such as castration fear, the phallic mother, and the synonymity of material success with sexual potency.[44] The ability of pantomime, burlesque, extravaganza, ballet, and melodrama to endure in fixed formats for decades testifies to the insatiability of the sexual appetite, the restricted gender access to the encodings, the suitability of these genres of popular entertainment to the hegemonic public taste, and their coherence with other sexualized contexts.

Not until the early years of the present century did the audience begin to become satiated and the formulas pall. At the same time, new photographic technologies were offering a different viewing experience to the readers of erotic magazines and viewers of kinematic images, creating an expanded occupational typology of sexually scandalous women. Access to these images was more easily attained by both sexes, who were assured voyeuristic anonymity. With social attitudes about sex becoming relaxed, fashion permitted all women to don individualized and flamboyant dress and makeup, and greater numbers of middle-class women joined actresses in training for and pursuing careers outside the domestic sphere. The mystique and sexual threat of the stage actress diminished as concern about her legitimacy waned in the popular culture, and belief in her scandalous life lost its status in folklore.

Notes

1. Because of its convenience and lucidity, and in order to avoid the issue of differentiation of pornography from erotica on

the grounds of explicitness, violence, or erotic "quality," I have adopted the definition of erotica developed by the cataloguers of the Kinsey Institute: "a type of pictorial or written material which is intended to produce sexual arousal in readers and viewers. Excludes discussion of artistic value—is always dealt with in a social, moral, or legal context."

2. Michael Ryan, *Prostitution in London* (London: H. Bailliere, 1839), 5.

3. *British Weekly,* 10 Feb. 1888, 278.

4. Ibid., 16 Mar. 1888, 365.

5. Rev. S. M. Vernon, *Amusements in the Light of Reason, History, and Revelation* (Cincinnati: Walden and Stowe; New York: Phillips and Hunt, 1882), 78, 73, 76–77.

6. *British Weekly,* 6 Mar. 1888, 365.

7. A few titles remain elusive: *Rose Pompon, the Dancing Girl Millionaire, a piquant Paris painted to the Life by the lively Lady herself* (advertised in H. S. Nichols, *A Catalogue of Old Books in Various Departments of Literature,* no. 8, March 1888); *Memoirs of Cora Pearl, The English Beauty of the French Empire* (in Nichols); "The Rehearsal," in *Memoirs of Private Flagellation and Luxurious Living* (publ. Charles Carrington; H. K. Browne, artist); *The Pretty Girls of London; Their Lithe Love Affairs, Playful Doings, etc.,* praised by Ivan Bloch for its excellent pictures, "freely, though not obscenely treated," including a lady in her loge and a ballet girl onstage (Bloch, *Sex Life in England Illustrated,* trans. and ed. Richard Deniston [New York: Falstaff, 1934], 358); *Queens of the Stage: A Record of Carnal Intimacies with some of the Greatest Actresses, French, English and German Now Living* (London: Biblioteca Arcana, 1882), noted in Alfred Rose, comp., *Register of Erotic Books,* 2 vols. (New York: Jack Brussel, 1965); George Thompson, *Amorous Adventures of Lola Montez* (in Rose, and H. S. Ashbee, *Catena Librorum Tacendorun*); *The Lady in Flesh Colored Tights* (Rose); *Cerisette, or, the Amours of an Actress* (Rose); *Little Thomas of the Opera Colonnade* (Rose); and *L'actrice chaste et le capitaine amoreux* (formerly in the Kinsey Library).

8. Andrea Dworkin, *Pornography: Men Possessing Women* (London: Women's Press, 1981), 201.

9. Mrs. Stewart [Beatrice R.] Headlam, *The Ballet: A paper read before the Church and Stage Guild* (London: William Poole, 1880), 11.

10. Edward J. Bristow, *Vice and Vigilance: Purity Movements in Britain since 1700* (Dublin: Gill and Macmillan; Totawa, N.J.: Rowman and Littlefield, 1977), 218.

11. Variations among the British Library and Kinsey Institute sets occur in early numbers. Instead of Vestris, the Kinsey Institute's first issue is "Compare all Things" (three women lift their skirts to show their lower legs); number 4 is definitely labeled Taglioni in the Kinsey Institute set, whereas in the British Library set the dancer is unidentified.

12. The significance of featuring Mrs. Honey twice is made clear by a quip in the contemporary erotic weekly *Gems for Gentlemen:* " 'What is good for stiffness in one's lower extremities?' inquired the Duke of Wellington of somebody at the Queen's Ball. 'Why,' observed Chesterfield, who stood near, 'I have found the application of honey to the parts removes it in a very few minutes' " ([c. 1850] 1.3:23).

13. Nisbet also appears in breeches on the first page of the *Crim. Con. Gazette*, 26 Jan. 1839.

14. *Days' Doings: An Illustrated Journal of Romantic Events, Sports, Sporting & Theatrical News at Home & Abroad*, 10 Feb. 1872, 1; 2 Sept. 1871, 87–88; and 23 Dec. 1871.

15. *Here and There*, 30 Mar. 1872, 92, 93.

16. *London Illustrated Standard*, 21 Dec. 1895, 5.

17. National Vigilance Association, *Eleventh Annual Report*, 1896, 10–11.

18. *Photo Bits*, 9 July 1898, 5.

19. "At An Empire Ballet" (*Photo Bits*, 9 July 1898, 11):

Londoner   — How are you enjoying yourself?
Country Cousin — It is like Paradise.
Londoner   — You must be having a good time, then?
Country Cousin — Not altogether, but the costumes remind
                  me so much of the Garden of Eden.

20. *Photo Bits,* 18 Feb. 1899, 2, and 17 Dec. 1898.

21. Ibid., 9 July 1898, 26.

22. *Crissie: A Music-Hall Sketch of To-Day* ([London]): Alhambra, 1899), 35. Charles Carrington delights in denouncing this work as "simply utterably filthy" and claims that it is based on the adventures of a real-life Crissie, written by a man "most cruelly treated by her, ruined and driven to drink." See Carrington, *Forbidden Books: Notes and Gossip on Tabooed Literature by an Old Bibliophile* (Paris: [Carrington], 1902), 147.

23. *Crissie,* 47–48.

24. *Pauline the Prima Donna; or, Memoirs of an Opera Singer* (London and New York: Erotica Biblion Society [Paris: Carrington], 1898). This is a loose adaptation of *Aus den Memoiren einer Sangerin* (1868–75), the autobiography of Frau Schroder-Devrient.

25. [George Reginald Bacchus?], *The Confessions of Nemesis Hunt,* 3 vols. (London: Privately printed, 1902–06), 2:4, 1:107, 2:91.

26. *Intrigues and Confessions of a Ballet Girl; disclosing startling and voluptuous scenes before and behind the curtain, enacted by well-known personages in the theatrical, military, medical and other professions; with kisses at Vauxhall, Greenwich, &c., &c., and a full disclosure of the secret and amatory doings in the dressing room, under and upon the stage, in the light and in the dark, by one who has had her share* (London: Rozez and Co. [c. 1870]), 8, 14.

27. [Edmond Dumoulin], *Memoirs of a Russian Ballet Girl,* two vols. in one (Monte Carlo: [Carrington], 1901). The advertisement for this volume, included in the *Biblioteca Carringtoniensis* at the Kinsey Institute, purports that Mariska, "formerly in the ballet of the Imperial Theatres," was born in 1840; her ballet training would consequently have occurred between 1855 and 1861.

28. *Memoirs of the life, public and private adventures of Madame Vestris: formerly of the Theatre Royal San Carlos; and now of the Theatres Royal Drury Lane & Covent Garden. With interesting and curious anecdotes of celebrated and distinguished characters in the fashionable world. Detailing an interesting variety of singularly curious and amusing scenes, as performed before and behind the curtain, both in*

public and private life, "at home" and abroad ([London]: John Duncombe [1836]), 7, 75.

29. Ibid., 75–76. The *Amatory Biography* extract is also bound into the Harvard Theater Collection's extra illustrated volume of Duncombe's edition. This reprint was published as *Memoirs of the public and private life, amourous [sic] adventures and wonderful exploits of Madame V*—([London]: Chubb [1830?]), 8.

30. *Memoirs of the Life of Madame Vestris of the Theatres Royal Drury Lane and Covent Garden. Illustrated with Numerous Curious Anecdotes* (Privately printed, 1830 [ca. 1840]).

31. *Confessions of Madame Vestris; in a series of letters to Handsome Jack* (n.p.: New Villon Society, 1891), priced at two pounds.

32. [George Reginald Bacchus?], *Maudie. Revelations of Life in London and an unforeseen denouement* (London: The "Chatty" Club, 1909), 32.

33. Examples include: *Théâtre Gaillard,* 2 vols. (Glascow [sic], 1782); [Lemercier de Neuville, et al.], *Le Théâtre Érotique de la rue de la Santé* ([1864–66]); *Lady Bumtickler's Revels. A Comic Opera, in Two Acts, as it was performed at lady Bumtickler's private theatre, in Birch-Grove, with unbounded applause* (London: Printed for George Peacock and sold at No. 66, Drury Lane [J. C. Hotten, 1872]); *Theatre Royal Olymprick. New and Gorgeous Pantomime Entitled Harlequin Prince Cherrytop and the Good Fairy Fairfuck or the Frig the Fuck and The Fairy* (Oxford, 1879); and E[dmund] D[umoulin], *Théâtre Naturaliste* (London: Collection des érotiques français du XIXe siècle publiée par la société des bibliophiles cosmopolites [Amsterdam: August Brancart], 1889). Secondary studies include G. Capon, *Les Théâtres Clandestins* (Paris: Plessis, [1905]); Henri d'Almeras and Paul D'Estrée, *Les Théâtres Libertins au XVIIIe siècle* (Paris: H. Daragan, 1905); and Henry L. Marchand, *The French Pornographers, including a History of French Erotic Literature* (New York: Book Awards, 1965), 134–41.

34. See the frontispieces to *Le Théâtre Gaillard,* 2 vols. (1865).

35. Malek Alloula, *The Colonial Harem,* trans. Myrna Godzich and Wlad Godzich (Minneapolis: University of Minneapolis Press, 1986), 18.

36. From advertisements in the *Days' Doings,* rpt. Peter Fryer, comp., *The Man of Pleasure's Companion. A Nineteenth-Century Anthology of Amorous Entertainment* (London: Arthur Baker, 1968), 57.

37. From the *Catalogue of Curiosa and Erotica* ([London], 1892), in the Private Case, British Library, London.

38. Reproduced in Fryer, 57.

39. See *Catalogue of Curiosa and Erotica.* Typical examples of the cards are reproduced in Jean-Pierre Bourgeron, ed., *Nude 1900* (New York: Morgan and Morgan, 1980). An "abonnetand" was a theater subscriber, typically from the upper class; the term also connoted raffishness.

40. Reproduced in Paul Hammond, *French Undressing: Naughty Postcards from 1900 to 1925* (New York: Pyramid, 1975), 102.

41. Susan Griffin, *Pornography and Silence: Culture's Revenge against Nature* (New York: Harper and Row, 1981), 204.

42. John Elsom, *Erotic Theatre* (London: Secker and Warburg, 1973), 26.

43. See Annette Kuhn, *The Power of the Image: Essays on Representation and Sexuality* (London: Routledge & Kegan Paul, 1985); Teresa de Lauretis, *Alice Doesn't: Feminism, Semiotics, Cinema* (Bloomington: Indiana University Press, 1984); and Griselda Pollock, *Vision and Difference* (London: Routledge, 1988).

44. David Mayer, "The Sexuality of Pantomime," *Theatre Quarterly* 4 (February-April 1974): 53–64.

5 / The Muscular Christian
As Schoolmarm

John C. Hawley, S. J.

In 1859 the *Saturday Review* was one of the first journals to associate Charles Kingsley with a "younger generation of writers of fiction" who fostered the sentiment that "power of character in all its shapes goes with goodness." "Who does not know," the reviewer asked, "all about the 'short, crisp, black hair,' the 'pale but healthy complexion,' the 'iron muscles,' 'knotted sinews,' 'vast chests,' 'long and sinewy arms,' 'gigantic frames,' and other stock phrases of the same kind which always announce, in contemporary fiction, the advent of a model Christian hero?"[1] After Kingsley's death in 1875, however, Henry James and others spoke up in his defense and correctly identified the novelist George Lawrence, considered by many to be Kingsley's literary disciple, as the real proponent of the brutes commonly called "Muscular Christians."[2] Kingsley himself had something much more human in mind, and it was an ideal he preached not only to men but also to women.

Mark Girouard has argued that among the various "textbooks" for the renewed interest in chivalry in the nineteenth century were Kingsley's sermons and novels. In a sermon at Windsor Castle in 1865, for example, Kingsley declared that "the age of chivalry is never past, so long as there is a wrong left unredressed on earth, or a man or a woman left to say 'I will redress that wrong, or spend my life in the attempt.' "[3] The chivalry that Kingsley and other Christian Socialists envisioned had little to do with moats, castles, or armor and was actually more dutiful than that of the medieval past; in fact, given their growing ethical concern, such men held popular "aesthetic" chivalry in contempt.

Despite this criticism of the nostalgic chivalry that fascinated many contemporary young men, Kingsley's conception of woman's role in the code he advocated had its own medieval overtones. He opens his 1857 novel, *Two Years Ago,* with a description of the new Lady of Shalott as a miller's daughter who reads Charlotte Yonge's novels and, instead of pining away amid castle ruins, is now "teaching poor children in Hemmelford National School." Her modern "fairy knight" lectures at mechanics' institutes, travels by rail, and fights in the Crimea. But later in the same novel, Kingsley's rhetoric strikes more disturbing chords that were to reverberate throughout his century, and into our own:

> To a true woman, the mere fact of a man's being her husband . . . is utterly sacred, divine, all-powerful; in the might of which she can conquer self in a way which is an every-day miracle; and the man who does not feel about the mere fact of a woman's having given herself utterly to him, just what she herself feels about it, ought to be despised by all his fellows; were it not that, in that case, it would be necessary to despise more human beings than is safe for the soul of any man.[4]

Saviors of men, transmitters of civilization, advocates of the heart working in conjunction with man's mind: these were the roles for woman in Kingsley's version of Muscular Christianity. "Ah, woman," he intones in the same novel, "if you only knew how you carry our hearts in your hands, and would but use your power for our benefit, what angels you might make us all" (chap. 11, 1:316).

Such views would lead Kingsley into the heart of the women's movement, especially in his enthusiastic advocacy of their right to a better education, but would also bring about his inevitable alienation from many of the movement's more forceful leaders. From our vantage point, his definition of the "true woman" was limited by his mid-Victorian fear of social instability. Nonetheless, an age that builds a "crystal palace" to house a lump of coal is clearly searching for a new mythology to explain its dreams, and this, too, is part of Kingsley's story: the story of competing images for the New Woman—Angel in the House, Angel out of the House, complete equal, Female Savior, and others.[5] In the same way that George Lawrence and other contemporary novelists (many of them women) later adulterated Kingsley's masculine ideal, conservative aspects of his feminine ideal were also stretched beyond Kingsley's recognition by the psychologist Henry Maudsley, who was himself something of a George Lawrence character. This usurpation of Kingsley's ideal role for woman in the later form of Muscular Christianity had more ominous overtones, more unfortunate consequences, and more enduring power than the relatively humorous "model Christian hero" skewered by the *Saturday Review* in 1859.[6]

In his role as pastor, Charles Kingsley no doubt encountered many young middle-class women who were, as he described them, "often really less educated than the children of their parents' workmen" (*Two Years Ago*, chap. 5, 1:206). This was a problem he sought to address at a particularly crucial period for the emancipation of schooling in England. The history of his involvement in women's education is interesting, therefore, not only in terms of the changes he may have hastened in some quarters, but also as a quite telling example of a reformer who shied away from revolution. What Kingsley wholeheartedly endorsed as a stabilizing development in education—the training of governesses—quickly got beyond his, or any man's, control. Like several other early enthusiasts, he found himself wondering whether he had unwittingly encouraged a restructuring not only of the goals of British education but of the ideals of Victorian womanhood as well.

As in other areas of concern to him—notably, his involvement with Christian Socialism—Kingsley's mind seemed pulled in two directions. He eventually became a notoriously enthusiastic proponent of marriage but was equally concerned that young Victorian women find a purpose in life beyond the attainment of a comfortable niche. In *Two Years Ago,* he inveighed against women who had become "sedentary, luxurious, full of petty vanity, gossip, and intrigue, without work, without purpose, except that of getting married to any one who will ask them." Such women, he felt, had talents to offer England that too frequently atrophied if left undeveloped, and he warned that until the country found a better method of educating women, far too many would be "fated, when they marry, to bring up sons and daughters as sordid and unwholesome as their mothers" (chap. 5, 1:206). In subsequent writings he argued that imposed ignorance had left young middle-class women no less victimized by society than were the children of the poor. Much of his anger is thus directed against those males who continued to obstruct educational reform. But "sordid" and "unwholesome" seem more embittered than righteous descriptions and suggest that by 1857 Charles Kingsley had cast himself as Lear, surrounded by daughters who would not be led.

His involvement in the education of women had begun ten years earlier. Frederick Denison Maurice, Kingsley's religious mentor, served on the Committee of the Governesses' Benevolent Institution; the Reverend David Laing was its honorary secretary. In 1848, with the help of some professors at King's College of London University, they established Queen's College, London, conceived as a training college for governesses. Maurice, who served as its principal from its founding until 1854, appointed Kingsley professor of English literature.

As Harriet Martineau kindly observed in 1861, "nothing short of heroism and every kind of magnanimity was requisite to make any man offer himself for a professorship in such colleges."[7] The conservative *Quarterly Review,* for example, immediately criticized the college's goals, arguing that such a scheme would merely inflame the imaginations of future governesses rather than adequately develop their mundane skills and common sense.[8] Maurice anticipated such objections, however, and in his "Introductory Lecture on the Objects and Methods of Queen's College" admitted that the word "college . . . has a novel and ambitious sound . . . [but] if any are offended by the largeness of the design they may be assured that . . . we found that any limitation would have made the education more artificial, more pretending, and less effectual for the class which we especially desire to serve."[9] The intention, obvious in Maurice's words and clear in the *Quarterly Review*'s aggressive response, was to broaden minds and open the eyes of young women to a larger world.

In any case, Kingsley's formal association with the college

was short-lived; having collapsed from nervous exhaustion while writing the novel, *Yeast,* he withdrew in December 1848 from teaching after offering only one course. But he continued to lecture on the subject of women's education and maintained an interest in Maurice's project. He advised his replacement, the Reverend Alfred Strettell: "We want to train—not cupboards full of 'information' (vile misnomer), but real informed women." One of the major areas of disagreement regarding women's colleges, of course, was the curriculum. Conservatives advocated traditional "feminine" subjects (music, foreign languages) that would make women more decorative. Progressives, on the other hand, proposed the same curriculum that young men had available to them. Kingsley's implied compromise endorses subjects that would turn out intelligent social workers rather than stereotypical bluestockings.

His letter to Strettell continues: "Don't be afraid of talking about marriage. We must be real and daring at Queen's College, or nowhere. The 'clear stage and no favour' which we have got there is so blessed and wonderful an opening, that we must make the most of it to utter things there which prudery and fanaticism have banished from pulpits and colleges."[10] What Strettell is to say regarding marriage is left unstated, but Kingsley's other writings resolve any confusion his successor may have felt. Marriage was a sacred office for women, far more important than any intellectual endeavor (although an "informed" wife was, of course, a better wife). Reviewing Tennyson's *The Princess* in September 1850 Kingsley warns that

> in every age women have been tempted . . . to deny their own womanhood, and attempt to stand alone as men. . . . Tenny-

son] shows us the woman, when she takes her stand on the false masculine ground of the intellect, working out her own moral punishment, by destroying in herself the tender heart of flesh . . . becomes all but a vengeful fury.[11]

Founding a college for women, therefore, was a good work, but becoming a wife, mother, and "saviour" even better.

Several later founders of women's colleges were inspired by this cautious hierarchy of female roles, while others emphatically rebelled against its double standard. In the late 1870s, after many battles that had improved educational opportunities for women, Lady Stanley of Alderley pointed to the establishment of Queen's as the real inspiration for all that came after: Bedford College, the Misses Buss, Beale, and Davies, and eventual admission of women to medical colleges and universities.[12] Frances Buss (1827–94) founded the North London Collegiate School for Ladies in 1850. Dorothea Beale (1831–1906) became headmistress of a similar school at Cheltenham in 1858. Emily Davies (1830–1921) chaired a committee that convinced the Cambridge Local Examinations Syndicate in 1865 to examine girls as well as boys. All three women were greatly influenced by Kingsley's mentor Maurice. Although not on especially good terms with Maurice, Harriet Martineau also offered similar praise for Queen's College and for Ladies' College in Bedford Square for the "new order of superior female teachers—issuing from these colleges to sustain their high credit and open the way to a general elevation of female education."[13]

Kingsley's own contribution to these developments did not go unrecognized. In 1859, in the second year of its publication, Bessie R. Parkes's *English Woman's Journal* praised his work, even citing the advice he had offered in "Practical Lectures to Ladies" to the effect that women should shock men into assuming social responsibilities by demonstrating their own willingness to sell their jewelry to help the poor. The journal argued that its readers needed to become more aware of social needs beyond their lintels and urged women to "free" their husbands to address these larger problems. To do otherwise, they scolded, would demonstrate three vices already far too evident in the nineteenth century: "self-ishness which wishes to merge the man and the citizen into the mere breadwinner for his own household; ignorance that cannot read the signs of the times, or understand what God is calling men to do; timidity which fears that He who feeds the raven, and providently caters for the sparrow, will not provide for those who sacrifice personal advancement to carry on His own work."[14] Kingsley expected, as did the women associated with this periodical, that most Victorian matrons preferred the familiarity of their home and hearth to the responsibilities of politics and empire. If that were the case, broadening their vision even enough to allow them to "liberate" their husbands to deal with that greater world was a large task in itself—and a relatively safe one for men.

But some women whose consciousness had already been raised were not unanimous in their praise for Kingsley, Maurice, and their associates. The philosophy of women's education that these men popularized persisted at Queen's long after Kingsley's formal connection with the school ended, if Harriet Martineau's reaction in 1861 to William Cowper, then dean of the college, is any indication. Despite her admiration for many aspects of the women's colleges, Martineau had already strongly condemned more than twenty years earlier the false notion of chivalry that she recognized as a justification for enfeebling women.[15] Specifically with regard to Queen's College, she now regretted that the majority of male friends of female education, like Cowper, still assumed that "the grand use of a good education to a woman is that it improves her usefulness to somebody else . . . as 'mothers of heroes,' 'companions to men,' and so on."[16] In private, she offered even harsher criticism. Richard Holt Hutton was to be professor of mathematics at Ladies' College from 1858 to 1865, but following his 1858 speech advocating less taxing academic subjects for women, Martineau wrote Fanny Wedgwood: "It seems to us that [his] Address at the College was so bad in spirit, manners and views that it ought to cost him the post. . . . It seems to incapacitate him for teaching in a Ladies' college at all. That whole narrow, insolent, prudish, underbred set of Unitarian pedants,—shallow, conceited and cruel,—are too disagreeable to do much mischief, unless they get into professorships."[17] There seem to be unmistakable rumblings here of the "vengeful fury" that Kingsley feared.

Even the *English Woman's Journal,* in a sign of things to come, published a letter from Emily Davies strongly advocating the training of women as physicians—just two years after the magazine had urged women to "free" their husbands for work in the world. Much later, in 1896, Davies wrote that efforts such as Queen's College were "only in a general sense pioneers in the movement for opening universities to women. They were self-contained, and there is no evidence that they were aimed at being attached to any university." She gave greater credit to individual women like Jessie Meriton White who in 1856 was the first to attempt (unsuccessfully) to obtain admission to a university.[18] Barbara Leigh-Smith Bodichon was also cautious in her praise. Maurice had advised against Bodichon's attempts in the 1850s to found a school that would draw from all classes, creeds, and nationalities. Even if he personally found such experimentation acceptable, he apparently considered it an assault on too many fronts at once, and bad strategy. This caution, characterized by some as cowardice and by others

as obstruction, was typical of the approach to female education that both Kingsley and Maurice took.

But in fact, Kingsley seems to have recognized the justice
in Davies's rather parsimonious praise for Queen's College.
He eventually argued that the real advances in education began around 1865, when Local Examinations for Cambridge,
Edinburgh, and Durham universities were opened to women.
(Oxford did the same in 1870.) In an 1869 *Macmillan's* article, he suggests how schools for governesses were just the
beginning: "A demand for employment has led naturally to a
demand for improved education fitting women for employment, and that again has led naturally also to a demand on
the part of many thoughtful women for a share in making
those laws and those social regulations which have, while
made exclusively by men, resulted in leaving women at a disadvantage at every turn."[19] As "natural" as these increasing
demands may have appeared to Kingsley in 1869, it was well
recognized by John Stuart Mill and others that supporters of
one set of demands, like education, might have great reservations about others, like suffrage. Kingsley's own increasing
hesitation seems to have arisen, however, less from specific
demands than from conflicting philosophies of the meaning
of "true womanhood." His ambivalent response to women
who fought against a wide variety of social regulations
amounts to a rejection of them as women. This is what led
to his eventual alienation from the movement for women's
rights and prompted some of the most high-pitched attacks
in his novels.

He did encourage women to become more fully educated
and to become actively involved in helping "the other nation," and his position in society no doubt assuaged the
fears of some men reluctant to see their wives engaged in
such work. Beyond his progressive interest in the social re-

sponsibilities of women, however, he continued to insist upon essential differences between men and women. In *The Roman and the Teuton* (1864), he writes that women's "influence, whether in the state or in the family, is to be not physical and legal, but moral and spiritual. . . . It therefore rests on a ground really nobler and deeper than that of man." A woman's main duty, whether she becomes educated or enfranchised, is to "call out chivalry in the man." He even views the enfranchisement of women in terms of the effect it will have on men—an effect he fears.

> The modern experiments for emancipating women, and placing them on a physical and legal equality with the man, may be right, and may be ultimately successful. We must not hastily prejudge them. But of this we may be almost certain; that if they succeed, they will cause a wide-spread revolution in society, of which the patent danger will be, the destruction of the feeling of chivalry, and the consequent brutalization of the male sex.[20]

Two years later, Emily Davies concludes her 1866 book, *The Higher Education of Women,* by directly addressing Kingsley's argument. She grants that female subservience may have occasioned male chivalry but asks, "Is it good for a man to feel that his influence rests on a ground less noble and deep than that of woman, and to satisfy himself with a lower moral position?"

> If the scheme of Divine Providence requires that there should be outlets for the protective energies, they are likely to be found for a long time yet, in the infirmities of age, of infancy, and of poverty, without encouraging morbid or affected weakness in human beings intended by nature to be healthy and strong. . . . The chivalrous spirit now shows itself in the abandonment of unjust privileges, in the enactment of equal laws, and in facing ridicule, opposition, and discouragement in behalf of unpopular ideas.

And she warns the preacher, "Let us take care lest, in cling-ing to forms from which the spirit has departed, in shutting our eyes to keep out the dawning day, we may be blindly fighting the battle of the Philistines, all unwittingly ranged among the enemies of the cause we desire to serve."[21]

An increasing number of women clearly were prepared to go farther than their lintels, and this made Kingsley skittish. It eventually dawned on him, for example, that there might be reasons other than religious celibacy or bad luck for some women's willingness to forgo marriage, and such ap-parent independence was not something he encouraged. Consequently, he readily caricatured women who would not allow men to lead the movement for their rights. The "true" emancipation of women, he claimed, was to be an emancipa-tion "not from man (as some foolish persons fancy), but from the devil . . . who divides her from man, and makes her live a life-long tragedy."[22] In *Two Years Ago*, he had pointedly condemned "that ghastly ring of prophetesses . . . [the] strong-minded and emancipated women, who prided themselves on having cast off conventionalities." Such exponents of the rights of women, he wrote, do more dam-age than good. They were

> women who had missions to mend everything in heaven and earth, except themselves: who had quarreled with their husbands, and had therefore felt a mission to assert women's rights, and reform marriage in general; or who had never been able to get married at all . . . and every one of whom had, in obedience to Emerson, "followed her impulses," and despised fashion, and was accordingly clothed and bedizened as was right in the sight of her own eyes, and probably in those of no one else. . . . They did not wish to be women, but very bad imitations of men. (Chap. 11, 1: 298, 300)

By 1869 he had concluded that these less patient "imitations of men" were in the ascendant; although he did support the campaign for women's voting rights, he failed to bring his customary energy to the cause.[23]

Some of his friends were troubled by this apparent break. Because Kingsley was presiding over the educational section of a Social Sciences Meeting at Bristol in that year, Maurice wrote asking him to reassert his conviction that women should be admitted to all the privileges of the other sex.[24] Mill was another correspondent on this issue. Although never fully in agreement on the Woman Question, he and Kingsley felt a mutual interest and Mill called him "one of the good influences of the age"; Kingsley, for his part, read *On Liberty* from cover to cover one day in a book shop and remarked as he left that it "affected me in making me a clearer-headed, braver-minded man on the spot."[25] Thus in 1870 Mill wrote to ask the reasons for Kingsley's alienation from the movement. Kingsley responded that he "depre-cate[d] the interference in this movement of unmarried women," and was particularly concerned lest the struggle for women's rights be discredited by "hysteria, male and female." He urged that "we must steer clear of the hysteric element, which I define as the fancy and emotions unduly excited by suppressed sexual excitement." In light of his many bouts of mental exhaustion and his concern with mastering his own sexual appetite, Kingsley himself had probably known such "hysteria." This would help explain his ultimate lack of trust in women, his fear that true equality would be "brutalizing": what had begun as a dream for training governesses threatened to become an Amazonian nightmare. His response to Mill, therefore, is not surprising: the movement should be led by matrons and should keep the questions of women's right to vote, work, and become physicians separate from "social, that is, sexual questions," such as the ongoing argument over the regulation of prostitution, as addressed in the Contagious Diseases Act. He suggests that women should avoid such "prurient" topics, which were fit only for men to consider.[26]

Mill immediately responded that the presence in the movement of "vulgar self-seekers" was unavoidable and even encouraging, because it signaled the movement's growing influence and popularity even among the lower classes who had access only to penny papers. Playing on Kingsley's anti-medievalism, Mill argues that

> too many of those whose influence will be of use . . . instead of joining in the work . . . are apt pusillanimously to withhold themselves altogether. Yet this is, in a manner, a monastic view of public affairs. If all the highminded shrink into the congenial privacy of their own homes (as in the middle ages into a convent) they leave none but the vulgar minded to occupy the public eye.

Regarding the "sexual questions" to which Kingsley refers, Mill argues that it is principally middle-aged women, "and most of them mothers of families," who have involved them-selves in this particular controversy, on the principle that "the connivance of virtuous women alone makes it possible for so-called decent men to call into existence the 'profession' which is in question."[27]

Apparently Kingsley did not find Mill convincing. It is telling, in fact, that in his advice to Mill he speaks of women as "our" advocates. Writing to Mrs. Peter Taylor during the same period regarding women's suffrage, he advises her to control rather than "excite" her friends: "By quiet, modest, silent, private influence we shall win."[28] But in Mill's letter to Kingsley it was precisely Mrs. Taylor's sort of upper-class aloofness that Mill criticized as unnecessarily exclusive. Fi-nally, therefore, Kingsley's advice to women seems to echo his Christian Socialist advice to working-class men: they are to convert their "masters" by offering an example of heroic suffering—and even martyrdom.

Listening to some of his own advice—and no doubt recognizing how far he had wandered from his earlier advocacy of "real informed women"—Kingsley defended his many hesitations as simple pragmatism. Again addressing Mill, he writes:

> I see how we must be tempted to include, nay, to welcome as our best advocates, women who are smarting under social wrongs, who can speak on behalf of freedom with an earnestness like that of the escaped slave. But I feel that we must resist that temptation; that our strength lies not in the abnormal, but in the normal type of womanhood. . . . Any sound reformation of the relations between woman and man must proceed from women who have fulfilled well their relations as they now exist, imperfect and unjust as they are. That only those who have worked well in harness, will be able to work well out of harness.[29]

He is not the first "liberal" thus to rationalize a fall from grace. The question of reform—allowing middle-class young women to develop their minds and educate the nation—was one to which Charles Kingsley could happily devote his energies. The question of revolution—deciding just what this "normal type of womanhood" was to be—was one that sent him into retreat.

A year before his death, Kingsley returned to the topic of the education of women, publishing "Nausicaa in London" in an 1874 issue of *Good Words*. He reaffirms there many positions he had argued with Mill, Maurice, and others. But he introduces as well the same sort of caution that he had already offered to young boys: that a sound mind, whether male or female, nonetheless depends upon a sound body.

Kingsley had once worried that sports might be too taxing for women's frail bodies. In 1841 he told his fiancée, Frances Grenfell, that as a woman she could not understand "the excitement of animal exercise from the mere act of cutting wood or playing cricket to the manias of hunting or shooting or fishing." He asked that she remember "the peculiar trial which this proves, to a young man whose superfluous excitement has to be broken in like that of a dog or a horse— for it is utterly animal."[30] Nonetheless, the point he attempts to make in "Nausicaa" thirty years later is the relatively important need for the "lower" education of women: "not merely to understand the Greek tongue, but to copy somewhat of the Greek physical training": in other words, the "full" Hellenism of the Muscular Christian. Here, however, as he had so often done before, what Kingsley concedes to the women's movement with one hand, he takes back with the other. The contemporary issue that led Kingsley to emphasize women's need to develop greater "muscularity" was the controversy over the relatively onerous physical demands that extended intellectual work imposed on women.

"Where is your vitality?" Kingsley asks young women. With overtones of Bram Stoker, he answers that it is draining into books they would do better to avoid, books inspiring emotions "which, it may be, you had better never feel." "And now," he worries, "they [who is this 'they'? No longer Kingsley, it seems clear] are going to 'develop' you; and let you have your share in 'the higher education of women,' by making you read more books, and do more sums, and pass examinations, and stoop over desks at night after stooping over employment all day; and to teach you Latin, and even Greek."[31]

In this account of Kingsley's increasingly fearful response to the women's movement, his earlier words of caution were political and strategic. The new element here, one that soon dominated late-nineteenth-century theory, is physiological and psychological. Too much scholarship for women, Kingsley warns, can "develop" them into "so many Chinese—dwarfs—or idiots." The women of London, Kingsley notes, are literally *shrinking:* there is "a general want of those large frames, which indicate usually a power of keeping strong and healthy not merely the muscles, but the brain itself." If true patriots do not take the necessary precautions, he ominously prophesies, the next generation of Englishmen will be sickly—just like Parisians.[32]

Such a near-hysterical view found other exponents throughout later Victorian society—and not only among men. In 1865, for example, English schoolmistress Elizabeth Missing Sewell had fretted over female fragility: "Any strain upon a girl's intellect is to be dreaded, and any attempt to bring women into competition with men can scarcely escape failure."[33] But Kingsley's reassertion of the physical (and mental) demands of childbearing was echoed with a vengeance by Henry Maudsley (1835–1918), the dominant influence in British psychiatry during the latter half of the nineteenth century.

Four months after "Nausicaa" appeared, Maudsley published a rather bizarre but influential article in the *Fortnightly Review,* entitled "Sex in Mind and in Education." He ignores Kingsley's nuances and his attempts to understand women as in some sense equal to Victorian men. Instead, he looks out into his society and sees "some women who are without the instinct or desire to nurse their offspring, some who have the desire but not the capacity, and others who have neither the instinct nor the capacity." It is this New Woman, he announces, who will "allow the organs which minister to this function to waste and finally to become by disuse as rudimentary in her sex as they are in the male sex."

This so-called woman (no doubt from the same group that Kingsley described as a "ghastly ring of prophetesses" and "very bad imitations of men") appears to Maudsley to be "a monstrosity—something which having ceased to be woman is yet not man."[34] These were strong words in the mouth of a novel-writing clergyman, but they take on an appalling and sinister finality coming from a respected physician of the mind.

Maudsley was goaded on by the example of three American physiologists, Edward Clarke (whose 1873 book, misleadingly titled *Sex in Education; or, A Fair Chance for the Girls,* created a sensation), Nathan Allen, and Weir Mitchell. These men, expanding on Augustus Gardner's 1860 article "Physical Decline of American Women," worry that "undue demands made upon the brain and nervous system to the detriment of the organs of nutrition" will make American women incapable of bearing children. American men, in consequence, "will have to re-act, on a magnificent scale, the old story of unwived Rome and the Sabines."[35] It seems incredible that this undisguised threat of rape comes from physicians claiming to have women's best interests at heart.

"After all," Maudsley threatens, "there is a right in might— the right of the strong to be strong. Men have the right to make the most of their powers, to develop them to the utmost, and to strive for, and if possible gain and hold, the position in which they shall have the freest play. It would be a wrong to the stronger if it were required to limit its exertions to the capacities of the weaker."[36] Georgina Weldon's *How I Escaped the Mad Doctors* (1878), Rosina Bulwer-Lytton's *A Blighted Life* (1880), and Louisa Lowe's *The Bastilles of England; or, The Lunacy Laws at Work* (1883) chronicle the results of this perversion of male dominance. The wrongful confinement that they knew, the real straitjackets, bolted doors, and painful rejection that threatened their contemporaries, found support in the images employed by their jailers—and "Muscular Christianity" was, unfortunately, one such image. In Charles Kingsley's lifetime, his arguments for a more balanced philosophy were only partially successful in finding an audience; they were even less so after his death.

Henry Maudsley's marriage and personal life were not without their problems,[37] and his apodictic pronouncements on women, lacking scientific objectivity, surely demand skeptical scrutiny. Unfortunately, quite the opposite happened in his lifetime. In fact, as Elaine Showalter has recently shown, Maudsley and his cohorts "set the model for the psychiatrists of his age. The psychiatrist's role would no longer be to provide an example of kindness, but rather one of manliness, maturity, and responsibility." In filling this role, "Maudsley and his cohorts were conspicuously and aggressively masculine in their interests, attitudes and goals. . . . They were athletic rather than literary; sportsmen and clubmen rather than stay-at-home fathers of a lunatic *famille nombreuse*."[38] As insurance against morbid introspection (what Kingsley elsewhere called "overmentation"), Maudsley recommended manly sport and games. But not for women—they were, thank God, still too weak for that, too easily unhinged.

Despite Kingsley's defense of the high ideals he saw in Muscular Christianity for men *and* for women, his own ultimate ambivalence on the Woman Question clouded the picture of "liberation" he painted for his readers. The year before his death in 1875, sounding like a calmer Maudsley, he wrote that "the woman's more delicate organisation, her more vivid emotions, her more voluble fancy, as well as her mere physical weakness and weariness, have been to her, in all ages, a special source of temptation."[39] This is the myth that threatened men sought to perpetuate, and it is little wonder that they saw its embodiments wherever they looked. A Maudsley could degrade women while a George Lawrence bestialized men, and the simplicity of their imagery would find large, enthusiastic audiences. It did not matter that Kingsley would insist again and again that woman typically rose *above* her "mere physical weakness" to "call out chivalry in the man." But in the world beyond Charles Kingsley's novels, in the classrooms where more and more women were acquiring the knowledge and certification necessary to change Victorian structures of perception, empowering myths were gradually replacing those that had shaped the way women might imagine themselves. To the chagrin of a Maudsley or a Lawrence—to the surprise of a Kingsley— some women had apparently decided to dispense with the Lady of Shalott. Perhaps some of their number trusted that a plucky Nausicaa could still overcome the specter of the Madwoman in the Attic; if it took a Boadicea, however, a growing number of women seemed prepared to welcome the new myth.

Notes

1. "Physical Strength," *Saturday Review,* 10 Dec. 1859, 701–02.

2. Henry James, review of *Charles Kingsley: His Letters and Memories of His Life,* ed. Francis Kingsley, *Nation* 24 (1877): 61. Reviewing the same book, G. A. Simcox wrote that Kingsley's "brain, or his personality, as we may choose to phrase it, was steadily on the side of the robust and active element, but was never impervious to the other. . . . Looking only to his strength, he was fit for an athlete; looking only at his temperament, he was fitter for

a monk." According to Simcox, those who knew Kingsley were struck by "the union of the most exquisite tenderness with a manliness that often seemed aggressive" (*Fortnightly Review*, 1 Jan. 1877, 16). See also James's review of Kingsley's novel *Hereward the Wake, Nation* 2 (1866): 115–16; E. L. Burlingame, "Charles Kingsley," *Appleton's Journal* 13 (1875): 204; J. K. Laughton's reivew of *Letters and Memories, Edinburgh Review* 145 (1877): 438; and T. H. S. Escott, "Charles Kingsley," *Belgravia* 26 (1875): 83.

3. As recalled by Dean Arthur Penrhyn Stanley in his eulogy at Westminster Abbey, 31 Jan. 1875 (see Frances Kingsley, ed., *Charles Kingsley: His Letters and Memories of His life*, 2 vols. [1877; rpt. New York: AMS, 1973], 2:466–68).

4. Charles Kingsley, *Two Years Ago*, collected in *The Novels and Poems of Charles Kingsley*, Chester ed., 12 vols. (New York: J. F. Taylor, 1899), chap. 13, 1:337–38. Chapter, volume, and page references to this edition hereafter will be provided in the text.

5. See Elizabeth K. Helsinger, Robin L. Sheets, and William Veeder, eds., *The Woman Question: Social Issues, 1837–1883* (New York: Garland, 1983), xiv–xvi.

6. Florence Nightingale was among Muscular Christianity's female critics; she complained to Benjamin Jowett, regarding two students in her charge: "What a bad thing the love of sport really is for the Upper Classes. These two youths are very much above the average in ability, but their souls as well as their bodies are absolutely given up to shooting and fishing, and more than half their conversation is on these subjects. It is quite weakening to them, this muscular Christianity of which Mr. Kingsley is the prophet." See E. V. Quinn and J. M. Prest, eds., *Dear Miss Nightingale: A Selection of Benjamin Jowett's Letters, 1860–1893* (Oxford: Clarendon Press, 1987), 99.

7. Harriet Martineau, *Once a Week*, 10 Aug. 1861, 177.

8. E. H., "Queen's College—London," *Quarterly Review* 86 (1850): 364–83.

9. Frederick Denison Maurice, quoted in Rosalie Glynn Grylls, *Queen's College 1848–1948* (London: Routledge, 1948), 2–3.

10. Kingsley to Alfred Strettell, [Spring] 1849, *Charles Kingsley: His Letters and Memories,* 1:201.

11. Charles Kingsley, "Tennyson," *Fraser's* 42 (September 1850): 250.

12. Lady Stanley of Alderley, "Personal Recollections of Women's Education," *Nineteenth Century* 11 (1879): 311.

13. Harriet Martineau, *Daily News,* 23 Nov. 1859, 4.

14. S. R. P., "The Details of Woman's Work in Sanitary Reform," *English Woman's Journal* 3 (1859): 323.

15. Harriet Martineau, *Society in America,* 3 vols. (London: Saunders and Otley, 1837), 3:116.

16. Harriet Martineau, *Once a Week,* 10 Aug. 1861, 175.

17. Harriet Martineau to Fanny Wedgwood, October 1858, in *Harriet Martineau's Letters to Fanny Wedgwood,* ed. Elisabeth Sanders Arbuckle (Stanford: Stanford University Press, 1983), 170.

18. Emily Davies, *Thoughts on Some Questions Relating to Women* (Cambridge: Bowes and Bowes, 1910), 160.

19. Charles Kingsley, "Women and Politics," *Macmillan's,* October 1869, 555.

20. Charles Kingsley, *The Roman and the Teuton,* 3d ed. (1864; London: Macmillan, 1901), lec. 10, 255.

21. Emily Davies, *The Higher Education of Women* (London: Alexander Strahan, 1866), 181–91 passim.

22. *Charles Kingsley: His Letters and Memories,* 1:453.

23. In an 1860 letter to John Stuart Mill, Florence Nightingale uses surprisingly parallel language to express her strong reservations over training women as physicians, because the ones she had seen in America had "only tried to be 'men' and they [had] only succeeded in being third-rate men." While making a living for themselves, they had not succeeded in improving the sorry state of medical education and "therapeutics" (see J. M. Robson et al., eds., *Collected Works of John Stuart Mill* [Toronto: University of Toronto Press, 1965—in progress], 15:710; this edition hereafter will be cited as *Mill*).

24. Frederick Maurice to Charles Kingsley, 22 Sept. 1869,

The Life of Frederick Denison Maurice, Chiefly Told in His Own Letters, ed. Frederick Maurice, 2 vols. (New York: Scribner's, 1884), 2:591–92.

25. Charles Kingsley to John Stuart Mill, 6 Aug. 1859, *Mill,* 15:633.

26. Charles Kingsley to John Stuart Mill, [Spring] 1870, *Charles Kingsley: His Letters and Memories,* 2:327.

27. John Stuart Mill to Charles Kingsley, 9 July 1870, *Mill,* 17:1742–44.

28. Charles Kingsley to Mrs. Peter Taylor, 27 May 1870, *Charles Kingsley: His Letters and Memories,* 2:326.

29. Charles Kingsley to John Stuart Mill, [Spring] 1870, ibid., 2:328–30.

30. Charles Kingsley to Frances Grenfell, February 1841, ibid., 1:51–52.

31. Charles Kingsley, "Nausicaa in London," *Good Words,* January 1874, 87.

32. Ibid., 88, 78, 80.

33. Elizabeth Missing Sewell, *Principles of Education* (1865; New York: Appleton, 1871), 451.

34. Henry Maudsley, "Sex in Mind and in Education," *Fortnightly Review,* April 1874, 477.

35. As cited in Maudsley, 474.

36. Ibid., 480.

37. On Maudsley's career, see Sir Aubrey Lewis, "Henry Maudsley: His Work and Influence," *The State of Psychiatry* (New York: Science House, 1967), 29–48.

38. Elaine Showalter, *The Female Malady: Women, Madness, and English Culture, 1830–1980* (New York: Pantheon, 1985), 117, 120.

39. Charles Kingsley, *Sanitary and Social Lectures and Essays* (London: Macmillan, 1880), lec. 9, 171.

PART THREE
(In)decorous Portraits

6 / George Eliot and the Journalists: Making the Mistress Moral

Teresa Mangum

By 1885, most Victorian readers knew that the names Mary Ann Evans, George Eliot, Mrs. Henry Lewes, and Mrs. John Cross signified the same person—a writer who presided over English literary circles as majestically as the Queen reigned over England, and yet a woman who lived with another's husband for decades, further outraging society by assuming his last name and the title "wife." Openly and unapologetically, Mary Ann Evans defied the moral edict central to the marriage plot she herself affirmed in letters and in fiction.

Gordon S. Haight's and Ruby V. Redinger's biographies of Eliot provide helpful reconstructions of Evans and Lewes's relationship.[1] By 1852, Evans had achieved professional success as the assistant editor, under John Chapman, of the *Westminster Review*. Her personal life, however, was less satisfactory. Living in Chapman's unusual household—which included his wife and an openly acknowledged mistress—Evans had painfully forged a friendship with Chapman that placated the jealousies of his wife and mistress, accommodated Chapman's vanities, and minimally satisfied her own longings for an affectionate and intellectual environment. At the same time, she began a long-term intimacy with Herbert Spencer, who could return only friendship for the deeper affection she offered.

In 1853, Evans renewed an earlier acquaintance with Lewes, a friend of Spencer's. By comparison with Lewes's domestic arrangements, Evans's chaotic circumstances seem trifling. His wife, Agnes, was about to give birth to the second child fathered by his best friend Henry Thornton Hunt, who had a wife of his own. True to his principles of Free Thought, Lewes not only acknowledged their relationship but also provided financial support and his name to Agnes and to children fathered by Hunt while Agnes and George Lewes still shared a household. Nevertheless, he withdrew from her emotionally, and on 20 July 1854, less than a year after Lewes and Evans fell in love, the two traveled to Weimar and Berlin. They returned to England in March 1855 amidst angry rumors that Evans had seduced Lewes from his family. Despite scandalous accusations and social ostracism, the two lived together, surviving literary fame as well as social infamy, until Lewes's death on 30 November 1878. Throughout their years together, both Lewes and Evans referred to themselves as husband and wife and demanded that would-be friends also acknowledge their "union" in name as well as deed. Evans continued to use the last name Lewes until she married John Walter Cross on 6 May 1879; she died Marian Cross on 22 December 1880.

Long after George Eliot achieved fame and acceptance in her public role as writer, her Victorian audience remained skeptical (and curious) about the scandalous private life of Mary Ann Evans. Mathilde Blind had produced a popular biography of Eliot in 1883, but *George Eliot's Life as Related in Her Letters and Journals*, published by Eliot's husband, John Walter Cross, in 1885, five years after her death, was considered the first authoritative life. Cross insists in the preface that the volume is an autobiography, yet his prudent hand is everywhere apparent. As Gordon Haight's research demonstrates, Cross not only censored whole letters, or large portions of them, but he also edited sentences, altered words, and reorganized passages. In addition, he began with an essay that refines Mary Ann Evans's childhood and suppresses reminiscences revealing the tempestuousness of those early years and her later adolescent flashes of anger and cynicism. He also introduces individual chapters and punctuates the letters with expository comments, reading instructions, and interpretations. From his Victorian audience's perspective, however, Cross's most important editorial decision was reflected in his silence. The same reviewers who reviled James Anthony Froude's volubility about Thomas and Jane Carlyle grumbled at Cross's refusal to comment on Evans's affair with Lewes. Although portions of letters in which Evans regally asserts her adopted title "Mrs. Lewes" are included, little else embellishes what reviewers and biographers still regard as one of the foremost "spectacles" of the later nineteenth century.

The preface to *George Eliot's Life* establishes Cross's editorial objectives. Confident that "on the intellectual side there remains little to be learnt by those who already know George Eliot's books," he hopes that instead these extracts "throw light on another side of her nature—not less important but hitherto unknown to the public—the side of the affections." More specifically—and revealingly—Cross writes, "I have been influenced by the desire to make known the woman, as well as the author, through the presentation of her daily life."[2] In the face of such romantic (and defensive) mythologizing, Victorian readers were first tentative, then exasperated, and finally resigned as they searched in vain for the "real" George Eliot.

An avalanche of notices, reviews, and retrospectives of course appeared in both British and American journals after Cross's volume was published. For twentieth-century readers these reviews constitute a study in Victorian ambivalence. Written for the *Athenaeum, Blackwood's Edinburgh Magazine,* the *Fortnightly Review, Temple Bar,* the *Westminster Review,* and others, the reviews reveal to us the nervous contradictions and compromises that characterized the late Victorian world—between forgivable weaknesses and damning errors for women, between the constraints imposed upon women and the allowances permitted to artists and intellectuals, between romance and "companionate marriage," and between definitions of realism as applied to art or to life. How, then, did Victorian readers and reviewers, when confronted with Cross's "autobiography"—which was, in fact, a heavily expurgated and mediated pastiche of letters, journal entries, and commentary of his own—countenance the contradictory life and career of Miss Evans, Mrs. Lewes, Mr. Eliot, and Mrs. Cross?

For reviewers, deciding what to call the relationship between Evans and Lewes posed the most immediate problem. Many writers openly condoned the affair by calling the pair Mr. and Mrs. Lewes or by electing to use Evans's own phrase, "blessed union," although an anonymous writer for the *Athenaeum* cautiously places the word union in quotation marks.[3] John Morley in *Macmillan's* gingerly refers to "the relation"[4] while a *Saturday Review* commentator tenders "the connexion."[5] Other reviewers go so far as to discuss their "marriage." In a column entitled "Mistakes about

George Eliot Corrected," a *Life* editor, identified only as "Droch," impatiently explains that the relationship was "a marriage which could not have been more solemnly regarded if sanctioned by the forms of law."[6] Edwin P. Whipple of the *North American Review* charmingly if absurdly disposes of the problem by announcing that Eliot "was married to him, we think, in some foreign city," which is "illegal rather than immoral conduct."[7]

For many reviewers their second problem was to redeem Eliot without precisely defending her, and certainly without endorsing her behavior. Most commonly, the writers countered the exoticism of the couple's scandalous conduct by demonstrating that a prosaically feminine Mary Ann Evans trembled behind the imposing mask of intellect and accomplishment known to the world as George Eliot. Cross's focus in his preface on the woman rather than on the writer encouraged the view that if Evans erred, her actions were the inevitable consequence of her womanhood.

In innumerable journals, reviewers took Cross's hint and embellished this highly feminized—that is, dependent, helpless, and indecisive—portrait of the writer. The *Athenaeum* critic explained that "manly intellect and girlish heart were united in her to an unusual degree."[8] In an *Academy* article, Edward Dowden describes her as an "eager, sensitive, frail, dependent woman." Dowden's representation of Eliot's womanliness reduces her from the role of temptress or genius to something more helpless than a child: "No child ever cared more to be cherished and petted, to hear kind words, to receive a motherly kiss, than George Eliot did as a grown-up woman."[9] The *Saturday Review* writer refers to Eliot's account of keeping a crucifix by her while she translated *Leben Jesu* as "an instance of feminine logic which is probably unparalleled." "Indeed," he pontificates, "the whole book shows how impressionable, how emotional, how illogical, how feminine she was."[10] Writing for the *Edinburgh Review*, Margaret Oliphant claims that Cross's text reveals a "conventional type of a woman—a creature all conjugal love and dependence, to whom something to lean on is a necessity, who is sure of nothing until her god has vouched for it, not even her own power." Despite Oliphant's ironic superiority not merely to Evans but to femininity generally, she grudgingly acknowledges society's responsibility for Eliot's damning dependency:

> This type of feminine character is one which has been much applauded in its day; it is perhaps that which at the bottom of our hearts, most of us like the best. . . . But it is not the type of character with which we connect the possession of powerful genius, nor should we have expected to find it in George Eliot.[11]

The awesome Eliot—profound philosopher and scientist; daring atheist; leading literary ethician; author of essays, novels, and poetry—shrinks into a mere woman.

The critics' dilemma arose in part from their belief in the dichotomy between male intellect and feminine sensibility, a gender stereotype that persisted through the 1880s. In some cases, however, we see a growing, nervous acknowledgment that the dichotomy itself may be an illusion, as evidenced in the strained sophistries that explain away Eliot's extraordinariness. In one startling reversal of conventional divisions of male and female powers, Oliphant argues that because Eliot is not a man she cannot think, yet because she is a woman who strives to emulate men, she cannot create. Combining these arguments, she concludes that on the basis of gender, George Eliot cannot be considered an "original" thinker. To the contrary,

> she was one instance the more, to be added to the many existing, of the want of the originative faculty in women. Had a man

possessed her weight of brain, her education, her mental capacity generally, he would have been the founder of a new school in philosophy or in literature—adding to the power common to both sexes the gift of construction special to his own.[12]

Once again, Victorian estimations of feminine ability defend a reviewer against the intimidating potency of a female intellect. But here Eliot is even stripped of the accomplishments Victorians believed themselves to idealize in women—creative, generative, constructive power. Instead, the men who shaped George Eliot out of Mary Ann Evans's clay, Lewes among them, are the true creators and constructors. In *Blackwood's*, E. B. Hambley's telling choice of words plays on this ultimate dismissal even of conventional feminine powers as he speculates about Lewes's importance to her work: "She might have searched all society through without finding a companion so fertilising to her intellect."[13]

In a different context, Hambley raises the specter of Eliot's femininity to discredit another group of intellectual women who also threaten the integrity of the male and female spheres. These "strong-minded" women, soon to be labeled New Women, were beginning to challenge social, educational, and professional constraints upon women. Hambley's description of Eliot as "a moral nature tender, sympathetic, impulsive, and womanly, possibly in some things womanish" distinguishes (and thus separates) her from other intellectual women:

> It must be noted here, out of regard for the prepossessions of the many who fail to give to those known as strong-minded women the admiration which their virile qualities might seem to merit, that George Eliot was never in that sense a strong-minded woman . . . and [was] liable to be convicted by the truly strong-minded of her sex of what they might think a thousand weaknesses.[14]

Throughout these essays we see Evans's scandalous behavior and Eliot's intellect tailored to fit acceptable standards for female behavior. Here, however, Hambley also asserts her womanliness as proof against suspicions that Evans was what we would today call a feminist, who would demand a radical reassessment of controlling social assumptions, including the supposedly polar concepts of femininity and intellectuality. As Marilyn J. Kurata's essay on wrongful confinement and Tracy C. Davis's discussion of Victorian actresses make clear, the threat that women themselves might control their own lives, much less assert control over social definitions, was one that provoked immediate punitive measures—in the forms of incarceration, accusation, or trivialization.

Other reviewers undermined Eliot's achievements by exaggerating her dependency not merely on Lewes but also on men in general. Her alleged emotional dependency becomes intellectual parasitism. This perspective throws into question her feminine power to love because her relationship with Lewes is recast as a product of chance rather than destiny. In *Temple Bar* and the *Saturday Review*, for example, the writers magnify Eliot's alleged feminine weakness into an undiscriminating, near-neurotic compulsion to be loved. This interpretation of her actions denies the particularity of her relationship with Lewes, arguing that her series of friendships with Charles Bray, Dr. Brabant, John Chapman, and Herbert Spencer prove her vulnerability to the approval and affection of any man of her acquaintance. Thus the *Saturday Review* essayist claims that Eliot would have been equally susceptible to any "masculine influence," whether the man were a churchman or a Lewes, adding: "The person whom superficial critics long took to be the most masculine of her sex was a very woman."[15] Writing for *Temple Bar*, Eliza Lynn Linton goes even further. Relying on the argument of Eliot's feminine dependency, Linton insists that

Eliot's work is "eminently the result of other men's teaching; and throughout her life she bore the impress now of one, now of another, of various masters."[16] Eliot's attachments to male relatives, friends, and mentors become *proof* of her womanliness; her unsuspected femininity provides yet another antidote to her imposing and intimidatingly "masculine" intellect.

Most writers felt compelled to address Evans and Lewes's relationship in their reviews of Cross's *Life*. In fact, many reviewers obviously delighted in revisionary retellings of the romance. Amusingly, the reviewers frequently congratulate Cross on his tasteful omission of the titillating details, then are seduced by his silence into revealing their own fantasies about the famous lovers. Those reviewers who acknowledged, even applauded, Evans and Lewes's affair faced a serious moral dilemma to which they responded in one of two ways. Either the reviewers subdued the scarlet overtones of scandal into a somber and respectable portrait of domesticity, or they enlarged the figures on the canvas into the hero and heroine of a transcendent romance.

Writers who extolled Evans and Lewes's complacent domesticity insisted that the relationship actually affirmed rather than embarrassed the middle-class reverence for the "companionate marriage." For these reviewers, Eliot's alleged femininity and the error to which it led her validated rather than contradicted marriage as an essential social form. They argued that her loving dependence on Lewes embodied the traditional notions of womanhood central to the institution of marriage that her life called into question. Idealizing the couple's ordinariness, these characterizations reassured readers that the roles of brilliant writer and notorious adventuress merely masked an "ordinary" and therefore acceptable woman.

Once again, we witness the power of Cross's editorial

impact, for he sanctions this reading in his preface by explaining that Eliot "cherished" the "reward of the artist: but the joys of the hearth-side, the delight in the lover or her friends, were the supreme pleasures in her life" (vii). He also breaks his usual reticence about Evans and Lewes by quoting a letter to Caroline Bray, written 4 September 1855, in which Evans insists, "If there is any one action or relation of my life which is and always has been profoundly serious, it is my relation to Mr. Lewes. . . . Light and easily broken ties are what I neither desire theoretically nor could live for practically" (167). These lines are quoted repeatedly in the reviews as evidence that this was a marriage indeed.

Many of the reviewers conflate domesticity with femininity, comfortably assuring Victorian readers that despite Evans's defiance of social conventions, her essential womanly nature—upon which the social form of marriage depends—remained inviolate. Thus an anonymous writer for the *London Quarterly Review* bemoans Evans's relation with Lewes as "the spectacle of a great and rich nature gone blindly and hopelessly astray" but consoles posthumous spectators with the notion that

> domestic life, a sphere of domestic activity and bliss, were quite as essential to her enjoyment as was the stimulus of intellectual society; and with all her mental audacity, she needed more than most women to be guided and upheld by masculine strength; she had as little individual enterprise as the shallowest and simplest of her sex.[17]

Temple Bar printed a reminiscence called "A Week with George Eliot" as a companion piece to its review of Cross. In this narrative, Mathilde Betham-Edwards never names their relationship, calls them Lewes and Eliot, places them in the neutral setting of a mutual friend's home, and then waxes nostalgic about their compatibility.[18] John Morley of *Macmillan's* defends them in part by desexualizing them: "A more perfect companionship . . . on a higher intellectual level, or more sustained mental activity is nowhere recorded."[19] Oliphant sarcastically indicts such apologists along with Lewes and Eliot as she describes the "kind of comfortable middle-class veil of retirement and warmth and common-place" which hallows these "blameless, virtuous bourgeoisie," concluding with a sigh: "Such perfect domesticity."[20]

In contrast, a second group of writers elevate Evans and Lewes's affair into a grand romance. These narrative portraits share the posed, majestic, otherworldly aura of "ennoblement" that Julia Margaret Cameron sought in photographic portraiture. In one reconstruction of the romance, E. B. Hambley of *Blackwood's* portrays the inevitability of their love:

> A womanly compassion at first counted for something in the intimacy, for his domestic circumstances were unhappy, his married home having been spoiled and broken up two years before. On his side the admiration amounted to a kind of worship. . . . As the intimacy progressed, her reciprocation of his complete attachment grew so strong as to impel her to cast in her lot with his.

The narrative concludes with the appropriate (if somewhat dauntingly academic) fairy-tale ending: "Henceforward the pair form a remarkable picture, working industriously in their home, each finding in the other not merely an acute critic, but one bending all the energies of the mind to the consideration of what the other laid before it."[21]

Often, as in the above version, the "romantic" narratives emphasize Lewes's role rather than Evans's. The more pathetic Lewes can be made to appear, the less culpable Eliot seems. In the *Nineteenth Century* Lord Acton invites compassion for Lewes and sympathy for Eliot's susceptibility to him by dramatically picturing the Lewes of 1853: "the mark of failure and frustrated effort was upon him . . . disaster has settled on his domestic life."[22] In its grammar and content, the phrasing in the *Athenaeum* suggests the convolutions that resulted when a writer tried to romanticize the affair by making Lewes the protagonist of the story: "She had evidently found in him some one to cling to amid the dreary solitude of life in London lodgings and Lewes took the responsibility of accepting her sacrifice." Then this writer undermines his or her own eloquence on Lewes's behalf by apologizing for the supposed intellectual inferiority of this romantic hero: "We cannot hope that every Elizabeth Barrett will find her Robert Browning."[23] Even Margaret Oliphant, who maintains throughout that Evans "was altogether wrong in decision as a question of morals" and "must be condemned," tells Lewes's story in tones of pathos.[24] Although she refuses to pity a man who followed Lewes's course, she assumes it is natural for Eliot, as a woman, to do so.

Relying on Victorian moralists' tolerance for the double standard, the reviewers sometimes shift attention from Lewes, and by association from Evans, to Agnes Lewes's scandalous and fruitful affair with Hunt. This twist of the romance sacrifices Agnes Lewes to appease the moralists and to excuse the relatively lesser sins of Lewes and Evans. Thus Edwin P. Whipple in the *North American Review* claims that Agnes had not only abandoned Lewes but she had also taken more than one lover.[25] In this version of the romance, readers are encouraged to admire Eliot for acting out of compassion and indignation in the face of such domestic outrage. Earlier, the double standard had been leveled against Evans when she and Lewes first returned to England. Despite the storm of gossip during their absence, Lewes continued to be invited to social events in London while Evans lived the reclusive life of the outcast.

After having digested such fabrications and evasions, one

begins to find rather refreshing the exasperated reviewers who testily dismiss these fictions. The writer for the *Saturday Review* snaps: "We shall only say that, when third persons speak of 'Mrs. Lewes,' of 'husband,' of 'wife,' and so forth, in reference to this connexion, they not only debase the moral currency, but, taking the matter out of debatable points, endorse a deliberate literary and historical falsification." This irascible Victorian concludes by reminding readers of Eliot's unveiling in 1859 when an imposter claimed to have written *Adam Bede:* "It is no more true that the author of *Adam Bede* was Mrs. Lewes than it is true that the author of *Adam Bede* was Mr. Liggins."[26] Similarly, Eliza Lynn Linton of *Temple Bar* unmercifully attacks the motives of these falsifiers. Noting that "all sorts of myths" grew up about the two, Linton speculates that the people who visited them in their later years of literary fame still "did not like to countenance adultery to the world at large" and so "did their best to salve over their consciences by pretending that there had been some kind of ceremony which sanctified and redeemed the union."[27]

The most extended protest appears in the *Edinburgh Review;* Oliphant cannot decide who annoys her more, Cross or Eliot. First, she provides the most trenchant, least romanticized portrayal of the conflict embodied in the example of Marian Lewes/George Eliot:

> It was not long before it become [*sic*] known that this purest preacher of domestic love, of fidelity, and self-sacrifice, had, in her own person, defied the laws and modest traditions that guard domestic life, and had taken a step which in all other cases deprives a woman of the fellowship and sympathy of other women, and of the respect of men. But the rule which holds universally from the duchess to the dressmaker, and which even the least strait-laced of moralists would think it dangerous to

loosen, was abrogated for her, and the world agreed to consider that permissible, or even justifiable in her special case which neither in that of the dressmaker nor the duchess there would be any question of tolerating.

Turning her frustration on Eliot's audience, she calculates that the "wide and voiceless public which speaks by purchase" has bought Eliot's respectability for her. Ultimately, however, Oliphant is more outraged by the dullness of Eliot's biography than she is by the scandal of Eliot's life. Recalling critics' "gasp of that unlooked-for disappointment" on reading the *Life*, she protests that "the biography of George Eliot as here given is a gigantic silhouette, showing how her figure rose against a dull background." Comparing Cross's volume to Froude's biography of Carlyle, Oliphant complains:

> Carlyle has been made out of his own mouth to prove himself a snarling Diogenes, a compound of spite, falsehood, and meanness; and George Eliot by the same fine process has been made to prove herself a dull woman. We . . . can only hope that the biographer of the future may be arrested in this strange new art of transformation.[28]

From a twentieth-century perspective, these cantankerous critics seem the most astute as they resist narrativizing an illegal relationship into a romantic fiction. Perhaps they realized that in imaginatively recasting Evans and Lewes's relation, the romanticizing reviewers removed the couple from the moral boundaries of "real life." Instead, readers of Evans and Lewes's story could only hold the idealized characters responsible for adhering faithfully to the requirements of the romance plot: she must remain dependent, dignified, and an English heroine of letters; he must remain adoring, protective, and faithful to her. And, of course, they did live happily ever after.

Even those reviewers who rejected feminine helplessness or romantic resolution as excuses for the union were often willing to accept George Eliot on any terms. In the *Edinburgh Review*, Oliphant explains why, using the practical terms of consumer benefit: "If ever the ends can justify the means, it may be allowed to have done so in the present case. It is a test to which it is hard to put our conscientious judgement, yet it has to be faced. . . . These people did well to defy the laws that bind ordinary mortals."[29] In other words, the novels sufficiently justify for George Eliot anything that Mary Ann Evans may have done. Often, these reviewers insist that without Lewes, Evans would never have written fiction at all. Thus Edward Dowden argues in the *Academy:*

> The George Eliot who enriched the world with a series of writings from *Scenes of Clerical Life* to *Daniel Deronda* was not Mary Ann Evans but Mrs. Lewes. . . . It is doubtful whether without the fostering sympathy and devoted comradeship of her husband, we should ever have possessed one of those writings for which George Eliot will be remembered.[30]

Obliquely praising the benefit of her love life to her fiction, Lord Acton suggests that her fallen state "enlarged her tolerance of error,"[31] and another reviewer surmises that "the lapse must be forgiven or forgotten which led to that fusion of the intellect and the emotions necessary to the artistic impulse."[32]

Eventually, the fame Eliot won for her much-loved novels and acclaimed "genius" outweighed moral protests against her personal life. Lord Acton explains that "reverence for her genius, for the rare elevation of her teaching, bore down the inevitable reluctance to adjust the rule to an exception."[33] For some reviewers, in fact, the novels supplied the intimate portrait of Evans that the biography denied. Still peevish,

Margaret Oliphant argues that we can only uncover the details of Evans's early years that Cross omitted by reading the story of Maggie Tulliver's childhood:

> The early life of George Eliot . . . is already well known, and by a very different method from that which discloses the actual circumstances of her existence in the present book. No one can have forgotten the wonderful pictures, so large, so noble, so small and sordid, so warm with humour and passion, so extraordinarily representative of the least attractive phase of English life, against which the fine figure of Maggie Tulliver rises before us . . . the visionary sensitive girl, full of contradictory impulses, with her unity and simplicity of soul, her capacity for great emotion.

Although Oliphant hesitates to take *The Mill on the Floss* as "an actual picture of the scenes which surrounded the child of genius," she insists that in this instance the fiction is truer to life than the biography is.[34]

Other reviewers turned to Eliot's plots and characters for evidence of shame over her life with Lewes that would contradict the portrait of a happy, satisfied, unremorseful life of love and work that the biography paints. To avoid the embarrassment of unqualified admiration for an illicit union, the reviewers exchanged her life's story for that of her characters, particularly Maggie Tulliver and Hetty Sorrel. Although the inconsistency between Evans's liaison and her fictional affirmations of marriage puzzled her readers, these same readers nevertheless defended her on the basis of her fiction. R. H. Hutton, in the *Contemporary Review*, disbelieves Evans's claims that she never "condemned herself for that step, or even repented it," explaining "it is clear to me that, on the whole, she intended her work as an authoress to be expiatory of, or at least to do all that was possible to counterbalance, the effect of her own example."[35] The *Lon-*

don Quarterly Review critic, true to that journal's Methodistical leanings, describes Maggie in particular as a sign of Eliot's "unquiet conscience," noting that "the figure of a woman under a social ban recurs rather frequently in George Eliot's vigorous representations of English life." He or she adds:

> There is a kind of cruelty in more than one of these pictures; little sympathy softens the hard lines, bitten in with sharpest satiric acid, in which the victims or their own wrongdoing are portrayed; while the suffering inflicted by the scorn of society on a certain class of sinners is so vividly depicted, that one would say this writer was herself too exquisitely susceptible of the suffering and too scornful of the sin ever to have exposed herself to the one or to have fallen into the other.

As examples of events and characters which reveal Eliot's "true" feelings, the reviewer cites "Maggie Tulliver's temptation, all sensuous as it is," and "the ill-starred Hetty." For this reviewer, "the guilty feeling itself is described far too glowingly, with too much luxury of circumstance" for the novel to be the product of a clear conscience. In all of Eliot's novels, the reviewer senses "a certain taint" and a "tendency to hover and circle about evil-doings more or less allied to her own great error."[36]

The above reviewer and others rationalized that at heart Eliot must have believed in the conventions of marriage that her life challenged. Maggie thus becomes the index to Eliot's morality and by extension to Evans's; as Oliphant puts it, "George Eliot had far too profound a sense of what is and is not permitted by art, ever to place any imaginary woman in a similar position." Ironically, Oliphant also shows that the Victorian willingness to read fiction as life could work in quite the opposite direction. She claims that when *The Mill on the Floss* was first published in 1860, "the facts of George

Eliot's history, which had by this time percolated through society," so influenced her readers that many ignored the novel's "central incident of a self-sacrifice" and instead considered it simply "improper."[37] In these essays we begin to see that Evans's action did not threaten Victorian mores nearly so powerfully as did her unapologetic conviction that spiritually, emotionally, and physically her relationship met the conditions of the ideal "companionate" marriage of the nineteenth century—even though love rather than law sanctioned the union.

What Victorian reviewers missed is that Mary Ann Evans or Marian Lewes or George Eliot or Mrs. John W. Cross eludes critical identification in part because she absorbed all these identities and others. Clearly, Evans understood the powerful and assertive act of self-naming. Although the adoption of pet names, pen names, and married names may not be particularly unusual, Mary Ann Evans repeatedly named herself in ways that do assume significance. Ruby Redinger records a number of names she accepted or adopted to define her relationships with important people: to a school girl friend she was Clematis, which means mental duty; to her early mentor Dr. Brabant, a Casaubon of sorts, she was Deutera. As a child she changed her name from Mary Anne to Mary Ann; as a young professional writer she assumed another name, Marian. As an adult, she demanded the names wife and Mrs. Lewes and mother. Among intimates, she was known as Polly or Polliane, "little mother," and Madonna. As a novelist, of course, she was George Eliot.

We can explain many of these changes in practical terms. Eliot must have known that her novels would be read in a lurid light, if read at all, had she published under the name Evans. She also believed that the books would not have been given such a respectful reception had readers known she was a woman. A pseudonym was necessary to her. She herself explained that the Lewes children called her "mother" or "mutter," and, by insisting on "Mrs. Lewes," she may have wanted to reassure them (as well as herself and Lewes) of the tenacity of their relationship as a family. Nevertheless, Evans's adoption of the names George Eliot and Mrs. Lewes represents a kind of confidence, control, and independence of character that the reviewers overlook. Intent on discovering the remorseful, dependent, domestic woman behind the names, they may have repeatedly ignored the woman who triumphed over the social, religious, legal, moral, and literary limitations of Victorian England in part because of her artful disguises.

If we accept the public George Eliot which Mary Ann Evans imagined, constructed, and sustained as the public image she wished to project—a moral paragon, a persuasive teacher, a powerful intellectual, and one of Britain's greatest novelists—then Cross deserves our commendation. He understood Evans's objections to writing an autobiography herself: she had been too painfully exposed to personal criticism and felt too generally misinterpreted even by her friends to risk self-exposure yet again. Cross conceived of *George Eliot's Life as Related in Her Letters and Journals* as a public memorial to the public figure of George Eliot, as indicated by his title. The book, therefore, admirably fulfills his responsibility to the public self Mary Ann Evans consciously constructed, and he retains a most impressive fidelity of silence to the private person she revealed to so few.

Notes

1. See Gordon S. Haight, *George Eliot: A Biography* (New York: Oxford University Press, 1968); and Ruby V. Redinger, *George Eliot: The Emergent Self* (New York: Knopf, 1975).

2. John Walter Cross, ed., *George Eliot's Life as Related in Her Letters and Journals* (New York: Thomas P. Crowell, n.d.), v. Further page citations will appear in parentheses in the text.

3. Review essay, *Athenaeum,* 31 Jan. 1885, 146.

4. John Morley, "The Life of George Eliot," *Macmillan's Magazine* 51 (November–April 1884–85): 244.

5. Review essay, *Saturday Review,* 7 Feb. 1885, 181.

6. "Droch," "Mistakes about Eliot Corrected," *Life* 5 (January–June 1885): 104.

7. Edwin P. Whipple, "George Eliot's Life," *North American Review* 141 (July–December 1885): 824.

8. *Athenaeum* review essay, 146.

9. Edward Dowden, "Literature," *Academy,* 7 Feb. 1885, 89, 90.

10. *Saturday Review* review essay, 181.

11. [Margaret Oliphant,] review essay, *Edinburgh Review,* 161 (January–June 1885): 551, 552.

12. Ibid., 514.

13. [E. B. Hambley,] review essay, *Blackwood's Edinburgh Magazine* 137 (January-June 1885): 163.

14. Ibid., 162.

15. *Saturday Review* review essay, 181.

16. [Eliza Lynn Linton,] "George Eliot," *Temple Bar* 73 (January–April 1885): 516.

17. Review essay, *London Quarterly Review* 64 (April–July 1885): 210–11.

18. Mathilde Betham-Edwards, "A Week with George Eliot," *Temple Bar* 73 (January–April 1885): 226–32.

19. Morley, 244.

20. Oliphant, 538.

21. Hambley, 162, 163.

22. [Lord Acton,] "George Eliot's 'Life,' " *Nineteenth Century* 17 (January–June 1885): 478.

23. *Athenaeum* review essay, 146.

24. Oliphant, 535, 536.

25. Whipple, 324.

26. *Saturday Review* review essay, 181.
27. Linton, 520.
28. Oliphant, 515–17 passim.
29. Ibid., 538.
30. Dowden, 90.
31. Lord Acton, 479.
32. *Athenaeum* review essay, 146.
33. Lord Acton, 480.
34. Oliphant, 519.
35. R. H. Hutton, "George Eliot," *Contemporary Review* 47 (January–June 1885): 381.
36. *London Quarterly Review* review essay, 208–9.
37. Oliphant, 537, 546.

7 / Froude on the Carlyles:
The Victorian Debate over Biography

D. J. Trela

In late 1845, Thomas Carlyle's *Oliver Cromwell* was published. The following year, in lauding the book, one reviewer praised the quiet domesticity of the author's life at Cheyne Row and implied that such bourgeois retirement made his creative work possible. How strange it was, he noted, that the great hypocrite and usurper Cromwell should suddenly be regarded as an equally great hero, "and this apparently in consequence of the secret exertions of a single literary man, living in a retired manner in one of the little quiet streets that run at right angles to the Thames river at Chelsea!"[1] Insignificant as it may seem, this is one of the few instances I have found of any public knowledge of Thomas and Jane Carlyle's private life or of its possible influence on Thomas's work. Indeed, our information about this home life has come almost entirely from posthumous publications of their letters and contemporaries' reminiscences. Clearly, the Victorian period was not an age of "in-depth" interviews or investigative exposés. The scant information available at the time suggests unruffled contentment, domestic bliss, and only the heartburning that results from heightened sensibilities and artistic genius.

In February 1881, H. R. Fox-Bourne confirmed this image in an obituary in the *Athenaeum* whose main points dozens of writers repeated in the coming weeks. Carlyle's "public attitude as a nineteenth-century Puritan" was in part only an attitude. According to Fox-Bourne, his "transparent honesty and genuine kindness . . . endeared him to all who were so favoured as to know him in private. He was most punctilious as a host, and singularly courteous as a guest, always falling in with the ways of those he was visiting, though sometimes with an energy that was startling." Many examples of "overflowing good nature, prompted and guided by wonderful good sense," seemed to jar with his public image but were actually in harmony with his character. Despite "occasional irritability," he "was hale and active in body, bright and cheerful in mind." His savageness was more apparent than real; almost excessively sympathetic, he had a "good heart" and a "clear conscience" at the time of his death. Fox-Bourne mentions Jane twice. We are told Carlyle married her in 1826 and that she died suddenly in 1866 after forty years as a "good and faithful wife." Although Cheyne Row from then on was "more than half-empty" to Carlyle, "he never allowed his abiding grief so to master him as to hinder any good work that he found to do."[2]

There is no mention here, and virtually no hint elsewhere, that the public perception of Carlyle as a growling, querulous, yet lovable, well-meaning Victorian sage conflicted in any essential way with his conventional private life. Yet this view was sharply different from the one Carlyle's biographer, friend, and literary executor, James Anthony Froude, would soon be perceived to offer in his four-volume biography, three-volume edition of Jane's letters, and two volumes of Carlyle's autobiographical reminiscences.

In these works, Froude claimed that the marriage had been largely unhappy and that Carlyle was mostly at fault for not paying more attention to his wife or treating her more like a lady. Froude even claimed they would have been better off had they not married each other. Carlyle was revealed as having a childlike incapacity to deal with everyday problems, from paying tax bills to remodeling the house. He was frequently irritable and took out his frustrations on his wife through verbal abuse; he neglected her by dallying with Lady Ashburton. After her death, he bitterly mourned her passing with a prolonged period of penance and remorse, recounted by Froude in detail.

And if Carlyle did not show the respect due a wife, he also disfigured the literary icons of his day, as Froude reported. He disparaged writers like Coleridge, Wordsworth, Shelley, Mill, and Jeffrey, as well as public figures like the now-obscure Montagus, the hapless Mrs. Edward Irving, and Harriet Martineau, the latter of whom Carlyle wrote:

> Her adorers, principally, not exclusively, "poor *whinnering* old moneyed women in their well hung broughams, otherwise idle," did her a great deal of mischief, and indeed as it proved were gradually turning her fine clear head (so to speak), and leading to sad issues for her. Her talent, which in that sense was very considerable, I used to think would have made her a quite shining Matron of some big Female Establishment, mistress of some immense Dress-Shop, for instance (if she *had* a dressing faculty, which perhaps she hadn't); but was totally inadequate to grapple with deep spiritual and social questions.[3]

Many readers considered these scathing yet often ludicrous assessments indecorous and offensive. Taken in conjunction with his revelations about the Carlyles' domestic life, Froude's writings produced a strong reaction against Carlyle, possibly a stronger one against Froude himself, and certainly a vigorous discussion of the nature of biography. The dozens of reviews of Froude show, in part, a strong ambivalence in late-Victorian thought regarding how far private life deserved to be made public property and to what extent such private details should be used to judge public figures.

In the August 1881 edition of *Temple Bar,* Allen Grant humorously described the debate and reaction that Froude's writings evoked. At Carlyle's death, Grant wrote,

> All was gush and adoration. Sweetness and light pervaded the atmosphere. Then it was announced that the "Reminiscences" were to be immediately published. Mr. Froude, the editor of these sacred deposits, departed for the island of Madeira, probably unconscious of the coming tempest. The publication took place, and literary society became like a cage of parrots upset. Everybody was shrieking at the same time. Gush and adoration were at an end; sweetness and light vanished into *Ewigkeit;* critics who had taken up their pens to bless, used them with deadly effect on the other side. . . . There never was such a change of opinion. When the veiled prophet exhibited his expressive countenance to his friends there was considerable disappointment; but the "Reminiscences of Thomas Carlyle" led to a frantic stampede of enthusiasts.[4]

Grant's ironic view notwithstanding, the real picture is far more complex. Although many reviewers were offended by the private details of married life, others were not. Some reviewers thought Carlyle egotistical, irascible, and unreasonable; some found him charmingly idiosyncratic. If one group felt distress or pain, another one was delighted by the Carlyle revealed, and yet a third was pleased that an overrated writer and borderline charlatan had at last been unmasked.

Some were appalled at the abuse Jane endured; others insisted the marriage was happy and downright normal. Some felt a sage and prophet could not suffer from having the truth about himself known; some found hardly a word of truth in what Froude wrote. Such a complex response defies pat generalization. Yet after reviewing this material I would offer the following conclusions.

First, Froude inadvertently destabilized the popular conception of Carlyle as a kindly, well-meaning, selfless Sage— inadvertently because Froude's work was, on the whole, carried out at Carlyle's request and with his blessing, and further, because Froude was a true disciple of his master, not a Wildean Judas. The biography was intended, and largely reads, as a sincere act of hero worship. Yet Victorian reviewers regularly ignored this fact, focusing instead on what to them was the dirt, the sensation, the titillating anecdote. An outgrowth of this emphasis was a growing willingness on the part of reviewers to publicize private life and to use such details to judge public actions. Yet "ambivalent" is the best, briefest way to describe the evolving Victorian response to such revelations as Froude made. Victorians wanted to know the truth but found they could not learn it without giving pain. They wanted their heroes to worship and emulate, but at the same time they set incredibly high standards for them and delighted in pointing out their shortcomings. In the end, the Victorians offered no consistent answer to the question of what authors of biographies could properly reveal. In this regard, the response to Froude simply mirrors the confused, shifting, yet evolving standards of the age. And that evolution, for better or worse, was toward greater openness in biography, the fruits of which we witness today.

Second, although Froude's interpretation of Carlyle's character and marriage is scarcely dissented from now, the

Victorians *did* dissent, often vigorously. Reviewers who accepted Froude's assumptions directly contradicted other reviewers who could claim the same intimacy with the Carlyles that Froude did. Scholarly neglect of their arguments is unfortunate because it has created a deceptive critical unanimity regarding Carlyle. The pervasiveness of Froude's interpretation has kept scholars from assessing additional primary evidence representing points of view as valid as Froude's.

Froude's destabilization of Carlyle's image as revered seeker after truth and destroyer of shams began with publication of the *Reminiscences* (1881) and the *Letters and Memorials of Jane Welsh Carlyle* (1883). It continued with the appearance of the biography *Thomas Carlyle: A History of the First Forty Years of His Life* (1882) and *A History of His Life in London* (1884). Gail Hamilton, writing in the *North American Review* after the first two volumes of the biography and Jane's letters had been published, was appalled by the shabby husband they revealed. She felt the husband's public authority was destroyed by his private neglect of his wife. At Carlyle's side, she wrote, "moved always a slight figure, the figure of a woman whom he loved, despised, trampled upon, lamented with unavailing tears: a woman who loved him, revered him, immolated herself to him, recorded him." She concludes, not without satisfaction, that "the heart that held him highest brought him lowest."[5] For at last Carlyle's "ferocious selfishness" was revealed through the letters of the woman most deeply wounded by his injustice.[6] In Hamilton's eyes, Carlyle was a moralist whose crime was hypocrisy: he did not practice his own beliefs and so made a good woman and other people miserable. He was also a snob whose professed hatred of shams was a charade because "no greater sham than he ever resounded through the world."[7]

Hamilton's points were repeated by many critics, who in

general believed that as authorized biographer and close personal friend of the family, Froude had access to documents few others would see. Further, a disciple could have no motivation to be untruthful; therefore, Froude had been painfully honest, however unpleasant that had been for him. Thus the *Times* refers to Froude's "excess of editorial piety," and a 9 May 1881 leader defends Froude's publication of the *Reminiscences*. Rejecting the charge that Froude was indiscreet, the *Times* took the high ground. To edit out potentially offensive matter—to "draw all these talons"—would have made a characteristic book much less interesting and truthful. With an eye toward Froude's planned biography, the article concluded, "We are anxious that no terrorism should fetter his judgement in the future."[8]

This belief was tested with the publication of Jane Carlyle's letters. Yet the *Times* again accepted Froude's conclusions and made no complaint about the explicit documents made public. Jane's bright future was "brought to shipwreck by the most unfortunate of marriages"; she was made a "hard-working drudge"; "Carlyle was to blame" for this and for treating her with "deliberate tyranny." The reviewer further noted that "similar conduct is precisely one of those pleas we see continually brought forward when a wife is suing for a separation on the score of cruelty." Carlyle was also scored for his parsimony. He gave Jane a small allowance and only one servant; while Jane spent holidays at friends' houses to save money, Thomas traveled extensively. The cruelest neglect of all was that Carlyle repaid Jane's sacrifices "neither with caresses nor with confidence." Alluding to Lady Ashburton, the reviewer concludes, "And what embittered [Jane's] grief was that, sage as he was, he seemed to have yielded to the seductions of fashionable society."[9] In reviews like this, Froude's courage and skill in revealing un-

pleasant information are fully credited. Carlyle's once favorable public image is shattered.

This process continued in other reviews of the letters. The
Spectator noted that Carlyle "not unfrequently treated" Jane
as "a mere detail of life." The reviewer analyzed the marriage
in detail, delving into the defects of personality in both husband and wife that caused such unhappiness. Jane's problem
was pride; Carlyle's, insensitivity. And so a married life,
once considered private, was now public property.[10] This
development enables the *Spectator's* reviewer to refer to the
"extreme repression of [Jane's] life with Carlyle" and to
offer Jane's own witty yet apparently bitter explanation of
why women marry: "They do not find scope enough for
their genius and qualities in an easy life." The article dwells
especially on Jane's virtually helpless anger about her husband's infatuation with Lady Ashburton. Paradoxically, this
reviewer closes with belated words of advice that lay most of
the guilt on Jane. If she "had been a little more reticent with
her friends and a little less reticent with her husband, he
would, doubtless, have made her a better husband."[11]
Whether one agrees with such a conclusion, this review is an
example of how easy it was for many to accept, analyze, and
comment on Froude's revelations as a matter of course. They
were discussed, analyzed, and pronounced upon as if they
were Gladstone's latest speech or some other form of public
property.

Responses to Froude's biography of Carlyle were similarly
judgmental. Because Froude was a friend who judged the
man sympathetically but the husband harshly, his interpretation was viewed as having greater authority. The *Critic and
Good Literature* did not feel Carlyle had suffered much from
the "exposure" in *Thomas Carlyle: A History of His Life in
London* and called Carlyle "as lucky in his biographer" as

Froude was "happy in his subject."[12] Sarah Hubbard in the *Dial* concurred: Froude performed his task as literary executor "with honorable fidelity and eminent skill," evincing "an honest and single-hearted desire to represent the man . . . impartially and faithfully."[13] Writing in the *Academy*, William Wallace thought the biography was Froude's best work and declared that the public had a right to learn the private details of a great teacher's life. Carlyle himself demanded the truth; therefore, Froude, doubly bound to tell it, created "an honest and even courageous study in the moral nude."[14] In an earlier review, Wallace had also noted, however, the decline in Carlyle's reputation that this truth-telling had wrought. If the man's ideas, private opinions, or personal life lost him followers, these defectors were untrue disciples who had never properly understood him. Carlyle's heritage was his "moral message" which survived him and had "quickened and sustained two generations."[15] Here Wallace draws a distinction between private life and public pronouncements with which many of his colleagues would not concur.

Clearly, some reviewers saw nothing wrong in revealing private details, analyzing a stormy marriage, or chronicling a flawed character. Perhaps they began from the assumption that all people were flawed. Revealing the truth about them, then, was no crime, but an honest confrontation of the facts. Whether the flawed hero could still provide instruction, however, was a disputed issue. Hamilton thought not, but Wallace distinguished between the teacher and the teaching.

These writers formed the minority. Yet all reviewers, whether they accepted Froude or not, were concerned about the disparity between the public and private man. Even those who disagreed with Froude found it hard not to admit that something was amiss in a relationship that could evoke such biting letters or pathetic journal entries. Because Carlyle's own marriage did not work, his entire character and the whole of his thought were called into question. The public image and the Froudian deconstruction/reconstruction could hardly be more different, or, to many, more shocking. It is precisely this disparity that most critics emphasized. The Carlyles were compared with some idealized couple and found severely wanting because they did not fit the public perception of how such spouses should act. Thus, many critics dwelled on what was most spiteful, sensational, dramatic, and revealing, even though Froude's writings are favorable interpretations of two people whose only misfortune was to marry each other.

Dissenting reviewers dealt with this material in part by attacking Froude's editorial and moral seriousness. Commenting on the *Reminiscences,* the reviewer for *Month and Catholic Review* noted that Froude was habitually dishonest and untrustworthy. Referring to his *History of England* (1856–70), the reviewer claimed that he "wrote his book with so much utter unscrupulousness" that no one could be sure his document transcriptions were accurate. Because he regularly manipulated his sources, who knew how well or fairly he was editing the material Carlyle had given him?[16] The *British Quarterly Review* felt Froude failed as editor of the *Reminiscences* by tastelessly printing the lamentations of a "broken heart communing with itself"—and then this same periodical excerpted several of those lamentations.[17] The *Saturday Review,* noting that the *Reminiscences* were not meant for the public, speculated that "it is impossible to guess to what extent matter undesirable for publication has been withheld." The implication here, as in other reviews, is that if what has been given us is so bad, how much worse must be the excised portions? In addition, the reviewer disapproved of an editor who allowed a figure "of the highest public honour and the greatest private esteem and regard to exhibit himself in some of his worst and most wayward and whimsical humours."[18] This reviewer explicitly raises the issue of shattering a *public* image. And, in a curious twist of logic not uncommon to these critics, Carlyle was not blamed for being uncharitable and a bad husband so much as his biographer was blamed for revealing this information. If the truth resulted in a broken icon, it was best to suppress the truth, at least for a time.

Although no great admirer of Carlyle, Robert Buchanan agreed. Writing in the *Contemporary Review*, he asserted that "it is not yet the time . . . to speak the whole truth concerning his career, or to dwell with undue emphasis on those points in his character which are least agreeable." The publication of the *Reminiscences* was "hasty," "ill-advised" and "deplorable." Yet Buchanan felt the "bane" of the *Reminiscences* had found an "antidote" in a biography of Carlyle, now almost forgotten, written by W. H. Wylie. Calling this book a "masterly" appreciation, full of hero worship yet not idolatrous, Buchanan implied that Wylie's volume was the sort of kindly, positive appreciation that a posthumous biography should be. Buchanan insisted that this work "simply purifies, with the honest oxygen of kindly humanity, the fetid memory of certain ignoble moods, and its representation of the man in his habit as he lived, tenacious, pugnacious, truthful, and not too generous, yet full of personal affection and genuine if somewhat provincial humour, is as good in its way as Carlyle's own presentation of those saturnine historical heroes with which he had most sympathy."[19]

If speaking ill of the famous dead was considered indelicate, publishing the letters of a private woman such as Jane was utterly improper—even though Carlyle had insisted Froude should agree to edit the *Letters and Memorials of Jane Welsh Carlyle* after his death.[20] While arguably, Carlyle intended his quasiautobiography for publication, or even as an act of atonement, Jane was not a public figure; therefore, no one, the reasoning went, including her husband, had any right to parade her lamentations or jealousies before the public. Besides, many added, after perusing what they thought should not have been published, it appeared that the problem was lack of communication and not infidelity. Froude had no business revealing private misunderstandings between husband and wife. Although these critics were not particularly consistent, they effectively questioned the accuracy of Froude's interpretation.

Writing in the *Gentleman's Magazine*, H. R. Fox-Bourne again insisted that Froude misunderstood the Carlyle marriage and so had "grievously misled" the public and "wronged the memory" of the couple. It was incorrect to call Jane a martyr to her husband; she was a wise woman who must have understood what she was entering into and seemed generally pleased with what she got. Fox-Bourne also offered the then-startling opinion that "most wives are martyrs, whether their husbands are geniuses or not" and that the world would be much better off if women were "as free as men are to make the best they can of their lives."[21] If the letters revealed anything, it was how *un*free Jane was, yet in a review written a year later, Fox-Bourne continued to maintain his belief in the soundness of the marriage and went on to denounce Froude bitterly for injudicious editorial procedure.

> By what rule of right, or of honour, Mr. Froude considers himself justified in printing the secret confidences of a dead woman, written for no eye but her own at a time of great bodily weakness and mental depression—confidences that her own husband chose to keep sacred, except that he made such extracts from them as seemed to him necessary to complete an act of penance which he thought incumbent on him—I need not here inquire.

Froude's "abuse of trust" was "sacrilegious," his disloyalty shocking, his action that of an assassin.[22]

The *Atlantic Monthly* concurred, lamenting the utter lack of "old-fashioned chivalrous feeling for women" that Froude exhibited. Granting that the marriage was "not an exceptionally unhappy one," the reviewer nonetheless saw Carlyle more as overabsorbed in his work than habitually neglectful of his wife.[23] Here again the unhappiness is Jane's fault for not making the best of her lot. Complaint was a sign of disobedience, an assault on the institution of marriage, an affront to decorum. However bad a husband Carlyle might have been, Jane to some readers became a worse wife for not putting up with him, and Froude worse still for making the matter public. In this spirit the *Dial* insisted that the marriage was relatively happy but spoke resentfully of Froude's "desecration" of marital privacy.[24]

The most vocal and articulate critic of Froude was Margaret Oliphant, who in two reviews totally disagreed with both his interpretation and his ethical standards. She was in a privileged position to judge, having been a friend of both Carlyles in their later years and having interviewed Jane for her own biography of Edward Irving (1862). She entertained a warm, lifelong regard for each of them and was intensely angered "against that Nemesis known amongst men by the name of Froude," a play on words recalling Froude's early novel (*The Nemesis of Faith*, 1849) and hinting that his factual productions were closer to the injudicious fiction he began his career by writing. Oliphant claimed, with much justice, that both Carlyles were unusually high-strung, irritable people who "had no skin to speak of upon their quivering nerves." Jane, among the proudest, most private of women, never asked for nor expected such public exhibition of her ephemeral complaints; moreover, she was a naturally dramatic woman who consciously heightened the color of her stories for effect. Froude did not realize this, Oliphant maintained, nor did he respect Jane's likely wishes. "She did not confide her reputation to Mr. Froude, or give him leave to unveil her inmost life according to his own interpretation of it." What Froude did was to make Jane a "heroine" in a "tragedy" wholly of his own writing and the product of his "artistic instincts." Oliphant makes Froude out to be a writer of fiction and, by extension, a liar.[25]

It is quite possible that, with her quickness of insight and literary experience, Oliphant grasped more clearly than many that Froude was constructing an artistic impression of the life based on such materials as he chose to use. Thanks to John Clubbe's study of the biography, we can easily accept the thesis that Froude tells his story in terms of Greek tragedy so far as it regards Jane, and Spenser's *Faerie Queen* in reference to Lady Ashburton. Froude also uses certain traditional biographical devices, including holy living and dying, in treating both Thomas and Jane. But structurally interesting as such methods of focusing his story may be, they force on the selection and interpretation of the documents a peculiar bias. The "plot" of the biography is foreshortened and distorted. The structure represents a kind of "truth" to Froude, but this is not how it appeared to others who were minor characters in the same drama. The parts these other figures played in the Carlyles' lives were often separately, and certainly collectively, as great as Froude's. So it is natural that Oliphant and others should often have felt that his grasp of the tale he was telling was imperfect, compellingly readable as his book might seem.

Oliphant wrote that the author-editor's conception of the marriage "is a mistake and misconception of the most fundamental kind." If it was difficult for the Carlyles to be together at times, she argued, it was far worse for them to be apart. This she expressed in the Scots vernacular phrase "ill to hae, but waur to want." Jane's letters especially proved the marriage was a happy one. But what of her pathetic diary kept during the height of the Lady Ashburton episode? Oliphant wavered a bit by admitting it was the only material Froude could offer in defense of his theory. "The discovery of this bit of writing," she wrote, "was a godsend to the biographer, who must have felt by this time that the mass of letters were by no means so conformable to his theory as might have been desired." Yet she dismissed this evidence by denying the authority of irritable words written in a state of deep depression. Carlyle himself "passed reverently over" these words; why could not Froude? The fact that more people were not outraged over the indignity merely meant that "public feeling and sense of honour must be at a low ebb indeed when no one ventures to stand up and stigmatize as it deserves this betrayal and exposure of the secret of a woman's weakness." Simply put, it was none of our business, even though publication allowed everyone, including Oliphant, to promulgate pet theories at will.[26]

Here Oliphant and her adherents were thrust into a dilemma. They could not unpublish what had appeared, however much they deplored it. They professed not to want to know about it but had to review it in order to present their own differing views. And they certainly must have hoped for more primary information supporting their positions, even though that hope contradicted their desire for reticence about private matters such as marriage. Oliphant came closest to resolving the dilemma by taking all the information Froude used and reinterpreting it. Her article, then, is perhaps one of the quickest revisionist biographies on record.

Most reviewers opposed to Froude were not so perspicacious or resourceful. They simply attacked rather than rein-terpreted the documents in the final volumes of Froude's *Life*. Thus, the *British Quarterly Review* thought Froude chose the "very worst" possible method of biography. He was guiltier than one who fabricated because he had dissected a "sensitive heart"; the result was a "mischievous book" that made another biography nearly "impossible." Froude "has exaggerated the mists and vapours, he has intensified and underlined every failing." He was false to the memory of Carlyle, uncaring of the feelings of living acquaintances, and vengeful.[27]

Two later friends of Carlyle, Frederic Harrison and David Masson, agreed that Froude was both unfit and inaccurate. Harrison maintained that biographers of literary men should concern themselves only with how their subjects wrote their books and not inquire into the details of married life. Be-sides, Harrison *had* inquired and had firsthand accounts that the marriage "was in the main the worthy effort after happiness of two just spirits." Also, he had known Carlyle in old age and found him a "generous, hearty, simple man of genius."[28] Masson had known Carlyle for nearly forty years and felt Froude's gloominess of character made him "consti-tutionally incompetent to understand" Carlyle's personality. Froude was "too uniformly like . . . a man driving a hearse" and hence misconstrued Carlyle's sense of humor.[29]

Many reviewers felt Froude was wrong, then, to reveal unpleasant details so soon after his subject's death, and oth-ers thought Froude's interpretation was at fault. Whether Froude's views were correct or not, reviewers asserted that he had done his job badly and in the process had hurt his master's reputation. A. G. Sedgwick was among those who berated but could not refute Froude. He wrote in the *Nation* that "there is . . . an art of biography which Mr. Froude would do well to pay some attention to before laying his hand upon any more dead reputations." Sedgwick apparently had in mind biographies that were respectful tributes composed in a spirit of fulsome hero worship. By not producing such a work, Froude himself offended standards of decorum and so, Sedgwick huffed, he "may congratulate himself on having very nearly destroyed the authority of his master."[30] In offending decorum, Froude showed bad manners; in destroying an icon, he became a revolutionary who swept away revered Victorian authorities and replaced them with nothing. To many, the flawed hero seemed an unworthy object of veneration, while the flawed hero worshiper became an eminently worthy subject for bitter execration. The opposition to Froude, therefore, was based on several significant assumptions: that Froude misinterpreted the information he chose to use, that biography was intended to memorialize and not disfigure, that a person's private life should stay that way, and that the loss of worthy objects of reverence was harmful to society yet was the inevitable result of excessive candor.

Froude had no public defenders for his views among Carlyle's friends. Presumably Geraldine Jewsbury would have stood by him, but she had died in 1880. John Ruskin privately supported Froude and planned his own biography of Carlyle but was never capable even of starting it. Every other writer who knew the Carlyles strongly disputed Froude. The impressive list includes William and Helen Allingham, Charles Eliot Norton, G. S. Venables, Julia Wedgwood, Moncure Conway, Masson, Harrison, and Oliphant. Modern critics have charged that the "Froude controversy" grew out of the narrowness or greed of surviving Carlyle family members.[31] Yet the evidence of so many friends is forceful and convincing. This dispute derives from differences of opinion regarding the Carlyles' lives and characters based on personal knowledge. If such a majority of the Carlyles' friends believed Froude to be wrong, scholars should examine the grounds for this belief, then revise their opinions accordingly.

This relatively narrow conclusion should not, however, obscure a more general observation about Victorian views of biography and its function. Many critics saw biography as a means of memorialization, as a secular saint's life. The hatchet job or "kiss and tell" biographies common today did not really exist yet as recognized literary forms (although some would unfairly point to Froude as originator). What did exist were straightforward "life and times" books that saw, spoke, and heard no evil except what it was impossible to ignore. Providing innocuous anecdotes, often tedious correspondence, and morally uplifting yet invariably dull lives, they were modest acts of hero worship usually written by friends or relatives. Such a method of biography seemed to have wide acceptance. The reviewer for the *Athenaeum*, in discussing Wylie's life of Carlyle, noted that the "appetite for biography must be greatly on the increase," because the moment any famous man died, "a dozen pens" and as many "paste-pots" and "pairs of scissors are busy producing a 'biography.' " Furthermore, "each biographer seems to think that in chanting the praises of his hero he is not only earning an honest penny for himself, but honouring the hero to boot."[32] Thus the function of such biographies is primarily to *exalt*. Yet the reviewer's reference to clip-and-paste books perhaps implies a growing weariness with the endless rows of fat, two-volume hagiographies.

Margaret Oliphant made the best case for old-fashioned decorum and the traditional style of biography in an 1883 essay entitled "The Ethics of Biography." She sought the origin of biography and, characteristically, found it in the Old

Testament stories of patriarchs and in the New Testament life of Christ, "the most perfect of lives and portraitures." She tellingly adds that "the faiths of the world are founded" on just such "biographical works." One also has faith, she adds, in the "legends of the saints in all ages . . . which hold every one a living soul of humanity, a human life commending itself to the admiration, the instruction, the following of men." Oliphant goes on to deplore modern biographical iconoclasm:

> The saints and heroes, however, if we believe what is now told us on every side, were neither heroic nor saintly to their valets, and it might have been, for anything we can tell, quite possible to deprive us of every noble name that now gives lustre to humanity, and to leave the past as naked of all veneration or respect as is the present. That fine St. George, who has given an emblem of spotless valour and conquest over the impure image of fleshly lust and cruelty to two great nations . . . turns out, they say, to have been an army contractor, furnishing the shoddy of his time to the commissariat; and a great deal the better we all are for that exquisite discovery. And St. Francis was a dirty, little half-witted fanatic and Oliver Cromwell a vulgar impostor with a big wart, and Luther a fat priest, who wanted to marry. How many more could we add to the list? till at the end nobody would be left towards whom we could look with any sentiment more reverent than that which we feel for our greengrocer. That this is not the true sentiment of humanity, nor in accord with any law of natural right and wrong, must be evident to the most cursory observer.

For Oliphant, the function of biography was to inspire, uplift, and even reform readers while simultaneously creating in them a reverence for the subject. If she recognized readers' (and biographers') natural penchant for gossip or their curiosity about private matters, she set against that the more noble human tendency to find and follow worthy role models. She insisted that for people recently dead, negative details should be suppressed. If a biographer was incapable of doing this, he or she should give up the project; literary and social morality unanimously required such a decision. Scandal can be investigated in the fullness of time. But in the main "it is impossible that a biographer could be compelled to criminate his friend, or to soil an established reputation entrusted to his care."[33] Oliphant deplored iconoclastic biography because she felt it unnatural. It bred cynicism, disrespect, and contempt; ultimately, it was subversive. She is an articulate spokesperson for reticence and respect in biography because if society was based on the principle of reverence—as she claimed it was—then a form of biography based on lack of it subverted that society by undermining *all* objects of veneration.

On the other hand, those who approved of Froude had their own motives. Many such defenders revered unvarnished truth rather than carefully constructed images; they were photographers rather than portraitists, scientists rather than theologians. And some who agreed with Froude's methods disliked Carlyle's thought, seeking to refute it by discrediting the man. On this latter point, it would be too easy to infer that liberal critics of Carlyle were more enlightened, even though they justly indicated the weaknesses in Carlyle's thought. Their advocacy of progressive, reformist government, praise of individual liberty, and opposition to authoritarian rule gave them strong philosophical grounds for disagreeing with Carlyle. Practically, they were annoyed with what they viewed as his obstinate irrationality and his frequent yet unquantifiable appeals to the "Destinies" and "Eternities" for justice. While Carlyle remained dubious or openly contemptuous about various articles of the liberal creed, his opponents could only regard him as a worthy, misguided adversary. Yet now that one of his closest friends—and, moreover, a conservative—showed that Carlyle was rather a bad, cross, mean-spirited person as well as a political reactionary, his philosophy suffered from guilt by association. Some critics fell prey to the logical fallacy that a bad man must be a bad thinker—or at least they found it a convenient assumption for their reviews.

One example of this line of reasoning came in A. J. Robertson's 1883 article titled "Carlyle: Smirching the Idol." After vigorously defending Froude's "impartiality," he adds: "Then it is said that there is no need for these details because they will not affect our estimate of the man as a thinker, nor our estimate of the value of his teachings. This is a mistake. All of us desire to know the fullest that can be known of any particular author or other celebrated man; and in proportion as our knowledge increases of what kind of man he was in his private character . . . our estimate of him is modified thereby." Rousseau's private "unparalleled meanness," for example, is impossible to ignore when studying his works. Thus Carlyle's own "selfishness" and "growling discontent" must lead to modified views of his writings. Robertson warns against setting "idol[s] on too high a pedestal" because inevitably they are toppled. He also advises against "expecting too much from poor human nature" (even though he earlier uncharitably calls Carlyle "one of the greatest of modern shams").[34]

Yet it does the majority who praised Froude's methods a disservice to imply that their motives were base or their reasoning flawed. Most writers believed that the whole truth needed to be known in order to judge impartially, and they too eagerly accepted as the whole truth what Froude wrote. To these reviewers, Froude deserved no criticism for making public the faults of another man. If he destroyed an icon, or gave a saint vices, then it was about time. For it was clearly common sense that all people were human, with faults to match their talents. Not to admit this was prevarication, a view put best by George Bentley in *Temple Bar:* "If biographers will put a mask over their hero they must be content with the consequences of robbing from us the sight of the human face." It was far better to show Carlyle's bad side along with what was positive because that was more truthful. "Give it and all the bad things with it," Bentley concludes, "and time will let them settle at the bottom, and the wine none the worse."[35]

In summing up, we must return to the large, probably unresolvable issue of public image and private lifestyle in Victorian biography and society. Although in fact Froude was a genuine worshiper of Carlyle, his sort of revealing adoration was not acceptable to most people because his golden image had *visible* feet of clay. And to undermine a hero was worse, to these people, than fudging facts or suppressing details to create a coherent, positive image of him. One can certainly sympathize with Froude for believing that his relatively balanced criticisms and modest revelations about both Carlyles were exaggerated by reviewers. His high regard for Carlyle was lost in reviews that distorted his generally positive depiction by emphasizing the seamy, steamy details of private life he revealed. On the other side were the reviewers who demanded that nothing be suppressed. Thus the tension between restraint and revelation was strong, the debate acrimonious. Neither extreme satisfied everyone; compromise satisfied no one.

Yet Leslie Stephen tried, and perhaps his inconsistent views can be taken as representative of the ambivalence of Victorian society on this subject. In an essay on Froude, Stephen

wrote, somewhat enviously, that the historian had "not become the victim of a biography" and added that "the world"
did not possess any inalienable right to biographies of its
famous. "If they or theirs prefer silence I am inclined to ap-
plaud the refusal to gratify curiosity," he added. Such a response seems a classic example of Victorian reticence, but in
a later essay, "The Browning Letters," Stephen acknowledged
the desire to know, making it appear something like a right.
"However gravely we may speak," he remarked, "we shall
read the next indiscreet revelation, and our enjoyment will
only have the keener edge from affectation of prudery."
Stephen now noticed as well a problem with reticence:
"There are cases in which it may cover a paltry regard for
conventional propriety."[36]

One suspects Stephen, and the Victorians, of bowing to
the inevitable. People did enjoy indiscreet revelations. Learning about lifestyles of the rich, famous, and possibly naughty
was as popular then as today. Good historian that he was,
Stephen had to see the value of all documents, especially
those that dealt with well-known people. He further seemed
to realize that one could not devise any satisfactory half-
measures for making such documents public. In revealing
information from them that was characteristic, one could
not logically omit what might be unpleasant.

However, the Victorians also seemed to realize that truth
was not merely an accumulation of all the facts but an interpretation of some of them. And the interpretation could be
incorrect. Indeed, the more unscrupulous the biographer
was toward his or her subject, the greater the likelihood that
it *would* be wrong. Surely Margaret Oliphant was correct in
making this point. Surely she had a further point when she
suggested that the more sensational a biographer's "revelations are, the more are they likely to amuse and please the

public."[37] In brief, this was the dilemma Victorian biographers faced: To tell or not to tell, and on what grounds? To reveal in part and keep silence in part? To leave the documents to posterity to interpret or unloose them on contemporaries or destroy them?

Modern readers and writers face the same issues and confront them in the same ambivalent way. Families or estates of public figures frequently refuse or limit access to important papers for decades. Destruction of vital documents is hardly uncommon. Authorized biographies are frequently puff pieces, and unauthorized exposés are just as often hatchet jobs. Carefully written, balanced appraisals are still regularly remaindered. Modern readers cannot resist the checkout-line gossip of the tabloids yet are unfailingly captivated by representations of genuine selflessness and nobility. But if we have come no closer to a neat resolution of the dilemma, we can nonetheless thank our predecessors for stating both sides of the issue so clearly, and at times eloquently, and for giving us authorities to cite when we defend our own inconsistent attitudes about what to tell.

Notes

I wish to thank Professor Rodger Tarr of Illinois State University for his generous assistance, encouragement, and free use of his files in my gathering information on this topic.

The "Froude Controversy" has been frequently studied over the years. The most significant publications on the matter are James Anthony Froude, *My Relations with Carlyle* (London: Longmans, 1903); Alexander Carlyle and James Crichton-Brown, *The Nemesis of Froude* (London: Lane, 1903); and Waldo Dunn's books *Froude and Carlyle* (London: Longmans, 1930) and *James Anthony Froude:*

A Biography, 2 vols. (New York: Oxford University Press, 1961–63). G. B. Tennyson provides a welcome synthesis of information and sources in "The Carlyles" in *Victorian Prose: A Guide to Research,* ed. David J. DeLaura (New York: MLA, 1973). Significant articles in support of Froude's position include Hyder Rollins, "Charles Eliot Norton and Froude," *Journal of English and Germanic Philology* 57 (October 1958): 651–64; John Clubbe, "Grecian Destiny: Froude's Portraits of the Carlyles," in *Carlyle and His Contemporaries: Essays in Honor of Charles Richard Sanders,* ed. John Clubbe (Durham: Duke University Press, 1976), 317–53, and Clubbe's introduction to *Froude's Life of Carlyle,* ed. John Clubbe (Columbus: Ohio State University Press, 1976). For comment critical of Froude based on new information, see K. J. Fielding's "Froude and Carlyle: Some New Considerations," in *Carlyle Past and Present,* ed. K. J. Fielding and Rodger Tarr (New York: Barnes & Noble, 1976), 239–69, and "Froude's Revenge, or the Carlyles and Erasmus A. Darwin," *Essays and Studies* 31 (1978): 75–97. See also Ian Campbell, "Froude, Moncure Conway, and the American Edition of the 'Reminiscences,' " *Carlyle Newsletter* 8 (Spring 1987): 71–79.

1. "Carlyle and Guizot on Cromwell," *Lowe's Edinburgh Magazine and Protestant Educational Journal* 1 (1846): 273.

2. H. R. Fox-Bourne, "Mr. Carlyle," *Athenaeum,* 12 Feb. 1881, 232–35.

3. *Reminiscences,* ed. C. E. Norton, Introduction by Ian Campbell (1887; London: Dent, 1972), 118.

4. Allen Grant, "The Carlyle Controversy," *Temple Bar* 62 (August 1881): 16–17.

5. Gail Hamilton, "The Day of Judgment, pt. 1," *North American Review* 137 (December 1883): 566–67.

6. Gail Hamilton, "The Day of Judgment, pt. 2," *North American Review* 138 (January 1884): 77. Hamilton concludes her review by describing Jane's fate in terms of Greek tragedy. A "rare and radiant maiden" lavished on Carlyle her "heart and soul and life. Iphigenia was found, and from the smoke of that most costly

sacrifice uprose the true Carlyle." In "Grecian Destiny," John Clubbe writes: "Critics . . . have completely overlooked [Froude's] use of Greek tragedy in depicting the drama of the Carlyles" (331). In my study, I have, on the contrary, found several such brief references to Froude's separate works and not only the biography. Yet these references are sporadic, not carefully developed. Clubbe's study remains the most complete analysis of this intriguing biographical device.

7. Hamilton, pt. 1, 573.

8. *Times,* 7 Mar. and 9 May 1881, 5, 11.

9. "Mrs. Carlyle's Letters," *Times,* 31 Mar. 1883, 4.

10. Compare Elizabeth Gaskell's famous *Life of Charlotte Bronte* (1857), which casts perhaps a gauzy veil over the protagonist's married life, while Froude insists no reserve should be practiced (yet does not directly confront his own belief in Carlyle's impotence).

11. "Mrs. Carlyle," *Spectator,* 7 Apr. 1883, 445–46.

12. "Carlyle's Life in London," *The Critic and Good Literature,* 25 Oct. 1884, 193–94.

13. Sarah Hubbard, "More of Carlyle's Memoirs," *Dial* 5 (November 1884): 172, 175.

14. William Wallace, *Academy,* 1 Nov. 1884, 282.

15. William Wallace, *Academy,* 15 Apr. 1882, 261.

16. "Carlyle's Reminiscences," *Month and Catholic Review,* N.S. 22 (April 1881): 457.

17. *British Quarterly Review* 73 (April 1881): 239–40.

18. *Saturday Review,* 19 Mar. 1881, 370.

19. Robert Buchanan, "Wylie's Life of Thomas Carlyle," *Contemporary Review* 39 (May 1881): 792–93.

20. Froude, *My Relations with Carlyle,* 12–13.

21. H. R. Fox-Bourne, "Carlyle and His Wife," *Gentleman's Magazine* 252 (June 1882): 687–88.

22. H. R. Fox-Bourne, "Carlyle and His Wife," *Gentleman's Magazine* 254 (May 1883): 530, 532–33.

23. "Jane Welsh Carlyle," *Atlantic Monthly* 51 (June 1883): 837, 840.

24. Francis F. Browne, "Briefs on New Books," *Dial*, May 1883, 17–18.

25. Margaret Oliphant, "Mrs. Carlyle," *Littell's Living Age* 158 (11 Aug. 1883): 673–74, 683–84.

26. Ibid.

27. "Thomas Carlyle," *British Quarterly Review* 81 (January 1885): 143–47.

28. Frederic Harrison, *The Choice of Books* (London: Macmillan, 1886), 198–99, 184, 185–86, 190.

29. "Masson's Interpretation of Carlyle," *Popular Science Monthly* 28 (December 1885): 225–26. The first quotation is the reviewer's summation; the second is a direct quote from Masson.

30. A. G. Sedgwick, "Froude's Carlyle," *Nation* 34 (1 June 1884): 466.

31. K. J. Fielding in "Froude and Carlyle," 239ff, carefully inquiring into the legal wrangling occasioned by Carlyle's death and imprecise will, vindicates niece Mary Carlyle's legal position and points out the extremely awkward moral dilemma into which she was thrust by Froude's lack of sensitivity, good judgment, and trustworthiness.

32. *Athenaeum,* 9 Apr. 1881, 488–89.

33. Margaret Oliphant, "The Ethics of Biography," *Contemporary Review* 44 (July 1883): 79–80, 90–91.

34. A. J. Robertson, "Carlyle: Smirching the Idol," *Progress* 1–2 (May/August 1883): 370–74, 47–51.

35. George Bentley, "Sincerity in Biography," *Temple Bar* 62 (July 1881): 334.

36. Leslie Stephen, "James Anthony Froude," *Studies of a Biographer,* 4 vols. (New York: Putnam, 1907), 3:205; "The Browning Letters," 3:1–3.

37. Oliphant, "The Ethics of Biography," 88.

8 / Julia Margaret Cameron and the "Ennoblement" of Photographic Portraiture

Joanne Lukitsh

THE association of Julia Margaret Cameron's portrait photographs with "Victorian scandals" may come as a surprise to readers familiar with her status as one of the canonical figures of nineteenth-century artistic photography, whose depictions of Thomas Carlyle and Alfred Tennyson are displayed in Room 21, "Victorian Writers and Artists," of the National Portrait Gallery in London. Cameron's twentieth-century status as an artist would seem to be confirmed by references to the contemporary reception of her work as, for example, a review published in the *Reader* on 18 March 1865, less than a year after the first public exhibition of her photographs. The *Reader* remarked of Cameron and her photographic mentor, the painter David Wilkie Wynfield: "while what is called photographic portraiture, under the direction of the professional practitioner, is almost invariably vulgar, leveling and literal, it becomes in the hands of these cultivated artists at once highly characteristic and deeply suggestive."[1] This opposition between "vulgar" professional and "cultivated" artist is familiar to students of Victorian culture, and positions Wynfield and Cameron within an established hierarchy of cultural value, a place Cameron's photography continues to occupy.

Yet the *Reader*'s contrast between professional and artist was marshaled over a dispute about "what is called photographic portraiture." The *Reader*'s characterization of Cameron and Wynfield as "cultivated artists" organizes the discursive limits of a practice, "photographic portraiture," whose terms are not fixed, and imposes a hierarchy upon that practice. To these ends, Cameron, who had not participated even in the limited institutional artistic activity available to contemporary women, was immediately recognized as an artist with Wynfield, who had exhibited at the Royal Academy. Although perhaps more paradoxical than honorific, Cameron's status as an "artist" enabled her to serve traditional cultural values while enjoying opportunities for the expression of individual power untraditional to women.

The *Reader*'s 1865 indictment of "vulgar, leveling and literal" commercial photographic portraiture was related to its long-standing complaint against the *carte de visite* photographic portrait, which became a national mania in England in the early 1860s. For the *Reader* and other supporters, Cameron, like Wynfield, established a standard of decorum in her photographic portraits by alluding to Old Master precedents and eschewing contemporary clothing. Yet this "artistic" alternative to vulgar professionalism was limited, in that *carte* portraits had transformed public expectations of portraiture. The short-lived involvement of Wynfield, a painter, with photographic portraiture was indicative of the dim commercial prospects for an aesthetic approach. Cameron's involvement, however, was different: because she was freed from the requirement to support herself through sales, her photographic production greatly exceeded Wynfield's in duration, range, renown, and sheer volume, as she availed herself of the status of artist. Cameron's sustained engagement with photographic portraiture suggests that her production of decorous portraits concealed an indecorous expression of power: a woman creating images of some of the most influential men of her society.

Cameron began to work in photography at the age of forty-nine, in January 1864, with a camera given her by her son-in-law—reportedly to distract her from meddling in his family activities. Before 1864, she had devoted her considerable energies to her husband, Charles Hay Cameron, a distinguished jurist; their six children; and the social activities revolving around the prominent salon at Little Holland House conducted by her sister, Sara Pattle Prinsep. A member of the Victorian intellectual aristocracy, Cameron was a particularly close friend of Henry Taylor and also of Alfred Tennyson, her neighbor on the Isle of Wight. In 1847 her translation of G. A. Bürger's "Lenore" appeared; she reportedly published other poems and began a novel.[2] Photography was Cameron's only known practice of the visual arts, and she credited Wynfield, who was part of her social circle, with inspiring her work.[3]

In 1863, Wynfield produced a series of fancy-dress photographic portraits of fellow artists, including John Everett Millais, Frederick Leighton, Edward Burne-Jones, and W. F. Yeames. (See fig. 1, Wynfield's "Self—Portrait [?] in Renaissance Costume.") Early the next year, Wynfield published the series as a portfolio, "The Studio," to rave reviews in the press.[4] The *Illustrated London News* exclaimed of Wynfield's portraits, "if they do not, they *ought* to revolutionize photographic portraiture, if not other branches of the art," and

Fig. I. David Wilkie Wynfield, "Self-Portrait [?] in Renaissance
Costume," 21 cm. × 16 cm., c. 1863–64; courtesy of the International
Museum of Photography at George Eastman House, Rochester, New
York.

the *Reader* described "The Studio" as "the best portraits that have ever been produced by photography."[5] The reviewers applauded Wynfield's willingness to place the camera "out of focus" in order to mitigate the literalness of the photographic lens; they also appreciated his visual allusions to Old Master paintings.

The great enthusiasm of these journals for Wynfield's modest series of photographs was generated by their hostility to what the *Reader* characterized as "the vulgarity of photographic portraiture at the present time," as exemplified in the popular *carte de visite*, a photograph on a cardboard mount, approximately the size of a visiting card, typically used for portraiture (figs. 2 and 3). The *Reader* deemed Wynfield's photographs a salutary alternative to

> the vulgarity, monotony and poverty of resource exhibited by common *carte de visite* portraiture. The distinctions so patent between a lady and her maid, between a statesman and a prize-fighter, between a poet and a performer on the tight-rope, are unknown to photography, chiefly because they are unfelt by the individual who undertakes the all-important duty of posing the sitter and arranging the background.[6]

Wynfield's portraits were soft-focus, bust views of male artists in fancy-dress homage to Old Master artists, contrasting greatly with the sharply focused detail of contemporary dress and studio setting that typified the *carte*. Yet implicit in the *Reader*'s complaint against the *carte* is a situation in which a lady and a lady's maid, a statesman and a prizefighter, all have access to the same photographic portrait format, an equality of opportunity unavailable in other forms of social representation. The general development of nineteenth-century photography in Europe has been associated with the growing social influence of the bourgeoisie, whose aspirations to the status of painted portraiture led to the invention of more

Fig. 2. A. A. E. Disdéri, uncut *carte de visite* portrait of a woman, 19.8 cm. × 23.7 cm., c. 1860–65; courtesy of the International Museum of Photography at George Eastman House, Rochester, New York.

mechanized means of portrait production and reproduction. The mass circulation and marketing of the *carte,* however, transformed expectations of the purposes and audiences for photographic portraiture, as articles about the *carte* mania in contemporary journals variously recognized.

In Britain, the apocryphal origin of the popularity of the *carte* portrait format was J. E. Mayall's album of *carte* portraits of the Royal Family, appearing in August 1860. This publication initiated a rage for collecting *cartes* and for the fashion of having one's own photographic portrait produced in this format.[7] The *carte* portrait, produced in Western Europe and North America predominantly from the mid-1850s until the late 1860s, was the first photographic portrait for-

Fig. 3. Unknown photographer, "Thomas Carlyle," *carte de visite*, c. 1861–64; courtesy of the Visual Studies Workshop, Rochester, New York.

mat that incorporated the principles of commodity production with photographic portraiture: the merit of the patent submitted in 1854 by Parisian photographic entrepreneur A. A. E. Disdéri was that eight or ten images could be printed in the same amount of time needed to print one sheet of photographic paper, thus reducing the unit cost per image. The full-length portrait pose (as shown in figure 2) that typified the format during this period allowed the rendering of maximum detail with the lens open at full aperture, thus reducing exposure time and cost. Moreover, this full-length pose not only effectively displayed fashionable costume and studio furniture but it also appropriated a pose that had connoted power and prestige in painting and was used for contemporary fashion plates.[8]

The scale of *carte* production during the early 1860s in England was estimated to be in the millions. It was reported that ten thousand *cartes* was a typical production run during that time for a famous person's portrait; seventy thousand *cartes* of the Prince Consort, for example, were sold in the first week after his death.[9] This industrial scale of photographic production had been employed for stereograph cards but was unprecedented in portrait photography. An 1861 *Art-Journal* article on the *carte de visite* celebrates its potential for unlimited expansion of current institutions of portrait display:

> These *cartes de visite* in themselves constitute what we may even entitle an Art. They multiply national portrait galleries *ad infinitum*. They produce the family portraits of the entire community. They form portrait collections, on a miniature scale, but with an unlimited range and in every possible variety—family collections, collections of the portraits of friends, and of celebrities of every rank and order. Nobody now needs to inquire what such-or-such a person may be like, or to be left to such

surmises as written descriptions may convey. An ubiquitous *carte de visite* can always find its way with certainty and speed, and it is the best of all possible introductions, as it is the most agreeable of reminiscences.

The article then explores the implications of the marketing of *cartes* in the shop windows of urban streets:

> These photographic miniatures are exhibited and sold by persons whose establishments have no other connection with works of Art. They are in universal request, however, and so everybody thinks that he may quite consistently take a part in providing the requisite supply; and, if these portraits thus often find themselves in unexpected association with objects between which and themselves there can exist no sympathy, still more singular is that association which is apparent in the portraits displayed by *cartes de visite,* where they stand at the windows in long rows, tier above tier . . . [where] the most curious contrasts may be drawn, and the most startling combinations effected. Of course all these combinations are purely casual; but it is their casual origin that constitutes their singularity . . . when even the most hurried of passing glances reveals to us fac-similie images of Lord Shaftesbury and Cardinal Wiseman, and of the French Emperor and Sims Reeves side by side, with those of Florence Nightingale and Blondin and Professor Owen forming a trio, we are reminded in a manner most impressive that *carte de visite* miniatures are creations of the present day, portraits of our own contemporaries.[10]

The potential for social disruptions was enthusiastically advanced by Dr. Andrew Wynter in an article published several months later in *Once a Week*. Proposing a political dimension to the "purely casual" arrangements of *cartes* in a London shop window, Wynter begins with a telling discussion of the contrasting accessibility between the newly established National Portrait Gallery, open for only a few hours a day, and the hundreds of shop-window *carte* portrait displays:

Certainly our street portrait galleries are a great success: no solemn flights of stairs lead to pompous rooms in which pompous attendants preside with a severe air over pompous portraits, no committee of selection decide on the propriety of hanging certain portraits. Here, on the contrary, social equality is carried to its utmost limit, and Tom Sawyer is to be found cheek-by-jowl with Lord Derby.

The physical proximity of a *carte* of a boxer and one of an aristocrat symbolically effaced social distinctions, which were further challenged by the psychological accessibility of the *carte* image: the man and woman on the street exchanged gazes with notables. For Wynter, these "street portrait galleries" could therefore alter traditional hierarchies of achievement and privilege: heroism could be transformed from a transcendent value into a transitory event, achieved by accident, and even available to women:

> The commercial value of the human face was never tested to such an extent as it is in these handy photographs. No man, or woman either, knows but that some accident may elevate them to the position of the hero of the hour, and send up the value of their countenances to a degree they never dreamed of.[11]

This larger context, then, importantly amplifies the *Illustrated London News'* and the *Reader's* enthusiastic commendation of Wynfield's photographs for restoring the presence behind the camera of an *artist*, someone who would reinstate traditional order to a photographic activity seemingly governed only by fashion. The *Reader's* 1864 attributing the absence of "distinctions so patent" in the *carte* portraits of a lady and her maid to the *photographer's* inability to recognize, and thus represent them, simultaneously offered the possibility for repair: place an artist with knowledge of social codes behind the camera. The *Reader's* faith in the continued authority of these traditional social distinctions was evidence, obviously, of its disinclination to recognize the existence of the different audiences comprising the market for *carte* portraiture.

Yet the photographer-artist could not completely redeem the unreliability of photographic portrait signification, for how could truthful photographic representation have failed to convey "distinctions so patent"? Wynfield's "out of focus" portraits were praised for rejecting the perfection of detail and tone which connoted middle-class values of art and industrial progress. Cameron's manipulation of focus, depth of field, and lighting greatly exceeded Wynfield's, and early reviews of her work which noted her indebtedness to him considered her technical manipulations deficient to his. Cameron discussed these in a December 1864 letter to Sir John Herschel, in which she urged him to write in support of her photography,

> in that spirit which will elevate it and induce an ignorant public to believe in other than mere conventional topographic Photography—map making & skeleton rendering of feature & form without that roundness & fulness of force & feature that modelling of flesh & limb which the focus I use only can give tho' called & condemned as "*out of focus.*"[12]

Cameron's contrast of "skeleton" renderings and the modeling "of flesh & limb" exceeds the simple antagonism of detail versus "out of focus" to oppose death to life. She nearly promises for her photographs what is impossible in representation: the simultaneous presence of the representation *and* its referent. Underlying Cameron's belief in the physical presence of the subject represented by her photographs was an expectation of photographic signification not subject to the workings of the market, and capable of communicating transcendent truth.

A successful example of Cameron's conception of portrait

photography is an 1867 portrait of Thomas Carlyle (fig. 4). The photographic historian Mike Weaver associates this portrait with a passage from the Victorian art critic Anna Jameson's *Commonplace Book,* in which she discusses "C": "He is a man who carries his bright intellect as a light in a dark-lantern; he sees only the objects on which he chooses to throw that blaze of light: those he sees vividly, but, as it were, exclusively."[13] In this portrait, light as a physical agent of the trace of the subject on the photographic negative, and light as the literal and figural illumination described by Jameson, reinforce each other to represent Carlyle as an intellectual force. A comparison of Cameron's portrait with a contemporary *carte* (fig. 3) of Carlyle (which Cameron might well have described as a "skeleton rendering of feature & form") suggests how Cameron's photography not only utilized Old Master precedents but also signified how the photograph's status as a truthful representation was subject to the idea of the artist.

Cameron's portraits were predominantly bust and head/shoulder images of men. Their shoulders typically swathed in dark drapery, they were posed against a dark background in profile, three-quarter, or frontal face. Cameron's frequent use of the strict profile denied access to the individual psychology of the sitter in favor of representing typical characteristics. Cameron called her 1865 portrait of Alfred Tennyson (fig. 5) "a fit representation of an Isaiah or a Jeremiah"—in preference to "portrait[s] of our own contemporaries."[14] But if Cameron achieved many expressive effects through lighting and focus (fig. 6), she nonetheless used a limited range of devices to represent the transcendent qualities of intellect and heroism—as conventional, in their turn, as the formulaic poses, lighting, and backgrounds of the *carte.* These portraits, however, met the expectations of her audience. In July

Fig. 4. Julia Margaret Cameron, "Thomas Carlyle," 30 cm. × 24.2 cm., 1867; courtesy of the J. Paul Getty Museum, Malibu, California.

Fig. 5. Julia Margaret Cameron, "Alfred Tennyson," 25.3 cm. × 20.1 cm., 1865; courtesy of the International Museum of Photography at George Eastman House, Rochester, New York.

Fig. 6. Julia Margaret Cameron, "Henry Taylor as Rembrandt," 25.3 cm. × 20.1 cm., 1865; courtesy of the J. Paul Getty Museum, Malibu, California.

1864 the *Athenaeum* praised her for "treat[ing] her subjects in a manner which suggests the appropriate character of each," emphasizing what an 1868 review in *The Queen, the Lady's Newspaper* described as "the reality of the sitter."[15]

Cameron's practice of photography included both portraiture and *tableaux vivants* subjects, but she took early steps to make her portraits available to the public. Between 1864 and 1875, Cameron actively entered exhibitions of photographic societies and international expositions in Britain and abroad, organized one-woman shows in London, and prevailed upon her famous friends to write reviews and pose for their own portraits.[16] She exhibited only portraits when she debuted at the Annual Exhibition of the Photographic Society of London in May 1864; she published them through the London printsellers Colnaghi and Company as early as July 1864, and in 1867 Colnaghi distributed a selection of Cameron's "large photographic portraits of eminent persons."[17]

Cameron's early sitters included not only visual artists George Frederick Watts (fig. 7) and William Holman Hunt (fig. 8) but also Henry Taylor (figs. 6 and 9), James Spedding, Alfred Tennyson (fig. 5), Robert Browning, and Aubrey de Vere. Later sitters included J. F. W. Herschel (fig. 10), Henry Wadsworth Longfellow (fig. 11), Henry Layard, George Du Maurier, Governor Edward Eyre, William Michael Rossetti (fig. 12), Charles Darwin, and Gustave Doré.[18]

Cameron's debut exhibition of portraits of Taylor, Watts, and Spedding at the 1864 Annual Exhibition of the Photographic Society of London created a controversy in the commercial photographic press which had not been visited upon Wynfield. The ostensible subject of this uproar was Cameron's photographic technique, but it was provoked by a favorable review of her portraits published in the *Athenaeum* on 16 July 1864, which asserted that "the productions are

Fig. 7. Julia Margaret Cameron, "G. F. Watts R.A. in His Studio," 26.2 cm. × 20.8 cm., 1865; courtesy of the J. Paul Getty Museum, Malibu, California.

Fig. 8. Julia Margaret Cameron, "William Holman Hunt," 22.9 cm. × 17.8 cm., 1864; courtesy of the J. Paul Getty Museum, Malibu, California.

Fig. 9. Julia Margaret Cameron, "Henry Taylor," 34 cm. × 28 cm., 1867; courtesy of the J. Paul Getty Museum, Malibu, California.

Fig. 10. Julia Margaret Cameron, "Sir J. F. W. Herschel," 27.9 cm. × 22.7 cm., 1867; courtesy of the J. Paul Getty Museum, Malibu, California.

Fig. 11. Julia Margaret
Cameron, "Henry W.
Longfellow," 35.2 cm. × 27.3
cm., 1868; courtesy of the
International Museum of
Photography at George Eastman
House, Rochester, New York.

Fig. 12. Julia Margaret
Cameron, "William Michael
Rossetti," 24.5 cm. × 19.6 cm.,
1865; courtesy of the J. Paul
Getty Museum, Malibu,
California.

made 'out of focus' as the technical phrase is, and although sadly unconventional in the eyes of photographers, give us hope that something higher than mere mechanical success is attainable by the camera."[19] The *British Journal of Photography*, a weekly with a commercial audience, picked up the gauntlet by reprinting a passage from the *Athenaeum* and commenting,

> The art critic of the *Athenaeum* in a recent notice of certain photographic portraits by Mrs. Cameron indulges in some observations which, seeing the quarter whence they came, are highly complimentary to the lady; but we think they will be received with a smile of incredulity by photographers generally. If the critic in question knew anything practically of photography he would not surely insinuate that photographs ought to be "out of focus" to be effective. If the principles he seems to advocate be true, surely we have no need of first class opticians to construct our objectives.[20]

By exhibiting portraits of prominent men and securing a prominent dealer for her work, "the lady" had entered the commercial market. But for the *British Journal of Photography*, the consequences of placing an artist behind the camera had less to do with restoring social distinctions between a lady and her maid in their respective portraits than with the anticipated consequences of having the art critic of the *Athenaeum* declare that technique was not a criterion for selecting a portrait photographer. Nonetheless, although Cameron's photographic technique was marked by class differences— and expressions of resentment on those grounds continued in reviews published by commercial photographic journals into the 1870s—it had ceased by 1868 to be a controversy in the commercial photographic press.[21] For despite the celebrity of Cameron's work, and despite the favorable reviews published by her friends in such fashionable journals as the

Pall Mall Gazette, her technique was not adopted by other photographers, and once she ceased to be a rival, her work was of comparatively little interest to them. Cameron's work continued to be popular among a select audience into the 1870s, but the circumstances of that popularity were too particular to inspire many others to imitate her.

Cameron's fierce and continued promotion of her photographs, however, suggests that other motives may have encouraged her sustained involvement with photography, and with portraiture in particular. Writing to Herschel in 1870, she acknowledged that she could make money by photographing professionally but did not do so, "fearing to lose my liberty in the choice of my sitters."[22] Although the prominence of Cameron's numerous sitters could not be attributed to a specific place or event, such as the fancy-dress activities of Wynfield's "The Studio," the assembly of Cameron's subjects before her camera was clearly based upon different premises than those of a fashionable studio photographer in London. As Coventry Patmore explained in an 1866 review of Cameron's photography published in *Macmillan's Magazine,* "her position in literary and aristocratic society gives her the pick of the most beautiful and intellectual heads in the world. Other photographers have had to take such subjects as they could get."[23] The two individuals cited most frequently in the copyright registrations deposited for Cameron's photographs are Henry Taylor and Alfred Tennyson, a fact indicative of their close friendships with Cameron as well as of the commercial prospects for the sale of their images. The large majority of Cameron's portrait subjects can be associated either with Little Holland House or with Freshwater and the distinguished visitors Tennyson received there.

Cameron's production of photographic portraits of the

members of her circle might seem to have offered promise in redrawing the distinctions between public and private, but her observation of conventional standards in the representation of women is indicative of the extent to which her portrait production supported traditional cultural values. Conspicuous in their absence are Cameron portraits of the women who were part of this society. According to Hester Thackeray Fuller, Cameron is said to have maintained that "no woman should ever allow herself to be photographed between the ages of 18 and 90."[24] Although Cameron did allow herself to be photographed during those years of her life, the observation is more accurate than not when applied to her own work, in which representations of women conform to conventional requirements of youth and beauty.

Yet the instability of the category of artist in relation to "what is called photographic portraiture" was utilized by Cameron in less conventional ways. Not only did her portraits commemorate her acquaintance with eminent men, but her self-aggrandizement through photography also pertained to her famed dominance over her sitters, both male and female, in the course of the often arduous photographic exposures. This tyranny was wryly epitomized in Tennyson's advice to Henry Wadsworth Longfellow as the American poet prepared to sit for Cameron: "I will leave you now, Longfellow. You will have to do what she tells you. I will come back soon and see what is left of you."[25] Implicit in such accounts is Cameron's exertion of power over her sitters, a power that was consistent with her conception of the portraitist's significance as a witness to human nobility. Recounting the experience of photographing Carlyle, she explained: " When I have had such men before my camera my whole soul has endeavoured to do its duty towards them in recording faithfully the greatness of the inner as well as the features of the outer man. The photograph thus taken has been almost the embodiment of a prayer."[26]

Cameron's portrait photographs celebrated both her sitters and her own worship of her sitters, an experience which took on additional grandeur with her recognition that her photographs would be given to the nation and be viewed by posterity. An important precedent from the fine arts would have been the contemporary series of painted portraits, "The Hall of Fame," which her friend George Watts began in the 1850s. Watts, who aspired to create High Art, produced portraits for income; with "The Hall of Fame," however, he reversed the usual relationship of painter and patron by asking people whom he admired to pose. The series of inspirational sitters was intended to serve the didactic and moralizing purposes that Watts aspired unsuccessfully to fulfill with mural programs; in 1861 he announced his intention to bequeath the portraits to the nation for the newly opened National Portrait Gallery.[27] Watts may have used Cameron photographs as studies for some of his portraits, but the more important example was the role of portrait artist as witness.

Yet Watts's transformation of portrait painting into a modern form of history painting, although striking in its reversal of the academic hierarchy of artistic achievement, was predicated upon a more general perception of the painter's importance. The expectation of artistic activity in photography was much less stable; thus Cameron was able to assume the artist's role in order to achieve a number of personal ends. Cameron discussed the role of artist as witness in a letter to Herschel, in which she asks him to sit for his portrait: "I often think I could then do a head that would be Valuable to all ages & I long to take your photograph with a longing *unspeakable*."[28] Cameron's entreaty embodies the interplay of personal desire, a sense of national duty, and pride of artistic accomplishment that operated in her photographic portrait of Herschel and, to different degrees, in her other portraits of Victorian men of mark.

Cameron's ennobling ambitions for photographic portraiture were fueled by many issues. Her response to the proliferation of photographic portraits addressed concerns with public image, but her terms were inapplicable to the changes in expectations of photographic portraiture that derived from their consumption by a mass market. Paradoxically, it was within the context of her particular audience that Cameron was able to exercise the power and influence that her "ennoblement" of portraiture did not achieve in the public sphere.

Notes

I wish to thank Debra Mancoff, Beloit College, for suggesting how Cameron's work addressed issues of decorum in Victorian representation.

1. "Mrs. Cameron's Photographs," *Reader,* 18 Mar. 1865, 186–87.

2. The standard biographical source on Cameron is Helmut Gernsheim, *Julia Margaret Cameron: Her Life and Photographic Work* (Millerton, N.Y.: Aperture, 1975); a more recent study is Mike Weaver, *The Whisper of the Muse: The Overstone Album and Other Photographs by Julia Margaret Cameron* (Malibu: J. Paul Getty Museum, 1986).

3. Julia Margaret Cameron to William Michael Rossetti, 23 Jan. 1866, collection of the Harry Ransom Humanities Research Center, University of Texas at Austin, reprinted in Gernsheim, *Cameron,* 35. Interestingly, Cameron did not give this credit to Wynfield in her account of her photography, "Annals of My Glass

House," written in 1874 and reprinted in Gernsheim, *Cameron,* 180–83.

4. See A. K. Garner, "David Wilkie Wynfield: Painter and Photographer," *Apollo* 97 (February 1973): 158–59; and Mark Haworth-Booth, ed., *The Golden Age of British Photography* (Millerton, N.Y.: Aperture, 1984), 120. Wynfield registered subjects from "The Studio" for copyright on 8 Dec. 1863 (Copyright Registrations, Public Record Office, Kew, England).

5. "Fine Arts," *Illustrated London News* 44 (19 Mar. 1864): 175; "Mr. Wynfield's Photographs," *Reader,* 30 Jan. 1864, 144–45.

6. "Mr. Wynfield's Photographs," 144–45.

7. Helmut Gernsheim, *The Rise of Photography: 1850–1880, The Age of Collodion* (London: Thames and Hudson, 1988), 193–94. Gernsheim reports that the retail price for a *carte* of a famous person in the early 1860s was one shilling, or one shilling, sixpence, depending upon the popularity of the sitter.

8. See Elizabeth Anne McCauley, *A. A. E. Disdéri and the "Carte de Visite" Photograph* (New Haven: Yale University Press, 1985) for an extensive account of the development of the *carte de visite* and its place within contemporary Parisian culture; also see William C. Darrah, *"Carte de Visite" in Nineteenth-Century Photography* (Gettysburg, Pa.: William C. Darrah, 1981).

9. A[ndrew] Wynter, *"Cartes de Visite," Once a Week* 6 (25 Jan. 1862): 134–37; see also "The *Carte de Visite," All the Year Round* 7 (26 Apr. 1862): 165–66, and "Photographic Portraiture," *Once a Week* 8 (25 Jan. 1863): 148–50. A useful source for these and other discussions of photography in contemporary literature is Helmut Gernsheim, *Incunabula of British Photographic Literature* (London and Berkeley: Aperture, 1984).

10. *"Cartes de Visite," Art-Journal,* October 1861, 306–7.

11. Wynter, *"Cartes de Visite,"* 135.

12. Julia Margaret Cameron to Sir John Herschel, 31 Dec. 1864, reprinted in Colin Ford, *The Cameron Collection: An Album of Photographs by Julia Margaret Cameron Presented to Sir John Her-*

schel (London and New York: Van Nostrand Reinhold, 1975), 140–41.

13. Quoted in Mike Weaver, *Julia Margaret Cameron, 1815–1879* (Boston: New York Graphic Society, 1984), 141.

14. Cameron, "Annals of My Glass House," reprinted in Gernsheim, *Cameron*, 180–83.

15. "Fine Art Gossip," *Athenaeum*, 16 July 1864, 88; "Mrs. Cameron's Photographs," *The Queen, the Lady's Newspaper* 43 (January 1868): 88.

16. For an analysis of Cameron's photographic career, see Joanne Lukitsh, " 'To Secure for Photography the Character and Uses of High Art': The Photography of Julia Margaret Cameron, 1864–1869" (Ph.D. diss., University of Chicago, 1987).

17. For reviews of Cameron's debut at the tenth Annual Exhibition of the Photographic Society of London, see "Photographic Exhibition," *Photographic Journal* 11 (15 Aug. 1864): 86–88; "The Photographic Society," *Athenaeum*, 4 June 1864, 88; and "Exhibition of the London Photographic Society," *British Journal of Photography* 11 (22 July 1864): 160–61. The publication of Cameron's photographs by Colnaghi and Company was noted in "Fine Art Gossip," *Athenaeum*, 16 July 1864, 88; the portraits were reviewed in "Fine Art Gossip," *Athenaeum*, 22 June 1867, 827, the contents being described as portraits of Alfred Tennyson, Thomas Carlyle, Val Prinsep (a painter who was Cameron's nephew), and John Herschel.

English amateur photography in the 1850s and early 1860s did not typically include portraiture, which was associated with commercial photography through the daguerreotype and later the wet collodion process. See Grace Seiberling, *Amateurs, Photography, and the Mid-Victorian Imagination* (Chicago: University of Chicago Press, 1985), 69. Lewis Carroll, who sold his portrait photographs, was a notable exception; see Helmut Gernsheim, *Lewis Carroll, Photographer*, rev. ed. (New York: Dover, 1979).

18. For a list of the sitters identified from copyright registrations of Cameron's photographs and other sources, see Lukitsh,

appendix E; Gernsheim also provides a useful list of sitters in *Cameron*, 173.

19. "Fine Art Gossip," *Athenaeum*, 16 July 1864, 88.

20. "Out of Focus," *British Journal of Photography* 11 (22 July 1864): 261.

21. See the discussion in Lukitsh.

22. Cameron to Herschel, 6 Feb. 1870, Herschel Papers, quoted by kind permission of the Royal Society, London.

23. [Coventry Patmore], "Mrs. Cameron's Photographs," *Macmillan's Magazine* 13 (January 1866): 230–31.

24. Hester Thackeray Fuller, *Three Freshwater Friends: Tennyson, Watts, and Mrs. Cameron* (Newport, England: Country Press, 1933), 36.

25. Alfred Tennyson, quoted in Gernsheim, *Cameron*, 35.

26. Cameron, "Annals of My Glass House," in Gernsheim, *Cameron*, 182.

27. See the exhibition catalogue, *G. F. Watts: The Hall of Fame, Portraits of His Famous Contemporaries* (London: National Portrait Gallery, 1975); for comparisons of Watts's portraits with Cameron photographs, see Lukitsh, 121–24.

28. Cameron to Herschel, 23 Oct. [1866?], Herschel Papers, quoted by kind permission of the Royal Society, London.

PART FOUR

The Wages of Sin

9 / The (Other) Great Evil: Gambling, Scandal, and the National Anti-Gambling League

David C. Itzkowitz

At the Mitcham Coroner's Court Mr. Percy Morrison held an inquiry into the circumstances attending the death of Richard Smith, aged 36 years, a commercial traveller engaged in the corn trade, lately residing at 1, Manor-gardens, Holloway, who was found dead with a revolver by his side, near the highway, at Fig's Marsh, Mitcham. Mrs. Lucy Smith, the widow, and Mr. John Wonfor, of 24 Yonge-park, Tufnell Park, N., an intimate friend of deceased, both agreed that he had a mania for *betting*. Mr. Wonfor received the following letter from the deceased: "Balham. Dear Wonfor,—I am enclosing you £7 in postal orders, which please use your discretion with. You are my only friend, and I am sure you will look after the affairs of my dear wife, as through my known mania I leave the world to-night. This with exception [*sic*], is my winnings of Saturday last, after your persuasion to abandon my failings and your always good advice. I must leave God to judge me. Trusting you will use your ever willing efforts to assure the world that my sorrowful dear wife never participated in my nefarious ways. Good-bye, Jack.—Yours sorrowfully,—DICK."—In reply to questions put by the Coroner, the witness said the "known mania" referred to in the letter was the deceased's habit of *betting,* from which he often tried to dissuade him.—Police Constable George Vine, 616W, who searched the clothing at the mortuary, discovered in an envelope bearing the words "I am R. Smith, 1 Manor-gardens, Holloway," the following letter, written with copying-ink pencil: "1, Manor-gardens.—When found, I am Richard Smith, of Holloway. This rash deed is through following the ruling passion, always with non-success until Burnaby, when my turning point came, and I did not take sufficient advantage, which has turned my brain, of which I possessed but little. I want the world to know that my sorrowing wife has never participated in this my failing, and her always good, sound, loving, and Christian advice I never heeded. May God protect her and my dear children, and may the sins of the father be never visited on them. Good-bye, good wife, good-bye. God will protect you. Your ever erring husband since I left God's services.—R. SMITH."—The Coroner asked what was meant by "Burnaby," and the witness said it was the winner of the Cesarewitch a fortnight before.—Dr. Henry Love, of Mitcham, said the deceased died from the discharge of two bullets into his brain. Witness did not think death had been instantaneous.—The jury returned a verdict "That the deceased committed suicide whilst in a state of temporary insanity."

THIS little Victorian melodrama[1] comes not from the pen of Dion Boucicault but from the "recent victims" column, a regular feature of the *Bulletin,* the organ of the National Anti-Gambling League, and illustrates one way that scandal and gambling intersected during the Victorian period.

Stories like Richard Smith's were seized upon by members of the league to point out what they saw as the inevitable end of gambling: ruin, scandal, disgrace, and death. It was not only lower-middle-class commercial travelers like Richard

Smith, however, who were seen to be in great danger. "Amongst the upper classes," warned the *Bulletin*, " 'Bridge' seems to vie with the Stock Exchange." "Young girls in their teens are preparing for a future not 'serene' and 'bright,' but like that of the hags at Monte Carlo . . . or the wife of a leading statesman, who announced, unable apparently to endure the mourning for the Queen, a small dinner, to be followed by 'Bridge,' to break the monotony."[2] For those who succumbed to the lure of bridge, a fate worse than the death of Richard Smith might await. "Not a few cases are on record, where young girls have been induced to play . . . [and] it is not without knowledge that even virtue itself has been sacrificed to satisfy the suggestion of male friends who have gallantly paid such debts on their behalf."[3]

As this last example shows, women were thought to be in special danger of falling prey to the risks of gambling, and working-class women were in even greater peril than the upper-class women who were victimized at bridge. The *Bulletin* had a special feature, "Women and Children," that detailed sad cases involving the most defenseless victims. Like the stories of Richard Smith and the unnamed victim of the West End bridge fiends, these were, of course, cautionary tales, warning society of the undoubted outcome to be expected from betting, the great evil that, according to the members of the league, ranked second only to intemperance in "filling our prisons, our poorhouses, and our lunatic asylums."[4]

Today we may wonder what all the fuss was about. Readers of George Moore's novel *Esther Waters* and those familiar with paintings such as William Powell Frith's *Derby Day* or Alfred Elmore's *On the Brink* are aware that betting was hardly absent from the Victorian world, but few of us can have suspected that Victorian England was in such danger of losing its moral character at the turn of a card or the running of a horse. Despite their publicly frowning on gambling, few Victorians suspected this danger either. That may be the main reason why the Anti-Gambling League had comparatively little impact on Victorian and Edwardian society. Only once were the scandalous stories spread by the league sufficient to influence any definitive action. In that case, the passage of the Street Betting Act of 1906, they succeeded because they reinforced current attitudes about the poor and the weak.

Antigambling activists had existed in England since at least the sixteenth century, but the National Anti-Gambling League was the first antigambling organization in the country. Founded in 1890, the league was a latecomer to the ranks of Victorian moral reform. Its announced object was "to offer a strenuous and uncompromising opposition to every form of Betting and Gambling, and to diffuse among young men and others useful information on the subject." In its early years, members of the league were expected to pay an annual subscription of at least one shilling, sign a declaration promising to abstain from all kinds of betting and gambling, and "do their utmost to develop a more healthy public opinion."[5] Such a vow was, of course, reminiscent of the teetotal pledge signed by many temperance activists; the similarity is hardly accidental. The league always liked to compare its work with that of the temperance movement and tried to link gambling with intemperance as the two great evils threatening the country. To compare the two movements, however, seems almost laughable. By any measure, the Anti-Gambling League was a pygmy next to the temperance movement. The league was able to command only a tiny fraction of the financial resources that were available to the temperance reformers.[6] More importantly, although the league boasted an impressive list of officers and committee members (including peers, bishops, deans, and other clergymen), the participation of most of them did not go beyond lending their names; the vast bulk of the league's work was done by a tiny handful of men, especially its indefatigable honorary secretary John Hawke.[7] Still, the existence of the league, and for that matter, its relative lack of success, is illuminating.

The league's opposition to gambling was complete. Although the betting habits of public figures like the Prince of Wales and Lord Rosebery were regularly deplored by the league and its spokesmen, no bet was too small to come within its view. The magistrate who fined three boys for playing cards for buttons was praised by the editor of the *Bulletin,* who declared, "buttons are of value, and that makes it gambling."[8] Even church raffles were decried, for they seemed "to give a sanction and therefore practically [did] give a sanction, to forms of gambling which are unquestionably wrong."[9]

An examination of the arguments used by the members of the league and those who associated themselves with its work reveals that the opposition to gambling comprehended a wide variety of stated motives, ranging from fear of the effects of betting on public order and morality to the belief that betting created a compulsion that would inevitably lead to ruin and poverty.[10] Central to the opposition, however, was the clear belief that gambling itself was essentially either depraved or sinful because it appealed to the worst instincts of humankind. On the one hand, claimed J. A. Hobson, the bettor was reverting to "a form of unreason which carries no sound instinct of direction with it."[11] On the other hand, gambling appealed "entirely to the greedy and selfish side of our nature."[12] Winning was every bit as dangerous as losing; indeed, the desire to win held greater moral dangers than the risk of losing. "The desire to take unearned gains," wrote Hobson, was itself immoral, "for such gains of necessity imply an injury to some other known or unknown persons."[13]

Opposition on religious or ethical grounds may have been at the core of league members' feelings but the main emotional appeal that the league made was not to such abstract moral sentiments. Instead, its publications were filled with stories meant to show that gambling, no matter how harmless it looked, was inevitably the first step along the road to crime, misery, and scandal, as in the unfortunate case of Richard Smith. Further, although the league opposed all forms of gambling with equal moral fervor, it decided as early as 1896 that it could attract the most attention by concentrating on what it called the "vile system of professional betting," which swept in "every racing season, hundreds of thousands of pounds from the incomes of the working population, contaminating youth, destroying true manhood, dishonouring age, and, by this pernicious commerce, enriching [those who were in charge of the 'vile system'] to such an extent" that they could bribe and intimidate their opponents in order to stay in business.[14]

By the "betting system," the league was referring to the commercialized mass betting industry, centered on horse racing, that made its first appearance during the Victorian period and flourished in England from the 1850s on. Two things were notable about this new industry, which had no real forerunners in England. The first was the appearance of professional bookmakers who were willing to take bets for as little as sixpence or a shilling from all comers. The second was the fact that on-course betting was only a tiny fraction of the total. Most of those who bet did so away from the course and probably never witnessed a horse race in their lives.

The emergence of these new bookmakers created a whole new milieu for betting, turning it from the sport of a specialized racing world into a pastime that could be followed by anyone willing to risk a few pence. Men, women, and children could pore over the form of horses running in race-meetings all over the country and then, depending on their station in life, place either a legal credit bet with a "turf accountant" or "commission agent," or—the more common practice—an illegal ready-money bet with one of the army of street bookmakers who regularly stationed themselves on corners, in public houses, and at factory gates; they even called at kitchen doors.[15] Most observers agreed that the development of this new kind of wagering was responsible for a vast increase in the number of people who bet.[16]

On the face of it, then, the decision to concentrate on professional betting made good sense for the members of the league who, by the mid-nineties, realized that the majority of the population did not share their zeal. In 1896, both the antigambling pledge and the minimum subscription had to be dropped as conditions of membership. The new concentration on the "system" was thus another tactic for rejuvenating the sagging fortunes of their cause, enabling the league to focus on how gambling affected those they portrayed as the weakest members of society—the poor, women, and children.[17] J. M. Hogge, who succeeded John Hawke as secretary of the league, was particularly interested in detailing "the real inwardness of the betting habit when it attacks the home through the housewife." Precisely because they seemed most respectable, Hogge argued, many women were not only in danger themselves but were also dangerous to others. Quoting a letter from "a reliable correspondent," he informed his readers of the case of a "perfectly clean and tidy" widow whom a bookmaker inveigled into becoming his accomplice. "Just because in all other ways she was respectable," he stressed, "the other women were snared into thinking less of the sin."[18]

Ironically, although this new concentration offered the league its greatest opportunities and contributed to its greatest success, it also ultimately prevented the league from striking the knockout blow against gambling that its members had always anticipated. In order to understand this apparent paradox, it is necessary to look more closely both at the league's activities and at some of the most important characteristics of the betting world that they attacked.

The lurid stories that the league circulated were, of course, intended to present a picture of "the system" as an evil, calculated conspiracy to fleece the people of England by leading them on into an ever-increasing frenzy of irrational behavior until they had few options left besides prison or suicide. But this picture was far from the truth. There were certainly compulsive gamblers in Victorian England just as there are today. Nonetheless, the vast majority of those who followed the progress of their favorite horses in the sporting press, who discussed the chances of the latest favorite or long shot at the public house or on the doorstep, and who risked their spare sixpence or shilling on the latest hope were engaging in neither irrational nor frenzied behavior. Most of those who bet on horses believed, with some justification, that they were not simply trusting to chance. Instead, they looked for ways to calculate their best odds of winning.[19] Further, the fact that most Victorian wagerers placed their bets away from the race-course had the unplanned effect of minimizing the element of uncontrolled excitement that could be aroused by the atmosphere of the course and the sight of horses thundering toward the finish.

The extent to which Victorian bettors strove to shift the odds in their favor may be seen in the development of several new institutions that sprang up to meet their needs. Aside from the bookmakers the most important was the new sporting press that arose around 1860. By the 1880s, sporting papers were being published daily in order to bring the latest "racing intelligence" to their readers. The field of sporting journalism soon became highly competitive.

Readers turned to the sporting press not only for the names of the horses entered in each race and their past performances but also for other information that they hoped would give them an edge over their bookmaker and fellow bettors. By the mid-nineteenth century, when most of those who bet did so away from the racecourse, it was no longer possible to pick up information on the basis of course gossip or direct observation. To meet the needs of this increasingly numerous kind of bettor, the racing tipster evolved, a "profession" that shaded imperceptibly into the other new calling, that of racing journalist. Each of the sporting papers, and many nonsporting papers as well, had one or more racing correspondents who regularly reviewed the major upcoming races and made predictions. But they were not the only people with "inside information" to sell. The pages of the sporting press were filled with advertisements from those who purported to have reliable intelligence for sale. Many tipsters were clearly dishonest, sending different predictions to different customers so that they could always claim to have picked the winner. Some were shameless in their self-promotion, such as the man who advertised his "extraordinary and unparalleled success" in advising his customers to bet on a "moral certainty" that was "only beaten by a neck."[20] Still others, however, did their best to provide their readers and customers with what they desperately felt they needed, that extra bit of information that would make the difference between winning and losing.

The new sporting press and the tipsters were an indication of the way in which bettors strove to shift the odds in their favor as much as possible. By reading the racing press, studying the predictions of the tipsters, discussing the horses in the public house or the workplace, and attempting to calculate rationally the outcome of the next race, the Victorian bettor completely denied Hobson's claim that wagerers regressed to "a form of unreason." In placing bets with the bookmaker, working-class or middle-class bettors were not abandoning themselves to chance—or at least that was the feeling of those who studied the pages of the sporting press.[21]

The failure of the league to convert public opinion to its cause, however, resulted not only from the fact that its description of the most popular form of gambling was unrealistic. Its tactics and strategy also severely limited the possibility of success. The league undoubtedly hoped that moral suasion would have a significant effect. But although it sponsored contests to produce antigambling hymns and printed antigambling leaflets and tracts,[22] the league soon realized that this approach was not reforming a public that merely viewed league members as uninformed extremists.[23] Therefore, the league had to turn to the courts to enforce existing laws against gambling, and to Parliament to pass new laws that would hit directly at the heart of the "system."

Although this strategy seemed more promising than a direct appeal to the public for moral regeneration and reform, there were still problems. Numerous laws dealing with gambling were already on the books, but enforcing them was a low priority for the police and magistrates, who believed that offenses against the gaming acts were not terribly serious unless they also menaced public order in other ways. For the members of the league, however, the fact of gambling was itself sufficient to threaten it. They could hope to embarrass and prod the authorities by undertaking private prosecutions; John Hawke, the league's secretary, did devote much of his energy to this. On one occasion he was, for a brief time, successful.

Although racing men had always assumed that the Betting-House Act of 1853,[24] which outlawed the keeping of a house or other place for the purpose of betting on horse races, did not apply to the betting enclosures at racecourses, antigambling activists claimed that it did. On-course betting was so inseparably a part of horse racing that few could imagine the continuation of the sport without it. Thus in the 1890s the National Anti-Gambling League brought several legal actions to force an end to betting at the racecourse as a way of destroying all horse racing.[25]

In 1897 a court held in the case of *Hawke v. Dunn*, a league-sponsored prosecution, that the betting enclosures were in fact "places" within the meaning of the act of 1853.[26] This ruling was a severe blow to racing, especially because no appeal was possible from the judgment of the criminal court in cases of this type. Within a month of the ruling in *Hawke v. Dunn*, however, a shareholder in the Kempton Park Racecourse Company, acting in collusion with the company and racing interests generally, sued the company over the presence of bookmakers on the course. The suit was, obviously, a legal maneuver to reopen the issue that seemed closed by *Hawke v. Dunn*, and it was successful. The Court of Appeals ruled that the betting ring at Kempton Park Racecourse, and by extension, at other racecourses as well, was not a "place" within the meaning of the act. The lord chancellor ruled further that because betting in the enclosure was carried on by bookmakers rather than by the course owners, it did not fall within the language of the act.[27] On-course betting was saved—to the fury of the league.[28]

The Kempton Park decision was, as everyone knew, based on a legal fiction, that the betting rings were not "places" within the meaning of the act. The fiction was no doubt convenient for the government, which was, in the words of legal writer Alfred Fellows, "neither obliged to pass a law to legalize ready money course betting in the face of the scandalized opposition of their serious-minded supporters, or to tolerate wholesale illegality, or to attempt to enforce a legal ruling against outraged racegoers."[29] The decision was going to force the courts to confront a series of future cases that addressed the question of precisely what apparatus a bookmaker had to have with him in order to transform the spot on which he stood in the betting ring into a "place."[30] That the courts were willing to make these distinctions is a clear indication of the way that the Victorian establishment, although accepting the notion that gambling was not a good thing, was nevertheless ready to distinguish among the various *kinds* of gambling, and to reject the absolute position of the Anti-Gambling League that betting, whatever the circumstances, was a moral evil to be stamped out.

Following its defeat in the Kempton Park case, the league changed its strategy. Although it continued to press for prosecutions in a number of cases, it realized that this approach was too piecemeal to have any real effect. The "system" had prevailed in the law court, and now it had to be defeated in Parliament. In November 1898, therefore, the league announced that it would push for legislation that would attack betting on many different fronts. It declared its support for a bill that would prevent newspapers from publishing the odds on horse races; give the authorities the right to imprison street bookmakers; curb newspaper competitions (which were little more than disguised lotteries); and, perhaps most controversially, allow the Post Office to examine and destroy letters suspected of being connected with gambling.[31]

This attack would also prove largely unsuccessful. Victorian society was clearly unwilling to accept the full contentions of the league as to the evils of gambling, and the remedies that the league offered were too extreme. The proposals to bar the publication of odds in newspapers and to allow the Post Office to open mail in search of betting material were simply unacceptable. The first could be seen as an attack on the freedom of the press, the second as conferring an unwarranted power on the Post Office to pry into the private communications of millions of ordinary people.[32] In the face of a national emergency, the government would have been willing to go this far. To the members of the league, of course, there *was* such an emergency, but not many Victorians were prepared to agree with them.

Only one part of the league's proposed legislative program had any real chance of success: strengthening already existing laws to limit betting on racing, and particularly to attack the large army of illegal street bookmakers with whom most working-class and poor bettors placed their wagers. This was a program that could appeal even to those who supported racing and betting as a sport for the wealthy and the middle class, because they accepted the vision of the victimized poor that the league and other social reformers presented. For example, Horace Smith, a London magistrate who assured a Select Committee of the House of Lords in 1902 that he did not think betting in itself either evil or immoral, went on to tell them that he supported national legislation to force the bookies off the streets. When pressed, he admitted that such a law would allow the wealthy to bet but would make it impossible for a poor man to do so. "I should be very glad if [the poor man] could not [bet]; that is just what I think is the mischief; I do not want him to have a shilling on at all."[33]

The support for this more moderate position was institutionalized in the Street Betting Act of 1906, which made a criminal offense of frequenting the streets or other public places for the purposes of betting or bookmaking.[34] This act represents the only victory for the National Anti-Gambling League in the years before the First World War and the only time that the scandals unearthed by the league's tireless propagandists moved influential opinion. But the Street Betting Act, which was the final step in a series of Victorian and Edwardian statutes that made it increasingly hard for the poor to bet while permitting the wealthy and the middle class to continue, also contained a clause specifying that the act did not apply to the racecourse on racing days.[35] No more cogent evidence for the limited nature of the support enjoyed by the league can be found. Although the act made prosecution of illegal bookmakers easier—at least theoretically—it also incorporated the position enunciated by the court in the Kempton Park case. Betting on horse racing was not to be made illegal; only *some* betting by *some* bettors in *some* circumstances was illegal. Even bookmakers, eager both to eliminate competition and to raise the status of their own trade, could support legislation of this kind.[36]

Ironically, in concentrating their attention on racing, the aspect of betting that affected the largest number of people in England, the league members and their fellow activists were backing the wrong horse. A more compelling alternative was available to them, and this brings us to perhaps the best-known gambling scandal of the nineteenth century, the Tranby Croft Baccarat Case of 1890–91. This case concerned allegations that Lieutenant Colonel Sir William Gordon-Cumming had cheated at baccarat while a guest at Tranby Croft, the home of the shipowner Arthur Wilson. On being accused by other guests at the party, Gordon-Cumming, in order to keep things quiet, agreed never to play cards again. When news of the accusation leaked out anyway, questions were raised as to whether Gordon-Cumming should be allowed to resign quietly from the army, whether there should be an army inquiry into his ungentlemanly conduct, or whether there should be a private inquiry at the Guards Club. Before any of these matters could be resolved, however, Gordon-Cumming sued his original accusers for slander. The trial that followed was a *cause célèbre*. The Prince of Wales, who had been one of the guests at the party, and who, it was well-known, liked to play baccarat, was called as a witness; his presence alone insured that the trial would be covered at great length in the press. In the end, the verdict was in favor of the defendants; Gordon-Cumming was ruined socially.[37]

It might be useful to ask just where in this rather unedifying story the scandal really lay. There were those, like Gordon-Cumming's accusers, who saw the greatest scandal in his ungentlemanly behavior. There were others who may have thought that the attempt to hush up Gordon-Cumming's behavior was itself scandalous. But to those who believed as the members of the league did, both of these issues were secondary; the greatest scandal was that baccarat was being played at all, especially in the company of someone like the Prince of Wales, who should have been expected to set a better example for society. The prince, whose popularity plummeted as a result of his involvement in the case, was induced to pen a letter to the archbishop of Canterbury in which he expressed his own views on gambling. "I have a horror of gambling," he wrote,

> and should always do my utmost to discourage others who have an inclination for it, as I consider that gambling, like intemperance, is one of the greatest curses that a country can be afflicted with.
>
> Horse-racing may produce gambling, or it may not; but I have always looked upon it as a manly sport which is popular with Englishmen of all classes, and there is no reason why it should be looked upon as a gambling transaction. Alas! Those who gamble will gamble on anything.[38]

Those who are familiar with the prince's love of games of chance may find this statement incredible. But he was presenting a view of gambling that many of his contemporaries shared: he was drawing a distinction between *betting,* which he enjoyed, and *gambling,* which he deplored. Gambling was defined as immoderate or compulsive betting, and especially as betting amounts of money that the bettor could not easily afford to lose. What the prince neglected to mention, of course, was that the game being played at Tranby Croft was baccarat, and baccarat is as unlike horse racing as it can be; it is a game that depends almost entirely on luck and one played in an atmosphere of escalating excitement.

In the last decade of the nineteenth century, baccarat became the rage, both among the fast well-to-do crowd that surrounded the prince and more generally among a small but noticeable middle-class London bohemia. In the year before the events at Tranby Croft, the English public was titillated by the reports of police raids on gaming houses and clubs in London and elsewhere. Players at the different clubs were drawn from many social classes, ranging from the aristocratic patrons of the Field Club in Park Place, St. James's, through the more middle-class bohemians and theatrical people at the Adelphi Club in Maiden Lane, to the lower-middle-class and working-class patrons of the Cranbourne Club in Leicester Square.[39] Ironically, it was they who most clearly exhibited the kind of "irrational" behavior that the league inveighed against through its lurid stories. Nonetheless, it would be difficult to argue that had the league devoted the bulk of its attention to suppressing this kind of gambling it would have enjoyed greater success. For one thing, it would have been attacking a kind of gambling that affected only a tiny number of people compared with those who bet regularly on horse races. For another, it would have run afoul of entrenched social privilege, as the response to *Hawke v. Dunn* suggested. Still, it is interesting to speculate about the kind of reaction the league might have received. The prince's unpopularity as a result of his gambling suggests that they might have struck a responsive chord, especially because it could be argued that the spectacle of wealthy gentlemen cheating each other at cards was inherently more scandalous and vicariously entertaining than the relatively duller picture associated with off-course race betting.

This speculation, then, leads to the final conclusions that can be drawn from the relatively unsuccessful crusade of the National Anti-Gambling League. Scandal can only exist when a particular kind of behavior is perceived as scandalous. In the end, the league was unsuccessful because by choosing to make scandal the center of its appeal, it was necessary for it to identify scandals that contemporaries were willing to accept as scandalous. It was possible to find such scandals, but the response to Tranby Croft as well as the relative failure of the league—compared to its one success—suggests that for gambling to be deemed scandalous it had to be accompanied by some other form of inappropriate behavior, such as cheating, as in the case of Tranby Croft, or betting by inappropriate people, as in the case of the street bookmakers. Betting by itself was at least tacitly accepted, in part because the most popular form of betting reinforced other Victorian ideals.

Only once was the league able to hit on the proper combination. The league's view of the poor as people who needed special protection from the designs of evil men and from their own weakness was one that could be shared by a substantial portion of the middle and upper classes. For the rest, if scandal is in the eye of the beholder, the members of the league and their contemporaries saw things with different eyes.

Notes

Research on this paper was made possible by support from the National Endowment for the Humanities. I would like to thank Vicki Itzkowitz for her careful reading of the manuscript and Sheldon Rothblatt, in whose NEH-sponsored summer seminar I first began to think about the history of gambling.

1. *Bulletin, The Half-yearly Record of the National Anti-Gambling League,* November 1893, 74.
2. *Bulletin,* May 1901, 218.
3. J. M. Hogge, *The Facts of Gambling* (London: Andrew Melrose, 1907), 31.
4. *Bulletin,* November 1893, 61.
5. Ibid., 67.
6. Between 1894 and 1904, for example, the league's annual income from donations and subscriptions, as reported yearly in

the *Bulletin*, fluctuated between £283 and £788. Although this income included several large donations, most contributions were very small, often under £1, and as little as one or two shillings. By contrast, the annual income of the United Kingdom Alliance between 1890 and 1900 was in the £15,000 to £20,000 range. See Brian Harrison, *Drink and the Victorians* (Pittsburgh: University of Pittsburgh Press, 1971), 230.

7. In 1896, for example, the league president, twenty of the twenty-four vice-presidents, and five of the six committeemen did not even subscribe openly to the league's funds (*Bulletin*, May 1896, 161, 174–75).

8. *Bulletin*, November 1893, 70.

9. *Bulletin*, May 1896, 166–67.

10. In 1905, for example, J. A. Hobson and Ramsay MacDonald joined with John Hawke and J. M. Hogge, the then and future secretaries of the league, to contribute to a collection of antigambling articles edited by B. Seebohm Rowntree and published by him under the title *Betting and Gambling: A National Evil*. The essays all opposed gambling but did so from a variety of perspectives. Included were an article on the ethics of gambling by Hobson, one on gambling and citizenship by MacDonald, and one by "A Bookmaker," who purported to have no moral or ethical objections to gambling at all but revealed the great disadvantage that the wagering public was under when betting with representatives of "the system."

11. J. A. Hobson, "The Ethics of Gambling," in *Betting and Gambling: A National Evil*, ed. B. Seebohm Rowntree (London: Macmillan, 1905), 7.

12. From a sermon by the Reverend Hugh Legge, as reported in the *Bulletin*, May 1898, 96.

13. Hobson, "Ethics of Gambling," 13.

14. *Bulletin*, May 1896, 149.

15. For more information on the growth of racing, see Wray Vamplew, *The Turf: A Social and Economic History of Horse Racing* (London: Allen Lane, 1976). For the development of bookmakers and off-course betting, see my "Victorian Bookmakers and

Their Customers," *Victorian Studies* 32 (Fall 1988): 7–30. Working-class betting during the late-Victorian and Edwardian periods is discussed by Ross McKibbin in "Working-Class Gambling in Britain, 1880–1939," *Past and Present* No. 82 (February 1979), 147–78.

16. McKibbin, 148–49.

17. *Bulletin,* May 1896, 161.

18. J. M. Hogge, "Gambling among Women," in Rowntree, *Betting and Gambling,* 75, 78–79. Hogge also devoted a chapter in *The Facts of Gambling* to "Betting Among Women."

19. In his book on the theory of games, Roger Caillois suggests that forms of gambling, like other games, can be analyzed according to the extent to which they arouse a number of different emotional responses in the participants. For gambling, one of the most important distinctions made by Caillois is between what he calls *aleatory* gambling, gambling in which the element of pure chance is stressed, and *agonistic* gambling, forms of gambling in which the participants maintain a certain amount of control, or at least the illusion of control, over the outcome on which they are betting. Most forms of casino gambling, like roulette and baccarat, are aleatory games. Betting on horse racing, on the other hand, is agonistic. See Caillois, *Man, Play, and Games* (Glencoe, Ill.: Free Press of Glencoe, 1961), 12. For further discussion, see McKibbin, 166–69, and Itzkowitz.

20. *Sporting Life,* 12 Mar. 1870.

21. For further discussion of this point, see McKibbin, 162–63, and Itzkowitz.

22. For some sample hymns see the *Bulletin,* November 1905, 121–24. The tracts included such titles as "A Blot on the Queen's Reign," "Some Plain Words on Gambling," "A Protest against Betting and Gambling," "What Is Gambling?" "Join the Crusade!" and "Don't Bet!"

23. League publications were intended to be bought in bulk by activists, who would then distribute them to the poor. In the fiscal year 1894–95, the league received twenty-eight pounds from the sale of publications, but in other years the figure was much lower.

By 1899, it was no longer including an entry for the sale of publications in the annual financial statements that were published in the May issue of the *Bulletin*. For the incredulous reaction of a later observer, see McKibbin, 158 n. 57.

24. 16 and 17 Vict. c.119.

25. See the *Bulletin*, November 1894, 93, 96–97; May 1895, 109; *Sporting Life*, 1 Aug. 1895; Ward Coldridge and Cyril V. Hawkford, *The Law of Gaming*, 2d ed. (London: Stevens and Son, 1913), 256–57.

26. For an account of the case, see the *Bulletin*, May 1897, and Alfred Fellows, *The Law As to Gambling, Betting, and Lotteries* (London: Solicitors' Law Stationery Society, 1935), 93.

27. *Powell v. Kempton Park Racecourse Co.*, Court of Appeal (1897) 2 QB 242; 66 L. J. Q. B. 601; S.C. House of Lords (1899) A. C. 143; 68 L. J. Q. B. 392. For a full account of the case, see Coldridge, 293–302.

28. See the *Bulletin*, May 1898.

29. Fellows, 95.

30. See, for example, the case of *Brown v. Patch*, in Coldridge, 305–6.

31. *Bulletin*, November 1898, 101.

32. Testifying before a Select Committee of the House of Lords in 1902, Sir Robert Hunter, solicitor to the Post Office, made it quite clear that the Post Office, at least, was very uncomfortable with the suggestion that employees might be allowed to open such mail. See "Report of the Select Committee of the House of Lords on Betting," 140, in *Parliamentary Papers*, 1902 (114), vol. 11.

33. Testimony of Horace Smith in "Report of the Select Committee of the House of Lords on Betting," 1902, 29.

34. 6 Edward VII, c. 43.

35. Coldridge, 359.

36. See the testimony of Frederick William Spruce and James Sutters in "Report of the Select Committee of the House of Lords on Betting," 1902, 40, 56.

37. The Tranby Croft case is discussed in Philip Magnus, *King Edward VII* (Harmondsworth: Penguin Books, 1967), 279–89.

For a fuller account of the case, see Sir Michael Havers, Edward Grayson, and Peter Shankland, *The Royal Baccarat Scandal* (London: William Kimber, 1977).

38. Quoted in Magnus, 289.

39. The raids were heavily reported in the press. See, for example, the *Standard*, 11, 14, 17 May, and 15 June 1889; *Pall Mall Gazette*, 13 May 1889; *Daily Telegraph*, 14 May 1889; *Penny Illustrated Paper*, 18, 25 May 1889. There are a large number of newspaper cuttings dealing with the raids in the Jessel Collection in the Bodleian Library, Oxford. Although gaming houses had never disappeared from London during the nineteenth century, they had become relatively uncommon by midcentury. In 1870, the antiquarian writer Andrew Steinmetz judged that his readers would find it "incredible" to learn that "within the memory of many a living man," gambling houses flourished in London. See Steinmetz, *The Gaming Table*, 2 vols. (London: Tinsley Brothers, 1870), 1: vii.

10 / "Sin of the Age": Infanticide and Illegitimacy in Victorian London

Ann R. Higginbotham

In 1844, Thomas Wakley, member of Parliament, London surgeon, and coroner, declared that "child murder was going on to a frightful, to an enormous, a perfectly incredible extent."[1] He was just one of many Victorians who pointed to infanticide as a growing problem. Reformers warned that parents, midwives, and childminders destroyed infants with impunity; London newspapers reported on the tiny corpses found in back passageways of the metropolis.

Much of this concern centered on the fate of illegitimate children because as W. T. Charley, parliamentary spokesman of the Infant Life Protection Society, warned, the "first born of unmarried parents are the class of infants most exposed to violent deaths."[2] The dangers facing illegitimate infants were thought to be particularly acute in London, where the anonymity of a great city enabled unmarried women to hide the births and deaths of unwanted babies. Indeed, during much of the nineteenth century, London alone accounted for about one-half of all the homicides involving children that were noted in the Registrar General's reports for England and Wales. Edwin Lankester, coroner for Central Middlesex at midcentury, claimed that about twelve thousand London mothers had murdered their infants without detection.[3] In 1862, reports of 150 dead infants found in the city's streets during the preceding year led the *Times* to lament that "infancy in London has to creep into life in the midst of foes."[4]

Victorian alarm over infanticide has been discussed by many historians, who have focused both on the vulnerability of illegitimate infants and on society's efforts to limit infanticide and improve the treatment of children.[5] Relying mainly on official statistics, parliamentary reports, and the work of groups such as the National Society for the Prevention of Cruelty to Children, these scholars provide valuable insights into the growth of reform movements and changing attitudes toward the value of infant life. But they have not dealt specifically with the actual cases that sparked Victorian concern. In order to understand infanticide more fully, it is useful to examine the circumstances surrounding suspected child murders and how these relate to the picture of infanticide constructed by the Victorians.

Agitation over infanticide arose from a variety of sources, but the most vocal group was undoubtedly the medical profession. Concerned about high levels of infant mortality, coroners (such as Wakley and Lankester), individual medical men, the Harveian Society, and the *British Medical Journal* all warned of an epidemic of infanticide. They advocated various reform measures, including supervision of childminders, increased police vigilance, and changes in the law to improve the treatment of illegitimate children.[6] Beginning in the 1830s and 1840s, opponents of the New Poor Laws also argued that the changes in poor relief, particularly those relating to the affiliation of illegitimate children, would encourage child murder. They deplored the limitation of a woman's right to seek support from the father of her illegitimate infant; they attacked the new workhouses as "Bastilles" that drove women to murder their infants rather than "come on the parish."[7] In the last half of the century, charity workers blamed increased infanticide on the lack of services for unmarried mothers, justifying their own efforts in shelters and homes as a means to prevent infant deaths. One early charity, the Home of Hope, explicitly identified its mission as preventing "the dark sin of infanticide."[8]

All the campaigners against infanticide concerned themselves with the vulnerability of illegitimate children. In 1867 a special committee on infanticide established by the Harveian Society reported that "the life of the bastard is infinitely less protected than that of the legitimate."[9] This judgment seemed well founded. Medical men, particularly coroners, provided convincing evidence of widespread crime. They pointed to the bodies of infants found in the streets of London and to the large number of murder verdicts in inquests on infants. In the mid-1860s, more than 80 percent of all coroners' reports of murder in England and Wales involved infants, many of whom were assumed to be illegitimate.[10] Lankester charged that his metropolitan district produced one case of probable infanticide every day, and Wakley claimed that two hundred child murders in London escaped detection each year.[11] J. Brendon Curgenven, a physician and member of the Infant Life Protection Society, argued that even the alarming figures from coroners' inquests represented only a fraction of actual infant murders.[12] These perceptions of the acute danger facing illegitimate children were supported by the knowledge that illegitimate infants had a crude death rate at least twice that of legitimate children. In 1871, the Select Committee on the Protection of Infant Life speculated that as few as 10 percent of illegitimate babies survived to adulthood.[13] Such findings helped not only to expose the dangers facing infants but also to buttress a widely held view that infanticide was one of the strategies by which unmarried mothers rid themselves of the burden of unwanted babies.

The association between infanticide and illegitimacy was based not only on coroners' reports and judicial statistics but also on certain broad assumptions about unmarried mothers. The unmarried mother, it was recognized, faced enormous difficulties. The New Poor Law ended outrelief for unmarried women and curtailed the availability of assistance from the father of an illegitimate child. Women with illegitimate children were often servants, sweated workers, or factory hands, with few resources to support a family on their own. England lacked the system of foundling institutions that the Continent provided for unmarried mothers.[14] As a result, it was argued, "those who have erred are almost necessarily driven by the pressure of want to rid themselves of children they cannot feed."[15] But the unmarried mother's situation was made perilous by more than simple economics. She also faced the shame of her fall: "the infant at her breast was her stigma, her burden, her curse."[16] The unmarried mother, it was assumed, would seek above all to conceal her fall from virtue by destroying the evidence of her sin, the illegitimate infant. Given the difficulties and limited options facing her, infanticide seemed inevitable: "There are only two courses before the unfortunate mother, either to kill her child or support it by sin."[17]

Implicit in much of this rhetoric about infanticide was the idea that mother and infant alike were victims. The mother's deed, though deplored, was blamed not just on her poverty but also on the child's father who had betrayed her. This attitude was reflected in two novels that appeared at midcentury during the early stages of the campaign against infanticide: George Eliot's *Adam Bede* (1859) and Frances Trollope's *Jessie Phillips* (1843). Although *Adam Bede* was set at the close of the eighteenth century, Eliot might have taken the details of Hetty Sorrel's crime and even the testimony at her trial from contemporary newspaper accounts of child murder cases. Hetty, a childlike farm girl, gives birth and abandons her baby to die. She commits the crime while she is a despairing, penniless wanderer, having sought in vain to locate Arthur Donnithorne, the heedless young heir who has seduced her. Found guilty of murder, she is saved from the gallows by a last-minute reprieve secured by a penitent Arthur.

Mrs. Trollope intended her novel as an attack on the New Poor Laws and provided a much more sensational view of infanticide. Frederick Dalton, like Arthur Donnithorne, is the son of the local squire. He feels free to seduce Jessie Phillips, a cottager's daughter, because the new law will protect him from the consequences of his act: "It is just one of my little bits of good luck that this blessed law should be passed precisely when it was likely to be most beneficial to me."[18] The pregnant Jessie, spurned by Frederick, enters a horrifying workhouse but escapes to give birth in a cowshed. Frederick kills the infant; Jessie, however, is accused of the crime and stands trial for murder. She is found innocent by reason of insanity but dies of shock when she hears the news that Frederick has drowned while attempting to escape his sister's accusation that he, not Jessie, is guilty.

These two novels identified mother and illegitimate infant as victims both of a censorious world and of the men who had deserted them. Each woman contemplates suicide as an escape from her shame. Although Jessie does not actually murder her child, the novel's twist simply emphasizes her helplessness. In Mrs. Trollope's novel, the blame is squarely placed on the man, but Eliot's Arthur Donnithorne is also shown to bear part of the guilt for Hetty's deed. When Adam Bede, who loves Hetty, hears the news of her arrest, he responds: "It's his doing . . . if there's been any crime, it's at his door, not at hers. . . . Is he to go free, while they lay all the punishment on her . . . so weak and young?"[19]

This ambivalent attitude about the guilt of fictional women accused of infanticide is reflected in the actual trials of suspected child murderers. Victorian women who were accused or even convicted of infanticide were treated with what seems a surprising leniency. Few women were convicted of infanticide, and those who were, routinely received pardons. After 1849, no woman was hanged for the murder of her own infant under one year old, legitimate or illegitimate.[20] Reformers argued that this was not an indication of the innocence of the suspects but rather a result of the overly sympathetic attitudes of judges, juries, and the general public. One barrister contended that juries "eagerly laid hold of every favourable scrap of evidence, and then brought in verdicts of 'Not Guilty' when there was no moral doubt that guilt did exist."[21] Thus, it was charged, unscrupulous unmarried mothers took advantage of the courts to commit murder, callously secure in the knowledge that they would not be punished.[22]

Although novels, official statistics, and reformers' rhetoric do suggest the vulnerability of illegitimate infants, they are not entirely reliable indicators of the extent and nature of infanticide. Despite the alarming numbers of infant murders identified by coroners, these officials may have overemphasized the extent of infanticide involving illegitimate children.

Coroners included among such infants those whose parents could not be identified even though some of these children may have been legitimate. Nor were coroners' inquests always accurate in identifying the causes of infant death. Witnesses before a parliamentary commission on capital punishment complained that the findings of inquests on infants often resulted in unsubstantiated murder verdicts.[23] Some over-zealous coroners' courts may well have identified natural or accidental deaths as child murder. Even Lankester came under attack from the *Times* for exaggerating the extent of infanticide in his district.[24]

Medical men, and especially medical coroners, had a possible stake in describing infanticide as a widespread problem. Infant mortality was one area in which they could demonstrate the social benefits of their technical expertise at a time when medical men were seeking wider recognition and professional status.[25] Medical coroners were also competing for office with lawyers. Suggestions that coroners without medical training might overlook serious crimes against infants would have supported the need for more medical men in those positions. Although the high level of infant mortality in the nineteenth century made concern for infant life a logical priority for the medical profession, an exaggerated emphasis on murder as an important component of such mortality may have provided a distorted picture of the connection between illegitimacy and death. Between the 1860s and 1890s, fewer than two hundred murders of children under age seven were actually reported each year in England and Wales. These cases represent a high proportion of all murders, yet they do not account for a significant proportion of the thirty thousand to forty thousand illegitimate infants born each year during this period.

An examination of child murder cases tried in the Central

Criminal Court in London—better known as the Old Bailey—suggests that infant murder cannot be understood simply as a common response to the problems of illegitimate motherhood. A search of all murder cases tried in the Central Criminal Court during twelve sample years between 1839 and 1906 produced forty-two trials (see table 1) of mothers accused of murdering illegitimate children under five years old, as well as ninety other cases involving crimes related to the deaths of illegitimate infants.[26] All but five of these suspected crimes involved at least one child under a year old.

These cases of suspected murder reveal a distinctive pattern in infanticides involving illegitimate children. In more than 70 percent of the murder cases, the victim was a newborn. The circumstances of these neonaticides were remarkably similar. Almost all the accused women had concealed

Table 1.

Women Tried for Murder and Related Crimes and Age of Victims: Sample Years 1839–1906

Charge	Age of Victim			
	Newborn	One Day to Eleven Months	Over One Year	Total
Murder	31 (73.8%)	10 (23.8%)	1 (2.4%)	42
Attempted Murder	1 (16.7%)	3 (50.0%)	2 (33.3%)	6
Manslaughter	3 (30.0%)	5 (50.0%)	2 (20.0%)	10
Concealment of Birth	74 (100%)			74

Note: Each woman is included under only one charge, the most serious, although twenty-eight women were charged with a second offense. In the two cases involving more than one child, the age of the youngest was used.

their pregnancies from families and employers. All had delivered their babies alone and unaided. Some gave birth in their homes or in lodgings, but at least half delivered themselves in the privies, cellars, and bedrooms of the houses where they worked as domestic servants. After giving birth, some of these women returned to their duties as if nothing had occurred. In one case, the accused woman testified that she had heard her mistress's bell while giving birth and went down to answer it as soon as she could.[27] A birth was most often detected when the woman's changed appearance, erratic behavior, or apparent illness aroused suspicion, or when the body of the child was discovered. In one typical case, Ellen Trollope, a young domestic servant, delivered an illegitimate child in her room in a home in Earl's Court. Another servant heard her groaning during labor and later searched her room, finding the body of a newborn infant hidden in a chest.[28] Fanny Young, a nineteen-year-old servant, became ill after delivering her child in her room. When a physician was summoned, another servant, probably suspicious about the cause of Young's illness, went to tidy her room and found the body of the child wrapped in a parcel.[29] Neonaticide was recognized as a pattern by at least some Victorians, a pattern that supported assumptions about the criminality of unmarried mothers and the connection between shame and infanticide. The Harveian Society report concluded that in cases of infanticide "no preparation for the confinement is made, for the discovery of the pregnancy involves the loss of character; and hence the temptation to destroy the child and to hide its body is strong, and often prevails."[30]

Although the Victorians often interpreted such secrecy as the simple prelude to crime, the cases provide little evidence of premeditated murder. The accused women had made no provisions for disposing of the corpse; many simply hid the bodies in their rooms or left them in convenient spots nearby. Their actions were improvised and hampered by the limitations on servants' movements; in their confusion, they sometimes made errors that insured discovery. Ruth Newman, a servant in a London hotel, concealed the body of her dead illegitimate infant in her room for a week. She then wrapped the body in a piece of paper and left it along an underground railway line. The body was quickly traced to her, however, because the paper bore the name of the hotel where she worked.[31] Another young servant, Christina Clark, wrapped her dead infant in a sheet that was marked with her employer's name, and placed the parcel on a nearby road.[32] Other women readily told police or physicians about the deaths of their infants. These women do not seem the cunning murderesses portrayed in some Victorian accounts. Their cases reveal fear, confusion, and perhaps an unconscious desire for discovery. This ambivalence is captured in Eliot's portrayal of Hetty Sorrel, who is arrested because she returns to the lonely woodlot where she left her child to die.

These cases also convey vividly the women's isolation. Few of the accused women had accomplices or witnesses to their guilt or innocence; most had revealed their condition to no one, although a few admitted to telling the child's father. Clark had hidden her condition from both her employer, for whom she had worked for five years, and her parents, whom she visited regularly. Most servants probably sought secrecy in order to preserve their positions until the last possible moment. A number of the women had been in their places of employment or their lodgings for only a few weeks or months, suggesting that they had left or been dismissed from more familiar surroundings. But some sought concealment among their own families. Alice Sargent, an eighteen-year-old matchbox maker, hid her pregnancy and the birth of her child even from her mother and sisters with whom she lived. She gave birth in the water closet and then threw the child over the back wall of the yard. At her trial she made no defense but stated, "I was not in my right mind when I did it, I was so frightened, and I did not mean to do it. I was in so much pain."[33]

This isolation, as one forensic scientist argued, could in itself lead to arrest and imprisonment: "Alone and unassisted, the mother of an illegitimate child may be placed under circumstances of the greatest suspicion, although innocent of any attempt to destroy the life of her child."[34] Assumptions about the interrelation between illegitimacy and infanticide would have insured that an unmarried mother whose infant had died would be suspected of murder: the secrecy surrounding the birth could only add to those suspicions. Such secrecy may indeed have presaged intent to murder, but often it stemmed from other factors. The woman may have sought to deny the pregnancy to herself as well as those around her. She may have feared dismissal from her employment and have lacked a network of family and friends. For example, in 1852 Matilda Bunn, a servant suspected of murdering her infant daughter, told a Marylebone Police Court that "if I had had friends to go to this would not have happened."[35]

Another crime closely associated with infanticide, concealment of birth, revealed a similar pattern of isolation and denial. The charge originated in a seventeenth-century statute that made secret childbirth a capital offense if the child died, even if there was no evidence of murder. The harshness of this statute was intended to discourage infanticide by identifying as a potential murderess any woman who sought to deny her pregnancy. The law proved impossible to enforce, and in 1803 the penalty was reduced to a maximum of two years. Ninety-one of the women in the sample were charged with concealment of birth, making it the most common crime connected with the death of an illegitimate infant. Of these women, fifteen were charged with concealment after being acquitted of murder charges, and two after being charged with manslaughter.

The parallels between neonaticide and concealment of birth are obvious. A charge of concealment meant that the child had been born in secret, that it had died, and that its body had been hidden. The decision of the Crown or the coroner's court to pursue a charge of concealment rather than murder certainly had important consequences for the woman, but the reasons for that choice are not always clear-cut. An initial charge of concealment would be understandable where there was evidence that the child had died from natural causes, but the decision may also have been made on the basis of a particularly affecting story or a convincing manner. Ann Spooner, a general servant, was charged with concealment after her mistress found the body of a dead infant in Spooner's box. Her employer did not realize that Spooner had given birth; she was searching Spooner's possessions for stolen items. Spooner testified that she had given birth alone in her room and then had fainted. When she awoke, the infant was dead.[36] Her story was accepted, and she was charged only with concealment, in part because the medical evidence pointed to death by natural causes. In other concealment cases, however, the evidence implied more complicity in the death of the child. In 1875, for example, the Metropolitan Police found parts of an infant's body and traced the remains to a house where they discovered the baby's head, along with a blood-stained nightdress. Despite the mutilation of the body and a police court finding of murder, Elizabeth Lewis, a lodger in the house and the infant's mother, was brought to trial only for concealment.[37] Such cases and the obvious parallels between concealment and infanticide led some Victorians to assume that the crimes were synonymous. Concealment was, according to a Scottish judge, simply a means of "bringing within the reach of the criminal law a few women who have improperly escaped the graver charge of intentionally killing the child."[38]

Neonaticide and concealment cases confirm the difficult circumstances and vulnerability of at least some unmarried mothers, but they provide less convincing evidence of the widespread criminality commonly posited by the Victorians. Even if concealment of birth is included with the murder charges, the cases in the sample averaged only ten a year in London—far short of the several hundred claimed by alarmists such as Edwin Lankester and Thomas Wakley. Nor is it clear that all these cases, or even all the suspected neonaticides, represented clear examples of infant murder. Not one of the women charged with murdering her newborn infant was convicted, although one woman was found guilty of manslaughter. Twelve of these accused murderers were found guilty of concealment of birth, but the rest were released. Did this low conviction rate indicate substantial doubts about each woman's guilt or merely the tenderheartedness of the British jury when confronted with a young woman charged with a capital offense? The evidence at Ellen Trollope's trial showed that her infant's throat had been cut and its skull fractured, but she was acquitted of murder. Fanny Young's infant died of strangulation, while another suspected woman had reportedly attacked her infant with a pair of scissors.[39] The infant of Maxwell Rae, a draper's assistant, was found dismembered in the yard of a friend's house, but she was acquitted of murder and the judge stated that she was "deserving of the greatest sympathy."[40] Such cases support the contention that juries were highly reluctant to convict women accused of murdering their illegitimate infants.

In other cases, however, the evidence of intentional murder was much less clear and the verdict reflected real questions about the woman's guilt. Ruth Newman was charged with murder, but the medical evidence presented at her trial showed that her child had been stillborn. Fanny Rosenburg, a twenty-two-year-old tailoress from the East End, was charged with murder even though her infant was premature and had apparently died of natural causes. The judge dismissed the case.[41] In several instances, the cause of death was given as neglect at birth; such neglect may have been a form of infanticide in which the mother took no action to save her baby, but it may also have resulted from her fear and lack of knowledge about newborns. Even when the child bore marks of violence, it was sometimes difficult to determine when these injuries proved deliberate intent to harm and when they were owing to the inexperience and fright of a woman delivering herself of her first child. In 1858, for instance, Ellen Stone, an unemployed servant, gave birth alone in her lodgings. She hid the body of her infant in the dust heap. The child had died from bleeding through the umbilical cord; the bleeding may well have been the result of an accident. She was charged with murder but the judge directed a verdict of not guilty.[42] Mary Ann Hicks, a servant, was charged with murder although a medical witness testified that "death might have occurred accidentally in the act of parturition."[43] In such cases, assumptions about the readiness of unmarried mothers to murder their infants may have sent women to the dock even when their infants died naturally or accidentally.

Table 2:

Verdicts in Sample Cases Tried in the Central Criminal Court, 1839–1906

Charge	Verdict			
	Guilty	Not Guilty	Not Guilty by Reason of Insanity	Total
Murder	4 (9.8%)	35 (85.3%)	2 (4.9%)	41
Attempted Murder	2 (33.3%)	4 (66.6%)		6
Concealment	62 (68.1%)	29 (31.9%)		91
Manslaughter	5 (38.5%)	7 (53.8%)	1 (7.7%)	13

Note: The figure for concealment includes seventeen women acquitted of more serious crimes (murder and manslaughter) and then tried for concealment. The figure for manslaughter includes three women acquitted of murder and then tried for manslaughter.

The judge's dismissal of the cases against Stone and Rosenburg was not unusual. Trial juries, tenderhearted or not, often had little to say about the guilt or innocence of the accused. Of the thirty-one neonaticide cases, sixteen were not fully tried either because the prosecution presented no evidence or because the judge directed the verdict. These court-determined verdicts occasionally reflected the judge's assessment of the evidence presented during the trial, as in the Stone and Rosenburg cases. More often, they indicated a rejection by the Crown or the grand jury of the findings of a coroner's court. At least nine of the sample neonaticide cases sent to the Central Criminal Court by a coroner's court were dismissed by the grand jury; in two others the prosecution simply ignored the murder indictment. Trollope, Stone, and Newman were all acquitted of murder when their cases were dismissed by a grand jury.

Such dismissals often resulted from problems with the medical evidence. In the Stone and Newman cases, the problematic evidence concerned the cause of death. But another difficult issue involved the timing of any injuries inflicted on the infant. British law required that in order to be counted a victim of murder, an infant had to be a separate person born alive and completely separated from the mother before death occurred. Various methods for testing the state of the child at the time of death evolved during the nineteenth century, including weighing the lungs for evidence of breathing and examining internal organs for signs of independent functioning. But none of these tests was particularly reliable. Given the limitations of their knowledge, some medical witnesses were therefore understandably reluctant to testify precisely about the death of an infant.[44] In 1882, Elizabeth Poyle, a twenty-three-year-old cook, was tried for the murder of her infant, found with its head severed in a parcel under her bed. The medical witness was unable to say if the child had been "fully born" at the time the injuries were inflicted; Poyle was acquitted.[45] The judge dismissed the murder charge against Emma Busch, a twenty-one-year-old servant, because despite testimony that the child had been strangled, he was dissatisfied with the prosecution's evidence that the injuries had occurred after the infant was born.[46]

The difficulties of convicting women accused of infant murder led to pressure for revising the criminal law. In the mid-1860s, barristers and judges appearing before the Capital Punishment Commission urged creation of a new category of crime for mothers accused of infanticide, one that would not be a capital offense and would not require medical evidence of separate existence. The Harveian Society also argued for the separation of infanticide from murder. Such advocates sought to increase conviction rates by decreasing the reliance on medical evidence and by removing the necessity of sentencing a sympathetic suspect to death.[47] In addition, they often provided a new definition of the crime of infanticide, suggesting that the crime of infant murder was somehow different from ordinary murder because of the unique relation between mother and child, the confusion of a woman who had just given birth, and the circumstances surrounding the crime. This view was stated in its most exaggerated form by James Fitzjames Stephen when he testified before the parliamentary commission that "the crime itself is less serious than other kinds of murder. You cannot estimate the loss to the child itself, you know nothing about it."[48] The proposals of Stephen and others did not become law until the twentieth century, but to a limited extent, judges and juries did find in concealment of birth a more flexible charge to use in cases of infant death.

Unlike murder, the concealment of birth charge presented few problems with evidence, and it did not involve the necessity of imposing a death sentence; thus the conviction rates were naturally higher (see table 2). Among women charged only with concealment, 68 percent were convicted. In cases where women were charged first with murder and then with concealment, 73 percent were convicted. These higher rates reflected not only the readiness of juries to convict women of this lesser crime but also the greater willingness of women to plead guilty to it. In the sample cases, more than 40 percent of the accused did not contest the charge of concealment. Sometimes these cases provide examples of an early form of plea bargaining; in 1906, the prosecutor agreed to drop the murder charge against Jemima Hoare, a cook who claimed to have been seduced by the butler, in part because she was ready to plead guilty to concealment.[49]

Table 3:

Sentences of Women Convicted of Concealment of Birth, Attempted Murder, and Manslaughter in the Central Criminal Court for Sample Years, 1839–1906.

Sentence	Charge		
	Concealment of Birth	Attempted Murder	Manslaughter
Released	9 (14.5%)		1 (20.0%)
One Day to Three Weeks	22 (35.5%)		
One to Six Months	26 (41.9%)	2 (100%)	1 (20.0%)
Seven Months to One Year	4 (6.5%)		2 (40.0%)
Over One Year	1 (1.6%)		1 (20.0%)
Total	62	2	5 (100%)

Note: The figures for concealment of birth and manslaughter include women acquitted of other charges.

Although they were more likely to be convicted, women accused of concealment similarly found a measure of leniency from the court. Despite the popular assumption that concealment of birth was simply disguised murder, women charged with concealment in the Central Criminal Court seldom received sentences that even approached the maximum of two years (see table 3). Fanny Young, who pleaded guilty to concealment after being acquitted of a murder charge, was sentenced to only five days' imprisonment; Ellen Trollope served two weeks without hard labor; Ruth Newman was released into the custody of a court missionary. Such sentences were not unusual. Half of the women convicted received sentences of less than one month in prison;

14 percent were released without serving any additional time after their trials. Fewer than 10 percent were given sentences longer than six months, and only one woman, Margaret Whitham, was sentenced to the full two years' imprisonment with hard labor.

Whitham's case reveals the extent to which a judge's response to circumstances surrounding the child's death could influence sentencing. A twenty-two-year-old woman living in her mother's house, Whitham was charged with both murder and manslaughter but was finally convicted of concealment. Her illegitimate infant had been found in the privy outside the house. During the trial, a neighbor testified that Whitham had thrown a brick or stone down after the child; other neighbors testified to hearing the child cry. The judge stated that the child's death may have been an accident but noted that Whitham had been remiss in not aiding the child after it had cried.[50] The woman's callousness—and perhaps a lingering suspicion that she had intended her child to die—may have provoked a more severe sentence. Clara Darvill, a laundress, was sentenced to eight months in prison for concealment, but she was charged with four separate offenses involving four illegitimate infants born between 1887 and 1893. The judge called this a "serious case."[51] Lena Smale, a cook, was acquitted of murdering her illegitimate infant but was found guilty of concealment. She was given a sentence of six months at hard labor, apparently because this was the second time she had been charged with concealment. The judge noted that "this is not like the case of a young woman who had given birth to a child for the first time."[52] Smale was not so clearly a victim and her sentence was correspondingly harsher. Her repeated pattern of concealment may also have left suspicions about the extent of her guilt.

Judges could use their sentencing power, then, to reflect their assessment of the character and motives of the accused and particularly the degree of her complicity in the child's death. The judge in Young's case may have given her a lighter sentence because she had prepared baby clothes for her infant, indicating at least the intention of caring for her child. Sir Samuel Martin, a witness before the Capital Punishment Commission, explained, "If you believe the child has been unfairly dealt with, you give a heavier punishment, than in the case of a young woman, who, the child having died, puts it in a secret place to conceal her shame, that is a very lenient offense."[53] Judges apparently created a secondary crime between murder and simple concealment by punishing more severely those women whose neglect or deliberate cruelty separated them from their more "innocent" sisters fitting the stereotype of a desperate victim acting in a moment's panic. The more unconventional the woman's behavior and background, the more likely she was to lose the sympathy of the court, a pattern also apparent in outcomes of trials of women whose infants were not newborns.

The few cases in the sample involving murder, attempted murder, or manslaughter of older illegitimate infants supplied less ambiguous examples of crimes against children. Most of the deaths in these cases resulted from violence, and the degree of the mother's complicity was evident. The cases often reflected the traditional motives ascribed to unmarried mothers who murdered their children. Adelaide Freeman apparently poisoned her illegitimate infant to disguise her infidelity from her husband, who was about to return after a five-year absence.[54] Kate Finlon, a twenty-five-year-old servant, was charged with the attempted murder of her nine-month-old son after the child was found lying in a tunnel on the underground railway line. She had fallen behind on her payments to the woman who cared for the child. The child-minder testified at the trial that Finlon "felt very keenly the shame of her position" and had sought to conceal the existence of her child from her parents in Ireland.[55] In the same year, Frances Pearch accidentally or deliberately drowned her month-old illegitimate infant when her mother, who already cared for an older grandchild, refused to give shelter to Pearch and a second illegitimate child.[56]

These cases all involved a crime reportedly committed at a time of immediate crisis. The circumstances again reflected the vulnerability of Victorian women left alone to support infants or young children. Although Freeman, Finlon, and Pearch faced special difficulties because their children were illegitimate, some of their problems were shared by deserted wives and widows. This can be seen in the case of Ellen Wallis, a twenty-seven-year-old woman accused of attempted murder after jumping into the Thames with her two children, a boy aged six months and a three-year-old girl. Wallis had cohabited for a number of years with a commercial traveler who was a married man and the father of her children, but he had left her for another woman. Wallis attempted the suicide-dual murder after meeting the man accidentally while out walking. At her trial she stated, "I did not wish to do my children any harm; but I did not like to part with them. He knows that I have neither father, mother, or relation, and I am not a married woman."[57] Her statement reveals the complexity of her motives. Wallis had been abandoned by the man who was in all but name her husband. She was concerned about her position as a deserted mother but also as one without even the status or legal position of deserted wife. She did not seem less attached to her children than a "legitimate" mother. She sought to end her own life as well as theirs, a pattern that may have been common among murders of legitimate children by their mothers. She acted out of the crippling emotional stress and fears that any deserted wife might feel.

Nineteenth-century juries were only somewhat less reluctant to convict women accused in crimes involving older illegitimate children. Four of the eleven women charged with murder were found guilty; three were sentenced to death and one was confined in an insane asylum. Two of the women acquitted of murder were found guilty of manslaughter; two more were found not guilty by reason of insanity and were institutionalized at "Her Majesty's pleasure." Adelaide Freeman was one of these; her crime was blamed on puerperal mania. The other woman found insane was Elizabeth Huntsman, a wet nurse, whose insanity was brought on by the "sudden absorption of milk."[58] Of the six women accused of attempted murder, two were found guilty and imprisoned for six months. Wallis was acquitted of attempting to murder her children but was found guilty of attempted suicide; Finlon was found guilty only of attempting to injure her child and was released. Five of the thirteen women charged with manslaughter were convicted; one was released, and the others received sentences ranging from a few months to two years in prison.

Of the three women sentenced to death, two had their sentences reduced to a term of penal servitude. The only woman in the sample who was executed was Louise Masset, a thirty-nine-year-old daily governess accused of murdering her three-year-old son in the lavatory of a London railway station. Masset's case received more sensational coverage than any of the others, and is the only one to have been included in a modern study of women's crime.[59] Masset faced few of the difficulties expected in a murder case involving an illegitimate child. She was financially secure and had a good relationship with her family. She had supported her son at a childminder's home since birth; he was fond of his caretaker. Masset visited him once a week until she removed him from the childminder in 1899. Her apparent maternal devotion was used as evidence in her favor. Masset was nonetheless convicted, although she claimed throughout the trial that she had not murdered the child but had left him with another woman. She reportedly confessed to the murder only shortly before she was hanged in January 1900. The Home Office gave no reason for denying a reprieve in Masset's case. Her nationality (French) and the seamier side of her story may have reduced sympathy for her both in court and afterwards: she committed the murder while on her way to a liaison in Brighton with a clerk twenty years her junior. The man testified that they had no intention of marrying.[60]

A less obvious but no less important factor in Masset's treatment may have been the mere fact that she had successfully taken responsibility for the child for so long. Women who could plead poverty, shame, or desertion may well have had a more sympathetic hearing than Masset, whose actions did not fit the stereotype of the victimized unmarried mother. Wallis, although not truly "innocent," could at least point to a man as the cause of her actions, a factor cited by one juror who made cutting remarks about the perfidy of the man who deserted her. Masset could make no such pretense. The lower conviction rates in neonaticide cases also imply that the courts were more sympathetic to suspected child murderers who acted in the first hours or days after confinement than to those who had successfully negotiated the period of anxiety following the birth of an illegitimate child. There was no confusion in Masset's case about who was the victim.

These cases from the Old Bailey suggest that the relation-ship between illegitimacy and infanticide was more complex than Victorians assumed. Infanticide was not the common reaction to an illegitimate birth. Indeed, many of these crimes resulted from very uncommon circumstances. Those women accused of neonaticide had concealed their condition and had given birth in secret. This combination of events some-times set the stage for murder, deliberate or unpremedi-tated, but at other times assured that the infant's death even from natural causes would bring the mother under suspi-cion of murder. The degree of guilt in these cases is some-times as difficult for the historian to assess as it apparently was for Victorian judges and juries. In some cases at least, the act of infanticide may have been more passive than ac-tive; the mother did not maliciously harm her newborn, but she also did not prepare for its arrival or succor the baby in the dangerous moments immediately after birth. In any event, most nineteenth-century women faced with illegiti-mate pregnancies either did not or could not conceal their condition or give birth in secret. They sought refuge in workhouses, charity institutions, and relatives' homes dur-ing their confinements. They faced difficulties but responded with resourcefulness rather than violence. They cared for their children, left them with family, or placed them with childminders.

Victorian assumptions about infanticide were part of a complex and changing response to illegitimacy. In some ways, the alarm over infanticide revealed a new sensitivity about the risks facing illegitimate infants—and indeed the vulnerability of all infant life.[61] The connection drawn be-tween illegitimacy and infanticide also meant recognition of the difficulties facing a single mother. References to the prevalence of infanticide were usually accompanied by proposals to improve the condition of unmarried mothers by establishing charities or reforming the Poor Laws.

But Victorian emphasis on infanticide also provided a way of avoiding the real problems of illegitimacy by offering a simple, even a comforting, explanation of high levels of infant mortality. It emphasized the actions of the individual mother and slighted the role of poverty, lack of extensive childcare, low wages for women, and poor social services. Medical men understood that the prime causes of infant deaths among illegitimate children were poor nutrition and improper care, but this understanding was lost amid the growing panic over murderous mothers. The Victorians could grapple with the problem of crime. Solving all the problems of illegitimacy, however, would have required rethinking fundamental assumptions about parental responsibility, the role of the state, and the allocation of resources. To change the condition of unmarried mothers would also have meant abandoning a fundamental Victorian principle: aiding the immoral simply encourages vice. In the end, infant deaths were easier to tolerate than easy virtue was.

The agitation over infanticide revealed as well some basic assumptions about women, particularly "fallen" women. The murdering mother's wild and emotional response to an unwanted birth reinforced ideas about the irrationality of all women. (This concept was institutionalized in the Infanticide Act of 1922, which declared all mothers to be potentially insane for the first few months after giving birth.) Infanticide and death on the gallows were only some of the dire fates predicted for the unmarried mother. She was commonly assumed to have little future beyond prison, the streets, or the river. Her fall condemned her to a life of degradation and crime. The terrible sin of infanticide served to isolate her from her respectable sisters and further high-

lighted the unacceptability of her first offense against purity
and the family.

Victorian accusations about the prevalence of infanticide
were plausible. There is no doubt that unmarried mothers
experienced economic hardship and a measure of social ostracism. As single mothers, their opportunities were limited
by the need to support an illegitimate child without help
from the state or the child's father. However, crime does not
inevitably result from a plausible motivation. In assuming
that widespread infanticide existed because unmarried mothers had good reason to conceal their condition, deny their
natural instincts, and murder their infants, the Victorians
confused deed with motive. Their sometimes melodramatic
claims about the extent of child murder overemphasized the
actions of a few women and ignored the special circumstances surrounding most cases of infanticide. It may be that
the heroine of George Moore's 1894 novel *Esther Waters*
provides a better model for understanding the experience of
an unmarried mother than do Hetty Sorrel and Jessie Phillips. Esther, a naive kitchenmaid who is seduced by a fellow
servant, gives birth to a son and raises him despite her poverty and the disgrace of her position. Moore's final scene
finds Esther, still a servant, welcoming home her grown
son, a soldier now, and thinking that "she had accomplished
her woman's work—she had brought him up to a man's
estate; and that was her sufficient reward."[62]

Notes

The research for this essay was funded by grants from the Social
Science Research Council and Eastern Connecticut State University.

1. U. K., *Hansard's Parliamentary Debates*, 3d ser., vol. 76 (1844), cols. 430–31 (Wakley).

2. W. T. Charley, "Infanticide," *Transactions of the National Association for the Promotion of Social Science* (hereafter cited as *Transactions*), 1877, 295.

3. "Infanticide and Illegitimacy," *Journal of the Statistical Society* 28 (1865): 420.

4. *Times,* 29 Apr. 1862, 8.

5. For one of the best accounts, see George K. Behlmer, *Child Abuse and Moral Reform in England, 1870–1908* (Stanford: Stanford University Press, 1982). See also his article, "Deadly Motherhood: Infanticide and Medical Opinion in Mid-Victorian England," *Journal of the History of Medicine and Allied Sciences* 34 (1979): 403–27; Lionel Rose, *Massacre of the Innocents: Infanticide in Great Britain, 1800–1939* (London: Routledge and Kegan Paul, 1986); and R. Sauer, "Infanticide and Abortion in Nineteenth-Century Britain," *Population Studies* 32 (1978): 81–93.

6. This concern has been well documented by Behlmer and Rose.

7. See, for example, G. Wythen Baxter, *The Book of the Bastilles; or, the History of the Working of the New Poor Law* (London: John Stephens, 1841), 571.

8. "Home of Hope," *Magdalen's Friend and Female Home Intelligencer* 4 (1863): 137.

9. "Report of the Committee of the Harveian Society on Infanticide," *Lancet* 1 (1867): 61.

10. Figures on coroners' inquests are taken from the "Judicial Statistics" found in the *Parliamentary Papers* each year beginning in 1852.

11. "Infanticide, the Sin of the Age," *Magdalen's Friend and Female Home Intelligencer* 3 (1862): 295; *Times,* 18 Oct. 1862, 12; see also William Burke Ryan, *Infanticide: Its Law, Prevalence, Prevention, and History* (London: Churchill, 1862), 19–20; and C. H. F. Routh, *Feeding and Its Influence on Life, or, the Causes and Prevention of Infant Mortality,* 3d ed. (London: Churchill, 1876), 238.

12. J. Brendon Curgenven, *The Wastage of Infant Life* (London: n.p., 1867), 12.

13. *Parliamentary Papers*, Select Committee on the Protection of Infant Life, Report, 1871, v.

14. See Rachel Ginnis Fuchs, *Abandoned Children: Foundlings and Child Welfare in Nineteenth-Century France* (Albany: State University of New York Press, 1984).

15. Committee for Amending the Law in Points Wherein It Is Injurious to Women, *Infant Mortality: Its Causes and Remedies* (Manchester: A. Ireland, 1871), 14.

16. "The Prevalence of Infanticide," *Magdalen's Friend and Female Home Intelligencer* 2 (1861): 34.

17. "Home of Compassion," *Seeking and Saving* 2 (1882): 73.

18. Frances Trollope, *Jessie Phillips: A Tale of the Present Day* (1843), chap. 9. See Sally Mitchell, *The Fallen Angel: Chastity, Class, and Women's Reading, 1835–1880* (Bowling Green: Bowling Green University Popular Press, 1981), 23–25; and George Watt, *The Fallen Woman in the Nineteenth-Century Novel* (London: Croom Helm, 1984), 41.

19. George Eliot, *Adam Bede* [1859], ed. John Paterson (Boston: Houghton Mifflin, 1968), chap. 39, 343.

20. William A. Guy, "On the Executions for Murder That Have Taken Place in England and Wales during the Last Seventy Years," *Journal of the Statistical Society* 38 (1875): 485; Fenton Bresler, *Reprieve: A Study of a System* (London: George G. Harrap, 1865), 55.

21. William Griffith, quoted in Charley, 306.

22. See "Infanticide," *Saturday Review* 20 (1865): 161; Curgenven, 11–12; "Baby Slaughter—Wholesale," *Sentinel* 12 (1890): 117; Ryan, 2–4, 10, 16; and "The Judge's Opinion upon Child Murder," *Spectator* 65 (1890): 44. This view also appeared in two major works on forensic medicine: Charles Meymott Tidy, *Legal Medicine*, 2 vols. (London: Smith, Elder, and Co., 1883), 2:248; and Alfred Swaine Taylor, *The Principles and Practice of Medical Jurisprudence*, 4th ed., 2 vols. (London: Churchill, 1894), 2:319, 432.

23. *Parliamentary Papers,* 1866, xxi, Report of the Capital Punishment Commission, q. 1807 (Avory); q. 2199 (Stephen); q. 1457 (Grey).

24. *Times,* 23 Aug. 1866, 8.

25. For a discussion of the search for professionalization, see M. Jeanne Peterson, *The Medical Profession in Mid-Victorian London* (Berkeley: University of California Press, 1978).

26. These cases were located by examining all cases involving women in the published sessions papers of the Central Criminal Court (hereafter cited as CCC, *Minutes*). The sample years were selected at six-year intervals beginning in 1839 and ending in 1906. The years included in the sample were: 1839–40, 1845–46, 1851–52, 1857–58, 1863–64, 1869–70, 1875–76, 1881–82, 1887–88, 1893–94, 1899–1900, 1905–06. Each court year began in November and ended in October. After a case was identified, additional details were taken from accounts of police court, inquest, and criminal court proceedings found in the *Times.*

27. CCC, *Minutes,* 1839–40, vol. 11, no. 953; *Times,* 15 Jan. 1840, 7; 10 Mar. 1840, 7. The woman was eventually charged with concealment of birth. She testified that the child died while she was answering her employer's summons.

28. CCC, *Minutes,* 1893–94, vol. 119–20, no. 699; *Times,* 25 July 1894, 4; 30 July 1894, 4; 6 Aug. 1894, 2; 13 Sept. 1894, 9; 14 Sept. 1894, 10.

29. CCC, *Minutes,* 1863–64, vol. 59, no. 132; *Times,* 30 Nov. 1863, 11.

30. "Report," *Lancet,* 61. This pattern has been noted in earlier periods as well; see R. W. Malcolmson, "Infanticide in the Eighteenth Century," in *Crime in England, 1550–1800,* ed. J. S. Cockburn (London: Methuen, 1977), 186–209; and Peter C. Hoffer and N. E. H. Hull, *Murdering Mothers: Infanticide in England and New England, 1558–1803* (New York: New York University Press, 1981).

31. CCC, *Minutes,* 1887–88, vol. 108, no. 823; *Times,* 17 Aug. 1888, 10; 18 Aug. 1888, 10; 25 Aug. 1888, 5; 20 Sept. 1888, 10.

32. CCC, *Minutes*, 1887–88, vol. 107, no. 7; *Times*, 27 Oct. 1887, 12; 4 Nov. 1887, 3; 18 Nov. 1887, 4.

33. CCC, *Minutes*, 1905–06, vol. 145, no. 645; *Times*, 15 Sept. 1906, 2; 27 Oct. 1906, 4.

34. Taylor, 2:388–89.

35. *Times*, 4 June 1852, 7; CCC, *Minutes*, 1851–52, vol. 36, no. 666. The murder charge against Bunn was dropped; she was tried only for concealment of birth.

36. CCC, *Minutes*, 1839–40, vol. 11, no. 532; *Times*, 12 Dec. 1839, 6.

37. CCC, *Minutes*, 1875–76, vol. 83, no. 127; *Times*, 9 Dec. 1875, 11; 16 Dec. 1875, 11.

38. John Dove Wilson, "Can Any Better Measures Be Devised for the Prevention and Punishment of Infanticide?" *Transactions*, 1877, 291.

39. CCC, *Minutes*, 1905–06, vol. 143, no. 28; *Times*, 8 Nov. 1905, 5.

40. CCC, *Minutes*, 1887–88, vol. 107, no. 282; *Times*, 5 Dec. 1887, 6; 9 Jan. 1888, 4; 16 Jan. 1888, 4; 4 Feb. 1888, 5.

41. CCC, *Minutes*, 1905–06, vol. 144, no. 344–45; *Times*, 2 May 1906, 3.

42. CCC, *Minutes*, 1857–58, vol. 48, no. 931; *Times*, 23 Sept. 1858, 11.

43. CCC, *Minutes*, 1845–46, vol. 24, no. 827.

44. This was the opinion of the forensic textbooks. See Taylor, 2:347, 381; Tidy, 2:246–47; Thomas Stewart Traill, *Outlines of a Course of Lectures on Medical Jurisprudence* (Edinburgh: Adam and Charles Black, 1836), 29–30.

45. CCC, *Minutes*, 1881–82, vol. 96, no. 28; *Times*, 6 Apr. 1882, 7; 12 May 1882, 4.

46. CCC, *Minutes*, 1900, vol. 132, no. 302; *Times*, 20 Mar. 1900, 3; 23 Apr. 1900, 14; 3 May 1900, 14.

47. *Parliamentary Papers*, Report of the Capital Punishment Commission; see the testimony of Lord Cranworth, James Fitz-james Stephen, Sir Samuel Martin, and Sir George Grey, the home

secretary, who was responsible for receiving requests for reprieves in capital cases ("Report," *Lancet,* 61); see also Wilson, 285–86; "Judge's Opinion," 44; C. A. Fyffe, "The Punishment of Infanticide," *Nineteenth Century* 1 (1877): 588–89. Fyffe suggests that the law as it stood tortured women unnecessarily by threatening them with the death sentence even though no conviction would ever result.

48. *Parliamentary Papers,* Report of the Capital Punishment Commission, q. 2193 (Stephen).

49. CCC, *Minutes,* 1905–06, vol. 145, no. 393; *Times,* 14 Sept. 1906, 10.

50. CCC, *Minutes,* 1851–52, vol. 36, no. 637: *Times,* 12 May 1852, 7; 18 June 1852, 7. The woman's name was given as both Whitham and Whitepen.

51. CCC, *Minutes,* 1893–94, vol. 119, no. 217; *Times,* 25 Jan. 1894, 10; 1 Feb. 1894, 8.

52. CCC, *Minutes,* 1905–06, vol. 143, no. 27; *Times,* 17 Nov. 1905, 4; 18 Nov. 1905, 5.

53. *Parliamentary Papers,* Report of the Capital Punishment Commission, q. 297 (Martin); see also qq. 2086–87 (Willes).

54. CCC, *Minutes,* 1869–70, vol. 71, no. 36; *Times,* 28 Oct. 1869, 9; 25 Nov. 1869, 11.

55. CCC, *Minutes,* 1893–94, vol. 119–20, no. 704; *Times,* 2 Aug. 1894, 13; 14 Sept. 1894, 10.

56. CCC, *Minutes,* 1893–94, vol. 119, no. 389; *Times,* 6 Feb. 1894, 4; 20 Feb. 1894, 14; 5 Apr. 1894, 3.

57. CCC, *Minutes,* 1869–70, vol. 72, nos. 509–10; *Times,* 10 June 1870, 10.

58. CCC, *Minutes,* 1845–46, vol. 23, no. 203; *Times,* 19 Nov. 1845, 7.

59. Patrick Wilson, *Murderesses: A Study of the Women Executed in Britain since 1843* (London: Michael Joseph, 1971).

60. CCC, *Minutes,* 1899–1900, vol. 131, no. 77; *Times,* 2 Nov. 1899, 14; 3 Nov. 1899, 6; 10 Nov. 1899, 10; 13 Nov. 1899, 16; 17 Nov. 1899, 7; 14 Dec. 1899, 12; 16 Dec. 1899,

14; 17 Dec. 1899, 12; 18 Dec. 1899, 13; 28 Dec. 1899, 9; 10 Jan. 1900, 7.

61. See Behlmer; Rose; and Deborah Dwork, *War Is Good for Babies and Other Young Children: A History of the Infant and Child Welfare Movement in England, 1898–1918* (London: Tavistock Publications, 1987), chaps. 1–3.

62. George Moore, *Esther Waters* [1894], ed. David Skilton (New York: Oxford University Press, 1983), chap. 47, 394.

Afterword:
Victorian Scandals,
Victorian Strategies

Thaïs E. Morgan

Each essay in this collection narrates the historical facts and controversies surrounding a "scandal" in the Victorian period. The main purpose of my essay will be to (re)open some questions about the significance of these scandals with reference to contemporary critical theories. The series of scandals that marked the Victorian period seem to converge on three areas: the construction of gender, the relationship between the social "body" and the individual body, and the strategic use of the mechanism of scandal by conflicting groups within Victorian society.[1]

Notably, most of the essays in this collection focus on "scandals" involving women. This reflects not only the well-documented importance of women's issues in the nineteenth century but also the rising interest in women's studies across the academic disciplines today.[2] Victorian women participated in controversies involving the medical profession, the law, the university, the family, the theater, the visual arts, and the literary scene. The chain of Victorian scandals involving women suggests a double process of thoroughly problematizing the feminine, yet highly valuing the feminine. Woman increasingly appears as both the "mystery" and the "key" to central Victorian socioeconomic, religiomoral, and scientific debates—all having political ramifications or "power-effects" that spread widely across class and gender lines.[3]

A prime example of the problematic valuation of the feminine in Victorian culture is the overcoding of the female body in the emerging life sciences, including biology, anthropology, and medicine.[4] The "feminization" of madness, which makes the female body into a paradigmatic site of physiological, moral, and social disorders, has attracted much recent critical attention.[5] Hysteria—the "feminine" disease par excellence—was defined as a microcosm of signs inscribed on the female body whose meaning and potential force were hidden, ambiguous, hence dangerous to family and society. By representing madness in this way, physicians gained the authority to cure, and thus to intervene directly, not only in the madwoman's body but also in the private lives of the woman, her husband, and her children.[6] The power of the medical profession as "moral managers" and as a political interest group was thus significantly established and maintained through its treatment of "female problems" and the "feminine" as "problem."[7]

In "Wrongful Confinement: The Betrayal of Women by Men, Medicine, and Law," Marilyn J. Kurata discusses several Victorian scandals centered on feminine madness, both in fact and in Wilkie Collins's novel, *The Woman in White*.[8] She makes the point that in each case of scandal, medical men, asylum keepers, and husbands cooperated in the effort to manage wives who dared to go beyond the proper sphere set for upper- and middle-class "ladies." Indeed, the insane asylum and the domestic interior eventually came to be used as interchangeable metaphors for the ideological containment of women's desires and rights, as in Charlotte Perkins Gilman's 1892 story, "The Yellow Wallpaper."[9]

In view of the scandal or public shame that attended any stay at an insane asylum, one would expect that most respectable Victorian wives would have been sufficiently intimidated and silenced by the mere threat of incarceration from husband or physician. Nevertheless, the scandal over the wife's madness in the Bulwer-Lytton family did not at all turn out this way. As Kurata recounts, after a legal separation in 1836, Rosina Bulwer wrote several novels highlighting the injustices done to women under the conditions of early-Victorian marriage. For a woman to criticize in print the sacred institution of marriage was in itself already a scandal, or a symptom of disorder in the very heart of the social body—the family. Consequently, Bulwer's retaliatory removal of their children from Rosina's custody was a strategic first step in the "hystericization" and control of his wife. Rosina was implicitly discredited as a sane, that is, morally fit because socially conformist, mother. Her ensuing self-imposed exile on the Continent may have been a defiant gesture of independence but was equally an acknowledgment of Bulwer's power to impose his will as patriarchal figurehead at home and in the public view. Indeed, the term of exile underscored Rosina's marginal position, with the Continent temporarily replacing the confined space of the home and ironically prefiguring her wrongful confinement in the insane asylum.

Bulwer's refusal to extend the name Lytton to Rosina upon his inheritance in 1844 is of a piece with his taking the children, for money and property were less at issue than the authority of gender and class invested in the patrilinear name itself. Here again, Bulwer hystericizes his wife by treating her as wholly "other"—in Victorian terms, unhealthy, insane, immoral—and hence too "improper" to be given the "proper" name of Lytton.[10] In this context, Rosina's courageous return to England in 1847 suggests that she was deliberately staging her own hysteria in order to embarrass and thus regain some power over Bulwer-Lytton. Her obscene letters to her husband manifest an aggressive use of scandal for her own purposes rather than the posture of the stereotypically passive and victimized Victorian woman.

With his own authority at stake, and symbolically that of the patriarchy, it is no wonder that Bulwer-Lytton called in the lunacy physicians in 1858 to assist him in managing his wife. Once again, though, Rosina seems to have been able to turn the attempt to certify her as a madwoman into a sort of counterhysteria, raising public doubts about her husband's intentions as well as causing controversy within the medical profession. Thus her appearance at a Bulwer-Lytton political speech, dressed in the colors of the opposite party, turned the force of scandal as much against him as against herself. For how could a man who could not rule his own wife rule in national government? Ultimately, what perhaps disturbed the Victorian public most about the Bulwer-Lytton scandal was the evidence it gave for fears about a slippage of power between the sexes.

Judging from the scandals precipitated by divorce cases in Victorian England, women suing for legal independence from their husbands were perceived as being every bit as dangerous as adulteresses and madwomen. However, in " 'Intended Only for the Husband': Gender, Class, and the Provision for Divorce in England, 1858–1868," Gail L. Savage demonstrates a significant disparity between the statistics, which show a moderate number of divorce suits actually filed, and the sensationalist way in which the supposed rise of divorce was reported by the Victorian press.[11] This contradiction prompts the question: What political agenda(s) did the production of scandal over divorce serve?

Savage points out that two social groups were in fact disadvantaged by the Divorce Act of 1857: wives of all classes and the lower-class poor. Besides regulating divorce itself, then, the Divorce Act had other power-effects, one of the most striking of which was the marginalization of women. Significantly, regardless of their real socioeconomic status, women were grouped by the Divorce Act into one large undifferentiated class, which was in turn legally aligned with the poor. Because "the poor" traditionally included all those without socioeconomic worth or of suspect moral status within Victorian society—vagabonds, the lazy, the disabled, criminals—women were implicitly placed outside the bounds of society proper and "proper" society by the discourse of this law.[12]

If we turn to the criticism voiced against the Divorce Act of 1857 for what was seen as its dangerous liberalism in regard to divorce rights for women and the poor, we find primarily men of the upper and middle classes concerned with the maintenance of the patriarchal and capitalist hegemony. Savage rightly remarks on the double standard that permitted husbands to indulge in extramarital affairs but that found adultery "a far greater injury to society when committed by women . . . in consequence of being attended with uncertainty as to the parentage of the offspring." Interestingly, this objection has little to do with class but everything to do with gender. In effect, any divorcing woman presented a strong challenge to the symbolism of male dominance gathered around the biological fact of paternity, with legal patrilinearity as its main discursive translation.[13] It is no accident that the standard Victorian marriage certificate included not only the occupation of the husband but also that of his father and wife's father. Marriage as an institution and a tropological system in Victorian discourse confirms the authority of fathers in particular and the male sex in general (as potential fathers). Similarly, it inscribes women into the system of sexual difference by appeal both to secular law and to biblical precedents. Ultimately, though, to be divorced by a woman is solely a man's scandal: divested of his paternal and patriarchal privileges, he finds himself repositioned as a "feminine" subject—the one being acted upon instead of the agent.

Viewed from this angle, the scandal surrounding Victorian divorce reveals a close connection to the "sin of the age," or infanticide. In " 'Sin of the Age': Infanticide and Illegitimacy in Victorian London," Ann R. Higginbotham examines the often-inconsistent juridical response to cases of infanticide from 1839 to 1906. She concludes that "a complex response to the whole problem of illegitimacy" was a major source of the legal and social controversy over infanticide. As with divorce, so infanticide raises the question of the distribution of power between the sexes. The child holds a special position at the intersection of the capitalist economy and the gender economy that structured Victorian society. Who produces, owns, and manages a child, and through the child, the future of society: the man or the woman? Also, like the marriage institution, the legal notion of "legitimating" the child's birth stems from the privileging of paternity over maternity within patriarchal thought. When the press reported that an increasing number of mothers were secretly delivering their own babies and taking the judgment of life or death into their own hands, their actions seemed to threaten a matriarchal insurrection against nature, God, and, of course, man.[14]

A brief comparison of the power-effects of the infanticide scandal, the Divorce Act, and the lunacy panics brings out a paradox about the positioning of the feminine within Victorian society. As a class constituted by gender alone, women are marginalized socioeconomically—for example, through property and divorce legislation—yet placed at the very center of society as the base of its reproductive economy, as recognized in the scandal over infanticide. Again, in both legal and medical domains, women who refused to conform to the restrictive ideology of the "True Woman" were declared mad and incarcerated. Yet, as Nina Auerbach argues in *Woman and the Demon,* the power of the feminine is reestablished elsewhere in Victorian culture, not only in literature and the arts but also in masculinist preserves such as political philosophy—witness Malthus's figuration of the social economy in terms of a fertile superwoman.[15] Finally, the crystallization of Victorian discourses and representations around "the feminine" generates power-effects that can be used almost interchangeably either by feminist interest groups or by their opponents. The outright contradictions and more subtle ambivalences that characterized the continuing Victorian debate over "the Woman Question" are perhaps the most salient example of this dialectic.[16] Each successive scandal that turned around women increased the space and power for co-optation by the other, competing or even hostile, subjectivities within Victorian society.

With this problematics of the feminine in mind, we can appreciate the Victorian actress's extremely precarious position, along with the fascination she held, and still holds. In " 'Come, Substantial Damages!' " Jane W. Stedman traces the rise and fall of Miss Fortescue (Emily May Finney), an actress of the lower class who dared to sue Lord Garmoyle for breach of promise after he broke off their engagement in 1884. More remarkable than the "scandal" of a marriage across classes is the fact that the press and public opinion in general came full circle from commiseration with to condemnation of the young actress.[17] What does this change in the public reception of Miss Fortescue signify?

Arthur Sullivan's remarks after auditioning Miss Fortescue hint at a disturbance within Victorian gender stereotypes. After describing her as "very intelligent, somewhat 'emancipist,' " he added: "Laf Haare auf den Zähnen" (she has hair on her teeth). Like many other young actresses, Miss Fortescue was a female head of household, with a bankrupt father, a mother, and a younger sister to support out of her earnings. The combination of her "grace of pose and demeanour" on stage with her independent style of talk and life offstage presented a quandary. Was she an alluring figure of "feminine" complaisance or a threatening figure of "masculine" will? Nina Auerbach has argued that apparently negative stereotypes of women in Victorian culture, such as the fallen woman, the prostitute, and the actress, actually exerted a subversive force on sexual difference.[18] But how, then, can we explain the abrupt fall of Miss Fortescue? If the Victorian actress in general enjoyed a special position that combined "womanly" desirability with "manly" independence, this ambivalent gender representation remains lodged within a discursive system whose ideological presuppositions are predominantly patriarchal, hence misogynistically defensive. The scandal over the inequality of social status between the partners in the Fortescue-Garmoyle case would seem, therefore, a smoke screen for anxiety over gender identity and its relation to power.

Interpretation of the fall of Miss Fortescue must also take into account the overlapping of two other stereotypes of the feminine in Victorian fiction, painting, photography, and journalism: the prostitute and the actress. Auerbach maintains that the sexist use of the phrase "public woman" for both prostitutes and actresses was offset by "the glamour of fallenness" which exerted a counterforce of its own. "The questionable social position of the . . . Victorian actress enhanced her mythic freedom."[19] In contrast, Tracy C. Davis documents the complex connections between the sign system of pornography and the sign system of the theater in "The Actress in Victorian Pornography." The Victorian actress violated the central tenets of the middle- and upper-class ideal for women: instead of domestic enclosure, the public stage; instead of full clothing, bare arms and legs; instead of socioeconomic dependence on her husband or father, financial independence and a profession of her own. In addition, the actress's relative freedom of body and speech suggested the disruptive presence of a distinctively feminine sexuality that did not at all coincide with either moral or medical definitions of women as instinctively modest, passive, and frigid.[20] Precisely because of her semiotic of desire and her "liberated" subjectivity, therefore, the actress as a powerful representation of the feminine could be re-encoded as a whore by those spokesmen in Victorian society interested in maintaining the inferior status of women. Miss Fortescue's "fall" as a "semiprofessional" was thus a strategic use of scandal, one aimed at foreclosing the theater as a legitimate career for women who wanted to move out of the domestic interior.

Julia Margaret Cameron offers an interesting example of the many strategies that Victorian women deployed in order to empower themselves and move beyond the enclosure of domesticity in spite of—and even by means of—the constraints on femininity operative in nineteenth-century Britain. A "respectable" wife and mother, Cameron created a stir by challenging the conventions of representation established in the male-dominated field of photography and by aggressively promoting her own individual talents as a photographer. As Joanne Lukitsh shows in "Julia Margaret Cameron and the 'Ennoblement' of Photographic Portraiture," the figure of a female photographer seemed to many of Cameron's contemporaries "an indecorous expression of power: a woman creating images of some of the most influential men of her society." There are several possible sources for the initial scandal that Cameron's photographs caused in the mid-1860s. Among these is the perceived threat that Cameron's abilities and status as a technician posed to the traditional socioeconomic division of labor between the two sexes, itself supported by the Victorian ideology of the two spheres. For example, with public action gendered as masculine and private feeling gendered as feminine, the production of photographic images—as an active process of representation and cultural definition—in the hands of a woman was scandalous in the sense of being "against nature," that is, against sexual difference as naturalized by Victorian ideology. Furthermore, as a professional artist who earned money for her work, an experimental photographer, and a married woman with children, Cameron demonstrated both the reproductive and the productive powers of woman—a sort of goddess of Domesticity Unbound.

Another possible source for the scandal raised around Cameron's photography has to do with relations between gender and class. As Lukitsh points out, Cameron's reforming ambitions did not pertain to the social impact of the widespread dissemination of portrait images, whether in the form of popular *cartes de visite* or copies of her own work. Perhaps in order to mask her disturbance of the Victorian gender hierarchy, Cameron chose her sitters from among the eminent men of the upper middle class, such as Alfred

Tennyson and Thomas Carlyle. In so doing, she managed to flatter the powerful of her own class, thereby gaining influence over them (her famed "tyrannizing" of her sitters), and also to position herself as an indispensable mediator between the public and their idols, thus ensuring her own personal fame. Cameron's combination of technological innovation and social conservatism (the latter further evidenced in the frequent allusions to the Old Masters of painting in her photographs) thus suggests a strategy of containment, whereby she was able to win eventual approval for her "unwomanly" desire to work outside the home precisely by idealizing or "ennobling" and re-legitimizing the authoritative men of her day.[21] In this political context, too, Cameron's particular style of focusing on the heads of her sitters but shooting them in profile suggests a compromise between acknowledging male superiority—man's greater intellect as supposedly reflected by his greater brain size—and feminizing photographic discourse by valorizing the closeup, the intimate and the private, thereby giving the Victorian viewer a peek at the great man's innermost feelings through his photo-portrait. Ironically, then, Cameron's intimate icons of famous men may have served to make the boundaries between the classes and the genders more rather than less porous. Instead of remaining inaccessibly aloof ideals, like the paintings on the walls of the National Gallery, Tennyson, Carlyle, and other national figures became widely—and promiscuously—accessible to the gaze of "the man and woman on the street," whatever their class or educational background. The scandal implicit in Cameron's photographs lies not only in her empowerment as a woman crossing over from the private into the public sphere but also in the circulation of desire which her photographs encouraged. A mid-Victorian inspecting a closeup photograph of Tennyson, author of "Mariana" and "The Palace of Art," might well look not for intimations of immortality but for hints of effeminacy in his face. As Cameron's comment to Herschel, one of her male sitters, reveals: "I . . . could then do a head that would be Valuable to all ages & I long to take your photograph with longing *unspeakable*."

The way in which Julia Margaret Cameron successfully negotiated a path between scandal and respectability might be compared with George Eliot's difficult positioning of herself in regard to conflicting Victorian representations of the feminine. In "George Eliot and the Journalists: Making the Mistress Moral," Teresa Mangum discusses the way in which gender expectations defined the relationship between the Victorian literary writer and his or her readership. More specifically, Mangum suggests that the personal lives of female writers were subjected to special scrutiny by reviewers, often for the purpose of discrediting their work as inferior to that of male writers.[22] The major strategy of diminishment used by the reviewers was to re-encode the author, who by definition had authority, into the woman, who by definition had none. This re-presentation enabled reviewers to fit Eliot back into contemporary biological, psychiatric, social, and theological truths about the "weaker sex." Moreover, the widespread resort to such *reductio ad feminam* not only in Eliot's case but in regard to other female writers of the period as well implies that Victorian aesthetic judgments reduplicated the gender bias operative in other domains.

Thus Eliot's essentially "feminine" nature, as seemingly proven by her monogamous relationship with George Henry Lewes, precludes her "possession of powerful genius"—that phallic force of creativity that Gerard Manley Hopkins considered the prerogative of the male sex.[23] Similarly, the reviewers' willingness to argue away the scandalous illegality of the Eliot-Lewes liaison in favor of romanticizing them as ideal lovers had the effect of muting Eliot's actual rejection of the marriage institution. Most insidious, however, are the critics' metaphors of sexual intercourse and even violence that limit the power-effects of Eliot's reputation as an author. For instance, a writer in the *Saturday Review* negatively refeminizes Eliot through a fantasy of her seduction by the professional men with whom she was associated during her career. Broadly susceptible to "masculine influence," Eliot is stripped of her authorial status as "the most masculine of her sex" and revealed as the good, if morally weak-kneed, daughter of the Victorian middle class—"a very woman." In a related scenario, her symbolic husband, Lewes, is seen as Eliot's indispensable better half, "a companion" "fertilising" her intellect in order that she might give birth, if not to children, then at least to novels. Because a Victorian woman is not able (not permitted) to write out of her own resources but must have male models to show her how, Eliot finds herself in a double bind, properly docile in learning her art from previous male authors but improperly promiscuous in learning from so many of them. As a reviewer for *Temple Bar* implies, not only Eliot's work but her very body "bore the impress now of one, now of another, of various masters."

The metaphorical association of the woman writer with sexual promiscuity here suggests that the representations of George Eliot and Miss Fortescue may have more in common than the two women's divergence in economic class, education, and career would indicate. To what extent was the female Victorian writer perceived as a "deviant" feminine subject, hence tropologically interchangeable with other "public women" such as actresses and prostitutes? And, from a slightly different angle, how might we compare the power-effects of Miss Fortescue's theatricalization of femininity with those generated by George Eliot's staging of multiple identities—"Marian," "George," "Mrs. Lewes," "little mother"? Auerbach reminds us of Eliot's imaginative involvement with the Victorian theater, as represented by the diva Alcharisi in *Daniel Deronda*. She sees Eliot's interest in theater and alternative self-representations as a positive assertion of the feminine in Victorian society: "For her . . . the art of translating oneself into a character was an act of devotion to the self's latent, and awesome, powers."[24] Yet perhaps Auerbach's vision of the possibility of women's self-empowerment through the creation of "character" in literature and the arts is overly optimistic in view of the countereffects of the misogynistic rhetoric of the reviewers and the masculinist ideological preferences of most Victorian arbiters of taste. At the same time, the ambivalent language of Eliot's own discourse must give us pause. For, like Elizabeth Barrett Browning—whose frank, "coarse" language concerning female sexuality in *Aurora Leigh* raised the eyebrows of many a scandalized reviewer in 1857—Eliot hesitates on the brink of asserting the superiority of a uniquely feminine order of knowledge and power.[25] Thus, in an early article, Eliot uses the dominant encoding of femininity in terms of the "True Woman" when she defends the intellectual woman for knowing what she knows—in silence. If in her novels Eliot is anything but silent in her criticisms of both men and women under patriarchy, the character Dorothea Brooke does, like Eliot herself, quietly (re)enter the middle-class social economy at the end of *Middlemarch*.[26]

The reviewers' insistence on reading George Eliot's books through her gendered body and treating her gendered body as a text to be deciphered also points to a larger structure characteristic of Victorian discourse: the practice of overlapping and even blurring metaphors and referents, fictions and facts. The "biographical fallacy" that characterizes Victorian literary criticism, as well as the practice of moralizing on life through literature, marks a "scandal" or crisis at the level of mimesis itself. Modern critics have noticed various forms of this disturbance in the norms for representation, such as the predominance of mirror imagery and the growing interest in the *doppelgänger* in nineteenth-century literature and painting.[27] With specific regard to gender, the body, and the body as text, the Victorian period may coincide with an "epistemic break" (Foucault) in which the gap between the truth of the mind or language is confronted and subverted by the truth of the body and its sexuality. This would manifest itself, for example, in the new and problematic importance given to the writer's body in relation to his or her works. Perhaps the recurrence of scandal in the Victorian period is a symptom of this deeper epistemological dis-ease.

James Anthony Froude's biography of Carlyle furnishes an interesting case of "scandal" in both the narrower moral and the broader representational sense. D. J. Trela discusses the uproar caused by Froude's disclosures about the private lives of Thomas and Jane Carlyle in "Froude on the Carlyles: The Victorian Debate over Biography." Here, the discourse of scandal is interdependent with at least two others: the discourse constituting the middle-class division of society into public spheres, and the discourse on the normative concept of "decorum," which in turn has both moral and aesthetic resonances. Specifically, in the writing of biography, "decorum" was taken by Victorians to mean a reticence about or actual omission of information concerning sexual and other bodily facts. Yet the controversy over the rules of decorum in regard to Froude's biography had the very opposite effect of what this term purports. Neither reticence nor propriety was observed as reviewers and general readers interpreted each bit of information about the Carlyles' domestic arrangement and sexual habits. Instead of laying this behavior down to yet another instance of Victorian hypocrisy, I would like to reconsider the connection between scandal, the dissemination of information, and the distribution of power.

In *History of Sexuality,* vol. 1, Michel Foucault criticizes "the repressive hypothesis," or the widely held view that the Victorians were prudish, censorious, and fearful when it came to acknowledging their own sexuality. On the related notion of decorum, Foucault argues that circumlocution and polite silence about matters of the body had a strategic effect. Instead of "repressing" or preventing general knowledge about sexuality, they valorized and encouraged a variety of "discourses concerning sex."[28] Turning to Froude's scandalous biography of Carlyle, it seems clear that the sexualization of the writer's life and works initiated by Froude was not counteracted by but rather supported by the controversy. Instead of a pattern of scandal and repression, the Froude case suggests that scandal is a major social mechanism for the dissemination of knowledge and the power which knowledge (of others) brings.

The close relationship between Christian confession and secular biography may offer some further insight into why Froude's biography of Carlyle created such a sensation. In theoretical terms, the "subject" of a confession, autobiography, or biography is "subjected" to the judgment of an audience invested with some degree of institutional or social power. At the same time, the "subject" of the discourse gains a certain position of delegated power within the ideological system he or she shares with the judging audience, and that he or she implicitly acknowledges by the very act of confessing. In this pact of knowledge/power, the values and beliefs held by the discursive subjects involved are not altered in the communicative exchange but instead reproduced and multiplied.

In Froude's biography, then, the textualization and "publication" of their private bodies and private words puts both Thomas and Jane Carlyle in the position of confessing—hence, already guilty—subjects on trial before the reader, who takes on the position of superior judge. By making the Carlyles into sexual and textual subjects, Froude also "subjects" them to our inspection as objects of knowledge and power. Not surprisingly, the language used by Victorian reviewers implies an acute awareness of the interplay of sexual knowledge and power. "When the veiled prophet exhibited his expressive countenance to his friends there was considerable disappointment," observed Allen Grant in *Temple Bar* (1881). The metaphor of the "veil" suggests that Carlyle has been transformed from authoritative guru to striptease girl: the sage has been disempowered, or "feminized." Likewise, even those who praised Froude for his revelations did so in eroticized language. In the *Academy* (1884), William Wallace called the biography "an honest and even courageous study in the moral nude." The Victorian sage translated into a titillating work of art underscores the inverse relationship between knowledge of the body and "truth" as constituted in a patriarchal culture. As the symbol of truth, the word of the sage is spectacularly subverted by the needs, desires, and weaknesses of his own body. Like Rosina Bulwer's "madness," Carlyle's impotence offers itself as another symptom of disorder in the social body. As A. G. Sedgwick concluded in the *Nation* (1884), "Froude may congratulate himself on having very nearly destroyed the authority of his master."

Recently, Victorianists have concentrated on the construction of gender "types," and in particular on the emergence of the "New Woman" and the "homosexual" as new social presences in the last two decades of the nineteenth century.[29] Like the category of the "feminine," the "New Woman" and the "invert" were both highly problematic and crucially functional within Victorian culture. The midcentury furor involving Charles Kingsley's on-again, off-again support of women's education offers a preview of the ambivalence and doublespeak of feminists as well as their opponents in the debate over the intellectual New Woman in the 1890s.

In "The Muscular Christian As Schoolmarm," John C. Hawley, S. J., presents the Reverend Charles Kingsley as a reformer who stopped short of endorsing a revolution in the status of women when the feminists themselves began to get "beyond his (or any man's) control." A close look at Kingsley's rhetoric, even in the days of his enthusiasm for the cause of women's emancipation from legal and economic strictures, reveals a mixture of misogynistic premises and liberal phrasemaking. In his 1857 novel, *Two Years Ago,* for instance, Kingsley advocates education for middle-class women but on the grounds that, if left untutored in their maternal duties by men, women will rear "sons and daughters as sordid and unwholesome" as themselves. In proposing to educate women as governesses at Queen's College, Hawley observes, Kingsley and F. D. Maurice were endorsing a "*stabilizing* development" in society that would actually perpetuate the socioeconomic marginalization of women.[30] The fundamentally conservative strategy behind Victorian liberal feminism can also be seen in an article in the *English Woman's Journal* in 1859. Praising Kingsley, the journal calls on women to "free" their husbands from the domestic sphere. Women are warned not to disturb the boundaries drawn between the two spheres, not to turn the true man and the citizen—the Muscular Christian—into a mere breadwinner and domestic adjunct. Yet whose "freedom" is asserted here? Besides preserving the mystification of sexual difference by upholding the doctrine of separate but equal spheres—the woman in her proper place and the man everywhere else— the identification of "man" alone with "citizen" implicitly excludes the woman from any rights under the British state.[31]

Arguably, a deep gender anxiety underlies Kingsley's love/ hate affair with the Victorian women' s movement—witness his very "muscular" indictment of radical feminists as women who "did not wish to be women, but very bad imitations of men." As Hawley also suggests, Kingsley's withdrawal from the suffrage movement in the late 1860s was motivated by a concern lest the freeing of feminine subjectivity lead to "hysteria, male and female," a sexualized hysteria released as a result of confusion over the proper roles of the "manly man" and the "womanly woman." In addition to feminist activism, Victorian homoeroticism, as represented by the discourse of Kingsley himself, must be considered as one of the chief irruptions into the traditional social order. In fact, the gospel of Muscular Christianity provided Kingsley and other men with what Peter Gay calls a "screen of . . . assertive masculinity" for their homosexual panic.[32] For instance, the stereotypical features of the "model Christian hero" of Kingsley's medievalizing fiction—"crisp, black hair," "pale but healthy complexion," "long and sinewy arms"—reappear in the androgynous beauty of Walter Pater's artistic heroes in *The Renaissance:* both texts have the effect of relativizing femininity and masculinity.

Kingsley's embattled relation to the emerging New Woman highlights an important link between femininity and modernity in nineteenth-century discourses.[33] Above all, the so-called New Woman operates as a figure of and in speech which is adaptable to a variety of ideological strategies.[34] Thus the "New Woman" trope was used by conservative men and women alike to ridicule and attack the feminist movement as a whole. Just as significantly, the New Woman is situated within the rhetoric of the gendered body which crisscrossed the domains of science, law, and aesthetics. The New Woman hence becomes the focus of anxieties concerning the crossing and even the dissolution of gender boundaries, with all the implications that this change holds for the patriarchal structure of society.

Cross-gendered metaphors abound in Victorian diatribes against the New Woman. She is figured in terms of war—an activity long reserved for men only—and the myth of the Amazon, advancing on society in "tumultuous battalions" with "drums beating and colors flying."[35] She is also figured as a mad scientist, a sort of feminine Dr. Frankenstein who practices vivisection, watching "with delight the struggles of the dying salmon." Both of these rhetorical codes depict woman as gaining new power through mastering what have traditionally been masculine preserves of knowledge, war, and science. At the same time, they refigure the feminine body in terms of phallic imagery. The castrating Amazon and vivisectionist are thus related through a sexualized metonymy to the bluestocking whose phallic nose is "too large for feminine beauty as understood by men" and whose hair is cut short. A third tropological intersection is that between the New Woman and the familiar Victorian stereotype of the spinster.[36] Both represent "insatiate" feminine desire but also evoke a "desexualized half-man." These figurations are not opposites but correlated defenses of the ideology of sexual difference that marks active desire as masculine, passive neutrality as feminine. In short, the "scandal" of the New Woman seems to be less that the feminine is changing into the masculine than that the feminine is appropriating and incorporating the masculine.

Victorians were equally if not more fearful of the new type of the "invert," which, like the New Woman, was associated with modernity, heralding dangerous changes in the patriarchal order for some Victorians, and viewed as liberating alternatives by others. The *Speaker,* a weekly paper, actually accused Oscar Wilde of leading the movement of New Women: Wilde's explicit rejection of the duty of reproduction in all its senses—sexual, aesthetic, and economic—made him seem a likely inciter of New Women dedicated to refusing marriage and motherhood for art's sake.[37] As a dandy and an aesthete, in his daily activities and in his writings, Wilde was a spectacularly transgressive, hence scandalous, figure. But Wilde's behavior and witticisms were in deadly earnest, as the famous trials organized around him in the 1890s—perhaps the best-known scandal of the entire nineteenth century—were to prove. Although critical attention has focused primarily on Wilde's challenge to traditional moral and social laws, and more recently on his representative role in wider changes within gender ideology during the late Victorian period, the Wilde trials also involved a redrawing of political power lines that implicated the class structure and the law at the state level. In *Between Men: English Literature and Male Homosocial Desire,* Eve Kosofsky Sedgwick argues that "in any male-dominated society, there is a special relationship between male homosocial (*including* homosexual) desire and the structures for maintaining and transmitting patriarchal power."[38] In fact, the Wilde trials were yet another instance of the recurrent "homosexual panics" among the ruling elite in Victorian Britain.[39] Because the continued dominance of middle- and upper-class males depended on their marrying and participating in the reproductive economy, homosexual desire had to be strictly regulated by the patriarchy itself. Scandal based on homophobia was the most effective strategy for the containment of homosexual desire because it reasserted the primacy of heterosexual norms and ensured the continuance of the status quo.

Ironically, however, the Wilde trials also served to increase the visibility of homosocial desire at the same time as, in the domain of science, sexologists were classifying the "invert" as a permanent psychosexual and social type.[40] The Labouchère Amendment (1885), by illegalizing homosexual intercourse and discourse, in public or private, acknowledged and inscribed the power-effects of "inversion" into the law itself. As with the Victorians' problematic overvaluation of the feminine, so the homosexual was both regulated and invested by the proliferation of late Victorian discourses and representations of the "effeminate" man. Finally, given the intense coverage of the trials in Victorian newspapers that reached literate readers of all classes, the Wilde scandal arguably had the effect of disseminating rather than suppressing knowledge about the homosocial structuring of Victorian Britain and its stronghold in the homoerotically directed high culture of literature and art. On one hand, the New Woman and what one might call the New Man combined to weaken the patriarchal ground of society. This outcome is exemplified by the breakdown of gender identities, marriage, and "truth" in Thomas Hardy's *Jude the Obscure* (1895), itself the source of another scandal. On the other hand, the increasing fluidity of boundaries of all kinds, and the treatment of each successive departure from traditional norms as a dangerous "scandal"—requiring containment of the irruptive forces along with reassertion of the old value system—had the effect of hystericizing the social body of mid- and late Victorian England itself. This paradoxical situation of enforced alarm actually established agencies of hegemonic power, such as the law and medicine, to intervene even more busily in people's daily lives.

We have been taught by such influential studies as Steven Marcus's *The Other Victorians* to presuppose a division of nineteenth-century society into "public" and "private," "underground" and "respectable." But to what extent are these categories themselves carried over from Victorian discourse, with its own ideological agenda?[41] Similarly, we have been accustomed to thinking of the "cause" of a scandal as deviant behavior and the "effect" of a scandal as the reimposition of social norms from above—in the present case, by the central and "repressive" authority of the middle class. Yet does this hierarchical view of power adequately explain the import of the scandals discussed in the present collection?[42] Rather than a cycle of revolt and repression, the itinerary of scandal seems to move from protest, to dissemination, and then to assimilation of dissenting opinions and deviant behaviors, making these, in turn, the next "norm" to be broken. The power of knowledge seems to move laterally, and within this dynamic, scandal takes place as spatial and temporal *drift* of conflicting ideologies and practices.

An example of the lateral drift of knowledge/power is the series of scandals involving gambling during the Victorian period. In "The (Other) Great Evil: Gambling, Scandal, and the National Anti-Gambling League," David C. Itzkowitz demonstrates that the league's attempt to suppress gambling as a moral vice and social danger succeeded instead in encouraging the development of a new industry. More specifically, the dissemination of information about gambling through several scandals involving the upper class had two major effects. First, the rapid professionalization of gambling enabled men and women at all socioeconomic levels to "play" at a distance, that is, to bet on horse races which they never attended. This mediated representation of the races allowed gambling to become democratized. The lower classes were given the chance to "play" at being aristocrats, which, in turn, served the conservative political agenda by deflecting economic discontent. Second, betting on the races confirmed the Victorian work ethic across all classes of society. As Itzkowitz points out, traditional moralistic discourse on gambling as sin and "unreason" shifted toward a purely secular rationalization of gambling as the victory of reason over chance. This alteration in ideology served the interests of the gambling industry, itself a product of the lower rather than the upper classes. The series of scandals over gambling, therefore, moved knowledge and power not only from the top down and the bottom up, but also diagonally across Victorian England.

What is our position today in the lateral drift of knowledge/power as we study Victorian scandals? Are we, like the "respectable" Victorians before us, perpetuating social and moral norms by focusing on those who break them? Are we, again like the Victorians, thereby implicitly agreeing to the necessity of intervention in our lives by a heterogeneous set of social agencies, each of which claims to be in possession of the truth, and each of which promises to restore social order to our diseased body politic? What finally are our own ideological investments in knowing about the "scandals" of others in the past century? As Jeffrey Weeks cautions: "There was no Golden Age of sexual propriety, and the search for it in a mythologised past tells us more about present confusions than past glories."[43]

Notes

1. In this essay, I will use "discourse" to mean verbal texts and "representation" to mean visual texts. In certain contexts, however, I will use "representation" in the broader sense of any mode of mimesis.

On the construction of gender, and the body as paradigmatic metaphor, see Susan Sontag, *Illness As Metaphor* (New York: Farrar, Straus and Giroux, 1978); Michel Foucault, *History of Sexuality*, vol. 1, trans. Robert Hurley (New York: Random House, 1980); various essays noted below from *Representations* 14 (Spring 1986); and Susan Rubin Suleiman, ed., *The Female Body in Western Culture: Contemporary Perspectives* (Cambridge: Harvard University Press, 1986). For the notion of discourse and representation as "strategies" that bind knowledge to power, I am primarily indebted throughout to the work of Foucault. See, for example, his conversations on the development of his theories in *Power/Knowledge: Selected Interviews and Writings, 1972–1977*, trans. Colin Gordon et al. (New York: Pantheon, 1980).

2. For documentation of the centrality of "woman" and the larger category of the "feminine" to Victorian thought, see the bibliographies in Martha Vicinus, ed., *Suffer and Be Still: Women in the Victorian Age* (Bloomington: Indiana University Press, 1972) and *A Widening Sphere: Changing Roles of Victorian Women* (Bloomington: Indiana University Press, 1977).

3. On "power-effects," see Foucault, *History*, 1: pt. 4, chap. 2 and chaps. 10–11 in *Power/Knowledge*.

4. See Jill Conway, "Stereotypes of Femininity in a Theory of Sexual Evolution," in *Suffer and Be Still*, 140–54; Thomas Laqueur, "Orgasm, Generation, and the Politics of Reproductive Biology," *Representations* 14 (Spring 1986): 1–41; Mary Poovey, " 'Scenes of Indelicate Character': The Medical 'Treatment' of Victorian Women," *Representations* 14 (Spring 1986): 137–68; and Ellen L. Bassuk, "The Rest Cure: Repetition or Resolution of Victorian Women's Conflicts," in *The Female Body in Western Culture*, 139–51.

5. See Michel Foucault, *Madness and Civilization: A History of Insanity in the Age of Reason,* trans. Richard Howard (New York: Random House, 1973), esp. 136–58 on hysteria as a feminine disorder; Vida Skultans, *English Madness: Ideas on Insanity, 1580–1890* (London: Routledge and Kegan Paul, 1979); and Elaine Showalter, *The Female Malady: Women, Madness, and English Culture, 1830–1980* (New York: Pantheon, 1985).

6. On the "hystericization" of the female body as a strategy of social control, see Foucault, *History,* 1:103–14. In *The Policing of Families,* trans. Robert Hurley (New York: Pantheon, 1979), Jacques Donzelot also offers a provocative critique of the role of madness and general health care in the "normalization" of women and children during the nineteenth century: "Functioning as a surface of absorption for the undesirables of the family order, the general hospitals, convents, and foundling hospitals served at the same time as a strategical base for a whole series of corrective interventions in family life" (25–26).

7. Skultans, 52–68.

8. Kurata's feminist interpretation of *The Woman in White* should be compared with D. A. Miller's analysis of both feminine and masculine "gender slippage" in this novel. (See "*Cage aux folles:* Sensation and Gender in Wilkie Collins's *The Woman in White,*" *Representations* 14 [Spring 1986]: 107–36.) Miller further suggests that the experience of sensational fiction made the Victorian reader into "the subject of a *body*" whose gender is as problematic and prone to hystericization as that of the fictional characters (111, 117, his emphasis).

9. On Charlotte Perkins Gilman's "The Yellow Wallpaper," see Annette Kolodny, "A Map for Rereading: Gender and the Interpretation of Literary Texts," in *The New Feminist Criticism: Essays on Women, Literature, and Theory,* ed. Elaine Showalter (New York: Pantheon, 1985), 46–62.

10. On the feminine and the mad as "other," see Foucault, *Madness,* esp. chap. 9. "The asylum . . . organized [guilt] for the madman as a consciousness of himself, and as a non-relation to the keeper; it organized it for the man of reason as an awareness of the

Other, a therapeutic intervention in the madman's existence" (247).

11. On the production of scandals by the way in which news was reported in the Victorian press, see Thomas F. Boyle, " 'Morbid Depression Alternating with Excitement': Sex in Victorian Newspapers," in *Sexuality and Victorian Literature,* ed. Don Richard Cox (Knoxville: University of Tennessee Press, 1984), 212–33.

12. The Victorian journalist and social historian Henry Mayhew classified the poor with social "undesirables" such as vagrants, prostitutes, and criminals. On the use of such classifications as a strategy of social control during the nineteenth century, see Foucault, *Madness,* and Donzelot.

13. For critiques of the ideology of paternity, see, for example, Sandra M. Gilbert and Susan Gubar, *The Madwoman in the Attic: The Woman Writer and the Nineteenth-Century Literary Imagination* (New Haven: Yale University Press, 1979); Jonathan Culler, "Reading As a Woman," in *On Deconstruction: Theory and Criticism after Structuralism* (Ithaca, N.Y.: Cornell University Press, 1982), 43–64; and Eve Kosofsky Sedgwick, *Between Men: English Literature and Male Homosocial Desire* (New York: Columbia University Press, 1985). As Culler wryly concedes, paternity is a "fact" that only the woman can know, and knowledge is power.

14. For a discussion of childbirth as a leading metaphor in several Victorian discourses on social control, see Loralee MacPike, "The Fallen Woman's Sexuality: Childbirth and Censure," in *Sexuality and Victorian Literature,* 54–71.

15. See Catherine Gallagher, "The Body Versus the Social Body in the Works of Thomas Malthus and Henry Mayhew," *Representations* 14 (Spring 1986): "The relation of the social theorist to the society . . . is that of an anxious lover to the body of the beloved" (85).

16. See Elizabeth K. Helsinger, Robin L. Sheets, and William Veeder, *The Woman Question: Society and Literature in Britain and America, 1837–1883,* 3 vols. (New York: Garland, 1983).

17. To an extent, marriages between actresses and aristocrats were popularly approved of as a sign of the democratic possibility of upward mobility, especially for women. See Christopher Kent,

"Image and Reality: The Actress and Society," in *A Widening Sphere*, 94–116.

18. Nina Auerbach, *Woman and the Demon: The Life of a Victorian Myth* (Cambridge: Harvard University Press, 1982), 185–86.

19. Ibid., 182, 205.

20. On women's own representations of their sexuality and erotic desires, in contrast to the mainstream ideology of the "True Woman," see Peter Gay, "An Erotic Record," in his *The Bourgeois Experience, Victoria to Freud*, vol. 1, *Education of the Senses* (New Haven: Yale University Press, 1984), 71–108.

21. Deirdre David borrows the concept of "strategies of containment" from Frederic Jameson in order to analyze George Eliot in *Intellectual Women and Victorian Patriarchy: Harriet Martineau, Elizabeth Barrett Browning, George Eliot* (London: Macmillan, 1987), 164. David also discusses a different attempt to resolve the conflict between the Victorian definition of femininity and intellectual ambition in Elizabeth Barrett Browning, whose situation is more closely comparable to Cameron's in that both set their artistic vocation squarely within the framework of True Womanhood.

22. For a discussion of sexual knowledge, authoring, and authority for the woman writer, see Susan Gubar, " 'The Blank Page' and the Issues of Female Creativity," in *The New Feminist Criticism*, 292–313. Judith Lowder Newton focuses on the ways in which women authors protected yet asserted their gender identity in *Women, Power, and Subversion: Social Strategies in British Fiction, 1778–1869* (Athens: University of Georgia Press, 1981).

23. Gilbert and Gubar show in *Madwoman in the Attic* how the dominant phallocentric metaphors for literary creativity pose special difficulties for women writers.

24. Auerbach, 205.

25. According to Cora Kaplan in *"Aurora Leigh,"* in *Feminist Criticism and Social Change: Sex, Class, and Race in Literature and Culture*, ed. Judith Newton and Deborah Rosenfelt (New York: Methuen, 1985): "Approved and taboo subjects are slyly intertwined so that menstruation, childbirth, suckling, child-rearing, rape and prostitution are all braided together in the metaphorical

language" (144). Still, this textualization did not prevent Victorian reviewers from accusing Barrett Browning of using " 'coarse' " and " 'unfeminine' " language (142).

26. See Auerbach, 54–62. "Despite what may have been George Eliot's conscious intention," Auerbach argues, "the shadow of female power determines the linguistic structure" of her discourse (55). But if female power is positive, then why use the negative term "shadow"? Less ambiguously, Wendell Stacy Johnson (*Living in Sin: The Victorian Sexual Revolution* [Chicago: Nelson-Hall, 1979], 82–95), and Phyllis Rose (*Parallel Lives: Five Victorian Marriages* [New York: Knopf, 1984], 197–237) approach Eliot as an exemplary Victorian rebel. Taking sharp issue with Rose, Gertrude Himmelfarb (*Marriage and Morals among the Victorians* [New York: Knopf, 1986], 3–22) argues that Eliot is conservative, if not reactionary, in her sexual politics: "In fact, Eliot's behavior . . . was calculated . . . to strengthen 'morality as it had been known' and to reestablish it on a more serious, a more *philosophical* basis" (17, her emphasis). Most recently, David has seen Eliot as "a 'man's' woman intellectual" (*Intellectual Women*, 171).

27. See Masao Miyoshi, *The Divided Self: A Perspective on the Literature of the Victorians* (New York: New York University Press, 1969).

28. See Foucault, *History*, 1: pt. 1, chap. 1. This section also compares the exchange of power/knowledge in the confessional situation to that in the publicization of sexuality.

29. See Jeffrey Weeks, *Coming Out: Homosexual Politics in Britain from the Nineteenth Century to the Present* (London: Quartet, 1979).

30. On the marginal socioeconomic position of the governess, see M. Jeanne Peterson, "The Victorian Governess: Status Incongruence in Family and Society," in *Suffer and Be Still*, 3–19.

31. Significantly, Kingsley uses a similar rhetorical strategy when discussing the equality of the sexes in a letter to John Stuart Mill, another famous supporter of women's education. "Any sound reformation of the relations between woman and man, must proceed from women who have fulfilled well their relations as they

now exist. . . . Only those who have worked well in harness, will be able to work well out of harness" (quoted by Hawley, above). Compared with runaway slaves earlier in the same passage, women are here metaphorized as work animals needing domestication and continual surveillance lest their "animal" instinct for freedom reassert itself "out of harness." Clearly, Kingsley intends men to remain in the position of mastery.

32. Peter Gay, *The Bourgeois Experience, Victoria to Freud,* vol. 2, *The Tender Passion* (New Haven: Yale University Press, 1986), 302. On the conflict between the "sacred bond" of marriage and for bidden homoerotic desire in Kingsley, see 297–309. Sedgwick discusses the connections between heterosexual marriage—of which Kingsley was a vociferous advocate—and homosocial relations (which could legitimate homosexual relations) in Victorian culture.

33. On the link between the feminine, modernity, and new forms of power, compare Christine Buci-Glucksmann, "Catastrophic Utopia: The Feminine As Allegory of the Modern," *Representations* 14 (Spring 1986): 220–29, with Gay, "Sexualizing Modernity," in *The Bourgeois Experience,* 2:312–28.

34. Jenni Calder gives a concise overview of the main political currents surrounding the figure of the New Woman in chap. 12 of her *Women and Marriage in Victorian Fiction* (New York: Oxford University Press, 1976). For a more recent study of the New Woman, see Lucy Bland, "The Married Woman, the 'New Woman,' and the Feminist: Sexual Politics in the 1890s," in *Equal or Different: Women's Politics, 1800–1914,* ed. Jane Rendall (Oxford: Basil Blackwell, 1987), 141–64. Helena Michie provides many insights into the system of tropes for the female body in Victorian culture in *The Flesh Made Word: Female Figure and Women's Bodies* (New York: Oxford University Press, 1987).

35. All the quotations from Victorian periodical literature in this paragraph are taken from "The Multifaceted Image of the New Woman: Enemy of Social Order," an unpublished paper by James M. Brophy.

36. On the powerful image of the spinster, see Auerbach, chap. 4.

37. As Regenia Gagnier explains Wilde's oppositional stance: "Wilde's homosexuality, contrary to mainstream notions of 'productive' or 'purposive' sexuality, likewise contributed to his particular formulation of aestheticism, including his explicit rejections of Victorian notions of the natural (as in 'Nature imitates art'), of the purposive (as in his stance of idleness), and of the productive (as in 'art for art's sake')." See her *Idylls of the Marketplace: Oscar Wilde and the Victorian Public* (Stanford: Stanford University Press, 1986), 139.

38. Sedgwick, 25, her emphasis.

39. For an analysis of gender, class, and the law regarding homosexuality in Victorian Britain, see Richard Dellamora, *Masculine Desire: Victorian Aestheticism, Sexual Politics, and Tradition* (Chapel Hill: University of North Carolina Press, 1990).

40. See Jeffrey Weeks, *Sexuality and Its Discontents: Meanings, Myths, and Modern Sexualities* (London: Routledge and Kegan Paul, 1985).

41. For a different criticism of Marcus and the "repressive hypothesis," see F. Barry Smith, "Sexuality in Britain, 1800–1900: Some Suggested Revisions" (in *A Widening Sphere*): "The impressive work of the 1960s by Peter Cominos, Steven Marcus, and Phyllis Grosskurth . . . has served to strengthen the received view that has come down to us" (184).

42. For a critique of the monarchical and patriarchal presuppositions in the hierarchical modeling of power, see Foucault, *Power/Knowledge.*

43. Weeks, *Sexuality and Its Discontents,* 16.

Contributors

Tracy C. Davis, assistant professor in theater and English, Northwestern University, is the author of *Actresses As Working Women: Their Social Identity in Victorian Culture,* and coeditor of Routledge's series on Gender and Theatre. She has published articles on nineteenth- and twentieth-century sexual politics, theater reception, the acting profession, historiography, popular culture, and feminist theater. Her current research focuses on the economic history of the Victorian theater.

Kristine Ottesen Garrigan is professor of English at DePaul University, Chicago. Author of *Ruskin on Architecture: His Thought and Influence* and *Victorian Art Reproductions in Modern Sources: A Bibliography,* she has published numerous essays and reviews on Victorian subjects.

John C. Hawley, S. J., assistant professor of English literature and women's studies at Santa Clara University, has published in *Victorian Periodicals Review, Nineteenth-Century Studies,* and *Children's Literature Association Quarterly.* A member of the Modern Language Association's Executive Committee on Religious Approaches to Literature, he is also vice-president of the Conference on Christianity and Literature.

Ann R. Higginbotham is associate professor of history at

Eastern Connecticut State University. Her essay, "Respectable Sinners: Salvation Army Rescue Work with Unmarried Mothers," is included in *Religion in the Lives of English Women, 1760–1914*. She is currently at work on a study of unmarried mothers in Victorian London.

David C. Itzkowitz, professor of history at Macalester College, St. Paul, Minnesota, is the author of *Peculiar Privilege: A Social History of English Foxhunting, 1753–1885*, and has published articles on the history of gambling in England. He is now undertaking a study of Victorian Anglo-Jewry.

Marilyn J. Kurata, associate professor of English at the University of Alabama at Birmingham, has published on Dickens, Hardy, Eliot, Tennyson, and detective fiction. Besides teaching Victorian literature and women's studies, she serves on the board of directors of the Alabama Humanities Foundation.

Joanne Lukitsh is a visiting lecturer in the Department of History of Art, Ohio State University. She is author of *Julia Margaret Cameron: Her Work and Career* and has been the recipient of a Rice University Mellon Postdoctoral Fellowship and an American Council of Learned Societies Grant-in-Aid for her research on the history of photography.

Teresa Mangum is assistant professor of English at the University of Iowa. She is currently writing a book to be entitled "Sarah Grand and the New Woman Novel."

Thaïs E. Morgan is associate professor of English at Arizona State University, where she teaches critical theory and interdisciplinary studies. Her most recent publication is the collection, *Victorian Sages and Cultural Discourse: Renegotiating Gender and Power*. She is now writing a book about the politics of gender and canonicity from mid-Victorian to early Modern poetry.

Gail L. Savage, assistant professor of history at George Washington University, is preparing a book about divorce in England from 1857 to 1937. Her articles on this subject have appeared in the *Journal of Social History* and *Historical Papers.*

Jane W. Stedman is professor of English emeritus at Roosevelt University in Chicago. She is the editor of *Gilbert before Sullivan,* her introduction to which helped to launch scholarly interest in W. S. Gilbert. Her work has appeared in *Suffer and Be Still, W. S. Gilbert: A Century of Scholarship and Comment, Shakespeare and the Victorian Stage,* and other collections, as well as in such journals as *Modern Philology, Brontë Society Transactions, Victorian Studies, Nineteenth-Century Theater Research,* and *The Arnoldian.* She is currently writing a biography of Gilbert.

D. J. Trela, assistant professor of English at Roosevelt University, is the author of *Carlyle Writing "Cromwell"* and editor of *Margaret Oliphant: Essays on a Gentle Subversive.* He is also editing Carlyle's *Historical Sketches* and Oliphant's uncollected short stories.

Index

19, 227–28, 299; opinions on
contemporaries, 182; public
image of, 181, 184–85,
189–90, 199–201, 305. *See
also* Carlyle, Jane; Froude,
James Anthony
Carrier, Norman, 26, 40n18,
41n19, 41n29
Carrington, Charles, 131n22
Carroll, Lewis (Charles Lutwidge
Dodgson), 231n17
Carte, Richard D'Oyly, 70,
75–76, 83
Cartes de visite, 7, 124–25, 208,
211–18, 298
Chant, Laura Ormiston, 127
Chapman, John, 159–60, 166
Charley, W. T., 257
Chesler, Phyllis, 43
Childbearing: and insanity, 278,
281; and paternity, 18,
293–94, 315n13; physical
demands of, 150–51. *See also*
Concealment of birth; Infanticide; Mothers, unmarried
Chivalry, 134–36, 141, 144–45,
153
Clarke, Edward, 151
Class distinctions: in cases of
wrongful confinement, 46,
58–59; disrupted by
photographic portraiture,
211–12, 214–17, 298–99;
among divorce petitioners,
12–13, 18–33, 293; and
gambling, 236–37, 247–52,
311–12; and marriage, 70–
77, 91, 295–96, 309–10,
315n17; scandal as challenge

to, 293, 295–96, 298–99,
309–10
Clubbe, John, 193, 204, 205n6
Collins, Thomas, 16
Collins, Wilkie: *The Woman in
White*, 52–59, 63, 67n18,
290, 314n8
Commission on Divorce, 14–15
Commissioners in Lunacy,
50–51, 61–62, 66n12
Concealment of birth: actual trials
for, 273–76; as alternate
charge to infanticide, 264,
267–69, 273; conviction rates
for, 268, 269, 271, 273–75;
judicial leniency in cases of,
274–76. *See also* Infanticide
Confessions of Nemesis Hunt, The,
113–14
Conolly, John, 52, 56–57
Contemporary Review, 174, 190,
197–99, 202–3
Conway, Jill, 313n4
Court Theatre (London), 85–86
Crim. Con. Gazette, 105
*Crissie, A Music-Hall Sketch of To-
Day*, 112–13
Critic and Good Literature, 187–88
Cross, John Walter: *George Eliot's
Life. . . . See George Eliot's
Life . . . (Cross)
Culler, Jonathan, 315n13
Curgenven, J. Brendon, 259

Daily Telegraph, 51–52, 58, 59,
80, 94n35, 256n39
Darrah, William C., 230n8

Darwin, Charles, 221
David, Deirdre, 316n21, 317n26
Davies, Emily, 140, 142–43, 144–45
Days' Doings, 107–8, 109
Defoe, Daniel, 65
de Lauretis, Teresa, 133n43
Dellamora, Richard, 319n39
Derby, Lord, 48, 51
Dial, 188, 192
Dickens, Charles: *Hard Times*, 38n4
Disdéri, A. A. E., 212, 214
Divorce, 11–37; access by social class to, 12–13, 18–33, 293; access by women to, 26–36, 293; actual cases of, 22–25, 30–33, 34–35; expense of, 12, 13, 22; grounds for, 12, 14–18; as husband's prerogative, 11–13, 16–18; incidence of, 11, 18–22, 36–37; *in forma pauperis* procedure for, 22, 32, 41n20; and the press, 19, 25, 36–37, 292–93; regional rates of, 33–36. *See also* Divorce Act; Judicial separation; Protection orders
Divorce Act (1857), 11–37; effects of, 19–37, 293; as favoring husband, 12–18, 293; parliamentary debate over, 11–18; and Victorian assumptions about women, 14–18. *See also* Divorce
Donzelot, Jacques, 314n6, 315n12
Doré, Gustave, 221

Dowden, Edward, 163, 173
Drummond, Henry, 16, 17
Dunn, Waldo, 203
Dwork, Deborah, 288n61
Dworkin, Andrea, 104

Edinburgh Review, 164–65, 171
Education, women's. *See* Women's education
Eliot, George (Mary Anne Evans), 159–79, 300–3, 317n26; *Adam Bede*, 171, 174–75, 261–62, 266, 282; biography of, 159–79; domesticity of, 167–69; and alleged emotional dependence on men, 163–64; *Daniel Deronda*, 302; as erring woman, 159, 160, 163, 168, 171–72, 174–75; and alleged intellectual dependence on men, 164–67, 300–1; marriage to John Walter Cross, 160; *Middlemarch*, 302; *The Mill on the Floss*, 174–76; novels interpreted as autobiographical, 174–76; as partner in "companionate marriage," 167–69, 176; as partner in "grand romance," 167, 169–70, 172, 300–1; and self-naming, 176–77, 302–3; reputation as writer, 159, 164, 172, 173, 177, 301. *See also George Eliot's Life* . . . (Cross)
Elsom, John, 125
English Woman's Journal, 140–42, 306–7
Entr'acte, 74, 79, 95n38

Gernsheim, Helmut, 229n2,
230n7, 230n9, 231n17,
232n18
Gilbert, Sandra and Susan Gubar:
*The Madwoman in the
Attic* . . . , 43, 315n13,
316n23
Gilbert, William Schwenk, 71,
77–83, 86, 90–91, 94n38
Gilman, Charlotte Perkins: "The
Yellow Wallpaper," 291
Girouard, Mark, 134–35
Gladstone, William Ewart, 11,
13, 16–17, 38n10
Good Words, 148
Gordon-Cumming, William, 249
Gounod, Charles François, 60
Governesses, 137, 138, 143,
278, 306
Grant, Allen, 183, 305
Graphic, 80, 83, 86
Grey, George, 14, 286n47
Griffin, Susan, 125
Grossmith, George, 71
Gubar, Susan, 43, 315n13,
316n22, 316n23

Haight, Gordon S., 159, 161
Hambley, E. B., 165–66, 169
Hamilton, Gail, 185, 188, 204n6
Hardy, Thomas: *Jude the Obscure,*
310
Harris, Frank, 76
Harrison, Frederic, 195
Harveian Society, 258, 259, 265,
272
Havers, Michael, 256n37
Hawke, John, 239, 241,
245–46, 251, 253n10

Headlam, Beatrice, 104
Here and There, 108
Herschel, John Frederick William,
217, 221, 223, 226, 228–29,
300
Hill, Robert Gardiner, 49–50
Himmelfarb, Gertrude, 317n26
Hobson, J. A., 239–40, 244,
253n10, 254n18
Hodson, Henrietta, 93n19
Hoffer, Peter C., 285n30
Hogge, J. M., 241–42, 253n10
Holcombe, Lee, 38n3
Homosexuality and homoero-
ticism, 306–7, 309–11,
318n32
Horstman, Allen, 38n3, 94n38
Houghton, Walter E., 39n13
Hubbard, Sarah, 188
Hunt, Henry Thornton, 160
Hunt, William Holman, 221, 222
Hunter, Robert, 255n32
Hutton, Richard Holt, 142, 174
Hysteria, 146, 290–92, 307,
310–11, 314n6. *See also*
Insanity

Illegitimate children. *See*
Concealment of birth; Infanticide; Mothers, unmarried
Illustrated London News, 92, 209,
216
Infanticide, 257–82; actual trials
for, 265–72; compared to
murders of older children,
278–79; incidence of,
257–59, 262–64, 269, 271,
274, 282; judicial leniency in
cases of, 262, 268–72, 279;

laws regarding, 272–73, 281; and medical profession, 258, 263, 272, 281; and New Poor Laws, 258–61, 280–81; novels dealing with, 260–62; typical patterns of, 264–67. *See also* Concealment of birth

Infanticide Act (1922), 281

Infant Life Protection Society, 257, 259

Insanity: certification of, 45–46, 49, 61–62, 64, 67n20, 290, 292; and childbearing, 278, 281; as "female malady," 46, 65n3, 278, 281, 290–92, 314n6; as grounds for social control, 63–65, 290–92, 314n6, 314n10; medical treatment of, 46, 57–58, 290–91. *See also* Hysteria; Lunacy panics; Wrongful confinement

Intrigues and Confessions of a Ballet Girl, 114–16

Irving, Henry, 95n38

James, Henry, 134

Jameson, Anna, 218

Jameson, Frederic, 316n21

Jessie Phillips (Frances Trollope), 261–62, 282

Jewsbury, Geraldine, 196

Johnson, Wendell Stacy, 317n26

Journal of Mental Science, 67n20

Judicial separation, 28, 44, 186

Judy, 87

Kaplan, Cora, 316n25

Kendal, Madge (Mrs. Kendal), 87–89

Kent, Christopher, 315n17

Kingsley, Charles, 134–56, 306–8; and founding of Queen's College, 138–43, 306; and John Stuart Mill, 146–48, 317n31; and marriage, 135, 137, 139–40, 145, 318n32; and Muscular Christianity, 134–36, 149–53, 306–7; "Nausicaa in London," 148–50; *The Roman and the Teuton*, 144; *Two Years Ago*, 135–36, 137, 145, 306; on women's nature, 135–36, 143–50, 152–53, 307, 317n31; and women's rights, 136, 143–48, 317n31; *Yeast*, 139

Kolodny, Annette, 314n9

Kuhn, Annette, 133n43

Labouchère, Henry, 76, 93n19

Labouchère Amendment (1885), 310

Ladies' College (London), 140, 142

Langtry, Lillie, 81, 85, 88, 93n19

Lankester, Edwin, 258, 259, 263, 269

Laqueur, Thomas, 313n4

Lawrence, George, 134, 136, 153

Leavy, Barbara Fass, 53, 67n18

Le Gallienne, Richard, 91, 96n50

Lewes, Agnes (Mrs. George Henry Lewes), 160, 170

Lewes, George Henry, 159–77; as creative influence on George Eliot, 165, 166, 173, 301; marriage to Agnes Lewes, 160, 169–70; as partner in "companionate marriage," 167–69, 176; as partner in "grand romance," 167, 169–70, 172. *See also* Eliot, George

Life, 162–63

Linton, Eliza Lynn, 166–67, 171

Littell's Living Age, 192–94

London Quarterly Review, 168, 174–75

Longfellow, Henry Wadsworth, 221, 224, 227

Lowe's Edinburgh Magazine, 180

Lowe, Louisa, 61–62, 151

Lunacy Law Reform Association, 61, 62

Lunacy panics, 43, 44, 52–53, 295

Lynhurst, Lord, 16, 17

Lytton, Robert, 51–52

Lytton, Victor Alexander, 47–48

McCauley, Elizabeth Anne, 230n8

MacDonald, Ramsay, 253n10

McGregor, O. R., 18

McKibbin, Ross, 254n14, 255n23

Macmillan's Magazine, 143, 162, 168, 226

MacPike, Loralee, 315n14

Madness. *See* Insanity

Magnus, Philip, 255n37

Maguire, John M., 41n20

Malcolmson, R. W., 287n30

Marcus, Steven, 311, 319n41

Marriage: across classes, 70–77, 91, 295–96, 315n17; Charles Kingsley on, 135, 137, 139–40, 145; and George Eliot, 160, 162–63, 167–69, 174–75, 300–1; as patriarchal institution, 14–15, 45–48, 55–57, 290–94, 309–10; as sacred for women, 135–36, 139–40, 291; of Thomas and Jane Carlyle, 180–95; wifebeating in, 28, 30–32. *See also* Adultery; Divorce; Wrongful confinement

Married Women's Property Act (1882), 63–64, 71

Martin, Samuel, 276

Martineau, Harriet, 138, 140, 141–42, 182

Masson, David, 195

Maudie; Revelations of Life in London . . . , 119, 121

Maudsley, Henry, 136, 150–53

Maurice, Frederick Denison, 138, 140, 142–43, 146, 306

Mayer, David, 127–28

Mayhew, Henry, 315n12

Medical profession: as certifiers of insanity, 46, 49, 61–62, 64, 67n20, 290, 292; and childbearing, 150–51; and infanticide, 258, 263, 272, 281; status of, 263; women's admission to, 142, 146–47, 155n23; on women's physical inferiority, 150–52; and wrongful confinement, 45–46, 49–50, 52, 61–64

Memoirs of a Russian Ballet Girl, 116–17

Michie, Helena, 318n34

Mill, John Stuart, 143, 146–48, 155n23, 317n31

Miller, D. A., 314n8

Mitchell, Sally, 284n18

Miyoshi, Masao, 317n27

Month and Catholic Review, 189

Moonshine, 72, 80, 90

Moore, George, 95n38; *Esther Waters,* 237, 282

Morley, John, 162, 168–69

Morning Post, 78

Mothers, unmarried: lack of support systems for, 259, 260–61, 266–67, 270, 277–78, 280–82; and New Poor Laws, 258–61, 280–81; novels dealing with, 261–62, 282; as threat to patriarchy, 294; Victorian perceptions of, 260–62, 265, 267, 270, 276, 280–82. *See also* Concealment of birth; Infanticide

Muscular Christianity, 134–36, 149–53, 154n6, 306–7

Musical World, 93n19

Nation, 195–96, 305

National Anti-Gambling League, 235–52; failures of, 241, 244, 245–47, 251–52, 311–12; limited successes of, 245, 248, 252; moral viewpoint of, 237, 239–40, 244, 249–50; and opposition to "betting system,"

240–41, 244–48; organizational structure of, 238–39, 241; publications of, 236, 240, 244, 254n22, 254n23. *See also* Gambling

National Portrait Gallery (London), 207, 215–16, 228

National Society for the Prevention of Cruelty to Children, 258

National Vigilance Association, 108–9, 127

Newspapers. *See* Periodicals

New Woman, 136, 150–51, 165–66, 306–9

Nightingale, Florence, 154n6, 155n23, 215

Nineteenth Century, 85, 169–70

North American Review, 163, 170, 185

Oliphant, Margaret: on George Eliot, 164–65, 169, 170, 171–76; on James Anthony Froude, 172, 192–94, 197, 202–3

Once a Week, 215–16

Pall Mall Gazette, 225–26, 256n39

Pater, Walter: *The Renaissance,* 307

Patmore, Coventry, 226

Pauline the Prima Donna, 113

Paul Pry, 105

Pearson, Hesketh, 94n38

Penny Illustrated Paper, 256n39

Periodicals: and divorce reporting, 19, 36, 37, 292–93; and *Finney v. Cairns* breach of promise case, 77–90, 95n46, 295–96; and infanticide, 257–58, 261, 294; pornographic, 105–11; as producers and disseminators of scandal, 4–7; reviewing of biography in, 161–76, 183–203, 300–5; reviewing of photographic portraiture in, 207–8, 209, 211, 214–17, 221, 225, 226; sporting, 243–44; theatrical reviewing in, 86–88; and wrongful confinement, 50–52, 64; as Victorian phenomenon, 4–5. *See also* titles of individual periodicals

Peterson, M. Jeanne, 285n25, 317n30

Photo Bits, 105, 108, 109–10, 121–22, 130n19

Photographic Journal, 231n17

Photography. *See* Portraiture, photographic

Pinero, Arthur Wing, 91, 93n19

Pollock, Griselda, 133n43

Poor Laws, 258–61, 280–81

Poovey, Mary, 38n3, 313n4

Popular Science Monthly, 195

Pornography, 99–128; actresses depicted in, 103–28; costume in, 105–7, 109–11, 115, 116, 117–19, 126; cross-dressing in, 105, 106–7, 117–19, 123, 124; female dancers in, 105, 111–13, 116–17, 124; lesbianism in, 109, 113, 124; periodicals, 105–11; photographs, 119,

121–26, 128; printed books, 111–21; sadomasochism in, 106, 112, 116–17

Portraiture, photographic, 207–29; of actresses, 7, 72, 106, 125–26; commercial practice of, 207–8, 211–17, 218, 225; disruption of social distinctions by, 211–12, 214–17; fancy-dress, 209–11; "High Art" practice of, 207–8, 211, 217–21; of Thomas Carlyle, 218–19, 227–28. *See also* Cameron, Julia Margaret; *Cartes de visite*

Potter, Beatrix, 69

Prince of Wales (Albert Edward), 239, 249–51

Progress, 200

Prostitution, 32, 116, 146–47; associated with actresses, 103, 109–10, 112, 121, 126–27, 296–97

Protection orders, 27

Punch, 88–89, 95n46

Quarterly Review, 138

Queen, the Lady's Newspaper, The, 221

Queen's College (London), 138–43, 306

Queen Victoria. *See* Victoria

Quilter, Harry, 95n38

Raleigh Club, 94n38

Reader, 207–8, 211, 216–17

Redesdale, Lord, 15

Redinger, Ruby V., 159, 176

Robertson, A. J., 200

Standard, 80, 256n39
Stanley, Lady, 140
Steinmetz, Andrew, 256n39
Stephen, James Fitzjames, 273
Stephen, Leslie, 8, 201–2
Stetson, Dorothy, 38n3
Stone, Lawrence, 38n3, 39n14
Street Betting Act (1906), 238, 248
Strettell, Alfred, 139–40
Suicide, 30, 235–36, 261–62, 277–78
Sullivan, Arthur Seymour, 70, 75, 296

Taylor, Henry, 209, 220, 226
Temperance movement, 238, 253n6
Temple Bar, 166–67, 168, 171, 183, 201, 301, 305
Tennyson, Alfred, 207, 209, 218, 220, 226–27, 299–300; *The Princess*, 139–40
Tennyson, G. B., 204
Terry, Ellen, 95n43
Terry, Marion, 78, 83, 84, 86
Theater: as depicted in pornography, 99–128; George Eliot's interest in, 302; and moral reformers, 99–102, 108–9, 127; moral reputation of, 85, 100–3. *See also* Actresses; Finney, Emily May; names of specific theaters
Theatrical Programme, 90
Thomas, Keith, 38n3
Thomson, Hale, 47, 49

Times (London), 36, 51–52, 64, 80, 186, 258, 263, 285n26
Tranby Croft Baccarat Case, 249–52
Trelawny of the "Wells" (Pinero), 91
Trollope, Frances: *Jessie Phillips*, 261–62, 282

Under the Clock, 77, 78, 86, 87
United Kingdom Alliance, 253n6
Universal Review, 95n38

Vamplew, Wray, 253n15
Venereal disease, 25, 101, 105
Vernon, S. M., 101
Vestris, Eliza (Madame Vestris), 105, 117–20
Victoria (Queen of England), 2, 4, 237

Wakley, Thomas, 257, 258, 269
Walkowitz, Judith R., 38n13
Wallace, William, 188, 305
Walpole, Spencer, 14
Watt, George, 284n18
Watts, George Frederick, 221, 222, 228, 232n27
Weaver, Mike, 218, 229n2
Weeks, Jeffrey, 312
Weldon, Georgina Traherne, 6, 59–64, 151
Weldon, Harry, 59–64
Westminster Review, 159
Whipple, Edwin Percy, 163, 170
Whistler, James Abbott McNeill, 73, 93n19

151–52; medical profession's role in, 45–46, 48–49, 63–64; and patriarchal power, 45–48, 55–58, 63–65, 291–92, 295; of Rosina Wheeler Bulwer-Lytton,

45–52, 151–52, 291–92; in *The Woman in White,* 52–59

Wylie, W. H., 190, 197

Wynfield, David Wilkie, 207–11, 217, 221, 226, 229n3, 230n4

Wynter, Andrew, 215–16

A NOTE ABOUT THE EDITOR

Kristine Ottesen Garrigan is professor of English at DePaul University, Chicago. Author of *Ruskin on Architecture: His Thought and Influence* and *Victorian Art Reproductions in Modern Sources: A Bibliography,* she has published numerous essays and reviews on Victorian subjects.